Unsung Heroines

Single Mothers and the American Dream

Ruth Sidel

UNIVERSITY OF CALIFORNIA PRESS

Berkeley   Los Angeles   London

University of California Press, one of the most distinguished
university presses in the United States, enriches lives around
the world by advancing scholarship in the humanities, social
sciences, and natural sciences. Its activities are supported by
the UC Press Foundation and by philanthropic contributions from individuals and institutions. For more information, visit www.ucpress.edu.

University of California Press
Berkeley and Los Angeles, California

University of California Press, Ltd.
London, England

Library of Congress Cataloging-in-Publication Data

Sidel, Ruth.
   Unsung heroines : single mothers and the American
dream / Ruth Sidel.
      p.   cm.
   Includes bibliographical references and index.
   ISBN 0-520-23826-5 (alk. paper).—
   ISBN 0-520-24772-8 (pbk. : alk. paper)
   1. Single mothers—United States—Social conditions.
2. Single mothers—United States—Economic conditions.
3. Welfare recipients—United States.   I. Title.

HQ759.915.S159   2006
306.874'32'086942'0973—dc22   2005016915

Manufactured in the United States of America

14   13   12   11   10   09   08   07   06
10   9   8   7   6   5   4   3   2   1

The paper used in this publication meets the minimum re-
quirements of ANSI/NISO Z39.48–1992 (R 1997) (*Perma-
nence of Paper*).

Praise for *Unsung Heroines*

"This pioneering new study by Ruth Sidel is an education for the nation. Sidel shatters all the old familiar negative myths and harsh stereotypes about single mothers, and gives us instead the unvarnished truth about their diverse lives, their courageous struggles to raise their children, and their genuine family values—values they share with millions of other Americans. Many of the larger patterns Sidel identifies—the constant search for a fair balance between work and family, the endless quest for decent jobs and fair pay and good schools and affordable health care—apply to all families as well. Hopefully, this excellent and eloquent volume will act as a wake-up call, and wiser federal, state, and local policies will enable many, many more of these hard-working mothers to find light at the end of the tunnel. This book offers a unique opportunity for every reader to walk in the shoes of single mothers and help find that light."

SENATOR EDWARD M. KENNEDY

Unsung Heroines

The publisher gratefully
acknowledges the generous contribution to
this book provided by the General Endowment Fund
of the University of California Press
Foundation

For Marilyn
a true heroine and a constant inspiration
and
for Rosie, Thea, and Andy
who are already helping to make this a better world

As our case is new, so we must think anew, and act anew.

Abraham Lincoln
Second Annual Message to Congress
November 1, 1862

Contents

Acknowledgments

To the wonderful women who were willing to share their thoughts, their feelings, and the story of their lives for this book, my deep gratitude. Their courage, warmth, generosity, and concern about the well-being of others are a true inspiration.

To Lynn Chancer, my profound appreciation for her enthusiasm for this project from the outset, her unflagging encouragement, her insight and wisdom, and, above all, her friendship. To Naomi Chase, Laurie Kramer, and Mindy Werner, my special thanks for reading part or all of the manuscript when it was in various stages of preparation and for giving me perceptive and invaluable suggestions. And to Kevin Sidel, who made cogent comments on the entire manuscript, my gratitude and my love.

To Vivyan Adair, Alice Axelbank, Aiyoung Choi, CarolAnn Daniel, Frances Falk Dickler, Dorothy Epstein, Sarah Greenblatt, Jerome Grossman, Steven Grossman, Margot Haas, Shawn Howard, Marilyn Jackson, Debi Sunhea Kim, Melinda Lackey, Suzanne Michael, Mary Murphree, Camille Murphy, Victor Perez, Janet Poppendieck, Margaret Raymond, Inge Sidel, Mark Sidel, Barbara Steed, Elizabeth Temkin, and Maria Terrone, my appreciation for their interest in the topic, their referrals to single mothers, and particularly for their warm wishes and support.

To my editor, Naomi Schneider, who reminded me to write the book I really wanted to write and gave me superb advice on how to do it, my admiration and appreciation. To Dore Brown, Sierra Filucci, Hillary Hansen, Barbara Roos, and particularly to Alice Falk, my thanks for their creative and painstaking work on all aspects of the book.

And finally, to Vic, computer maven and all-round advisor extraordinaire, my love and gratitude for all you do and all you are.

Introduction

The denigration and demonization of single mothers has deep roots in American culture. Mothers without husbands have been looked upon with suspicion and hostility since the time of the earliest settlers. Today's concerns about the weakening of the traditional family and about related issues such as single motherhood, divorce, sexual permissiveness, teenage pregnancy, and abortion have formed a central theme in American society for generations. Both the early Settlement Laws and the Colonial Poor Laws of seventeenth-century America punished husbandless women and unwed mothers, differentiating between the "deserving" and the "undeserving." During the early years of the twentieth century, programs to help the poor stated that only "fit and worthy" women would receive help; these generally were white widows.[1]

The recent period of intensified concern about single motherhood was spurred by the ascendancy of conservative ideology in the United States as marked by the election of Ronald Reagan as president. Rapid social change during the 1970s and 1980s—increasing numbers of single mothers, especially women having children outside marriage; a significant increase in teenage pregnancy and birth; a continuing high divorce rate; and fundamental changes in the roles and status of women—contributed to the anxiety about social issues. Reagan's infamous labeling of poor women as "welfare queens" was accompanied by significant cutbacks in essential social services, particularly for poor women and children. In the early 1980s Medicaid, Aid to Families with Dependent Children, the food stamp program, maternal and child health services, and day care were all slashed. These cutbacks increased the number of poor people and had a particularly devastating impact on female-headed families. Consequently, during this period there was a significant increase in both the "feminization" and the "minoritization" of poverty.[2]

Since the early 1990s, single mothers have continued to be systematically stereotyped and stigmatized. Poor single mothers have once again been vilified as being lazy, irresponsible, dependent, deviant, and, above all, living off the hard work of others. Single mothers, particularly those who have children outside of marriage, have been blamed for virtually all the nation's social problems—the "breakdown of the family," the crime rate, drug and alcohol addiction, illiteracy, homelessness, poverty, and students' poor academic performance. Perhaps the most denigrating and dehumanizing attacks on single mothers occurred in 1995 on the floor of the U.S. House of Representatives when, as part of an effort to reduce the money spent on social welfare programs, two members of Congress compared welfare recipients to animals. This campaign was fueled by conservative Republicans, spearheaded by Newt Gingrich and buttressed by the work of the social scientist Charles Murray, who labeled out-of-wedlock births "the single most important problem of our time" as he railed against the "culture of illegitimacy."[3] Bill Clinton seemed to support the negative view of welfare recipients when he made his now-famous promise in 1991, during the presidential campaign, to "put an end to welfare as we know it."[4]

In 1992, the then vice president, Dan Quayle, set off a firestorm by condemning Murphy Brown, the central character in a popular television sitcom, for having a baby outside of marriage. Interestingly, during the episode in which Murphy Brown decided to have the baby, she debated between having an abortion and bearing a child. Quayle was surely not calling for her to terminate the pregnancy; he was clearly criticizing her for not being married before becoming pregnant. In the same speech, Quayle also suggested that unmarried women with children were at least partially responsible for the "lawless social anarchy" that erupted in the May 1992 riots in Los Angeles following the acquittal of the four police officers who brutally beat Rodney King. Several months later, an influential and widely read article by Barbara Dafoe Whitehead titled "Dan Quayle Was Right" was published in the *Atlantic Monthly*. Whitehead claimed that studies show that children who grow up in single-parent families are at significantly greater risk than children raised in two-parent families for a variety of problems, such as developing emotional and behavioral difficulties, dropping out of school, becoming pregnant as teenagers, abusing drugs, getting into trouble with the law, and being victims of physical or sexual abuse. Whitehead stressed, moreover, that children of divorced, separated, or never-married parents are far more likely to live in poverty, fail in school, commit crimes, and engage in "aggressive, acting-out behavior" and in "assaults on teachers, unprovoked attacks on other children, [and] screaming outbursts in class."[5]

"Family values" became a ubiquitous slogan, instantly signaling an ideology that adamantly opposes abortion, promotes heterosexual marriage, criticizes the divorce rate and its effects on children and on the larger society, and generally looks back, nostalgically though not accurately, to earlier eras of traditional family and gender relationships. In a speech in March 1995, Newt Gingrich, then the Speaker of the House of Representatives, recommended returning to the values, norms, and social sanctions of Victorian England in order to modify antisocial behavior: "They [the Victorians] reduced the number of children born out of wedlock almost by 50 percent. They changed the whole momentum of their society. They didn't do it through a new bureaucracy. They did it by reestablishing values, by moral leadership, and by "being willing to look at people in the face and say, 'You should be ashamed when you get drunk in public; you ought to be ashamed if you're a drug addict.' "[6] Of course, Gingrich was also saying that American society must send the message that people should be ashamed to have children out of wedlock and that we should not be afraid of using shame to change behavior. One is reminded of Hester Prynne in *The Scarlet Letter*, stepping out of prison into the Massachusetts marketplace with that "mark of shame upon her bosom," so that "she will be a living sermon against sin, until the ignominious letter will be engraved upon her tombstone."[7]

The relentless stereotyping, stigmatizing, and demonizing of the poor, especially poor women, during the early to mid-1990s culminated in the passage of the Personal Responsibility and Work Opportunity Reconciliation Act. This legislation was signed into law by President Bill Clinton, a Democrat, on August 22, 1996. Euphemistically praised as "welfare reform," the act ended the sixty-one-year-old federal guarantee of aid to poor children. This legislation was based on the assumptions that welfare benefits lead to debilitating dependency; that jobs are indeed available for those who wish to work; that these jobs would provide a road out of poverty; and that only through work outside the home can the poor become responsible citizens worthy of respect. Such views, not so long ago considered the harsh and punitive positions of those on the extreme right, have become mainstream ideas in the United States over the past two decades. Poverty is seen as the result of personal failings rather than as a consequence of the U.S. social and economic system, and therefore government-supported efforts today are frequently aimed at modifying individual behavior rather than at making fundamental changes in the social structure. Since the passage of the welfare legislation, millions of poor women have been forced to work outside the home, often in jobs that pay poverty wages and without regard for the availability of decent, affordable child care.[8]

With the election of George W. Bush as president in 2000, an increasingly conservative agenda has once again taken center stage. The federal government has provided more and more resources to establish programs for young people that simply encourage abstinence from sex until marriage rather than teaching the facts about reproduction, contraception, and sexually transmitted diseases. Instead of investing significant amounts of money in job training, higher education, and child care, the Bush administration has encouraged poor women to marry as a strategy for moving out of poverty. The ideology underpinning much of the Bush agenda is that the individual has the power to succeed if only she or he works hard enough and makes the personal decisions deemed correct by the administration and its ultraconservative supporters. Accompanying this emphasis on individual responsibility and traditional values has been a marked disinclination to see a role for government at any level to provide support and services for individuals and families. Thus, while life has become increasingly difficult and complex over the past decade, as more and more jobs have disappeared, as those that remain often pay far less than a living wage, as millions must survive without essentials such as health insurance, and as the gap between rich and poor widens to Gatsbyesque proportions, families have largely been left to fend for themselves. Mother-only families have not only had to withstand a relentless barrage of criticism but have also seen social and financial support diminish significantly.

Who exactly are single mothers today? First, it must be emphasized that women become single mothers in a variety of ways: through separation from their husbands, through divorce, through widowhood, and through having children outside of marriage. No one scenario or set of circumstances explains the diverse, complex lives of single mothers. It must be stressed as well that millions of single mothers never intended to live their lives raising their children without the support of a partner. When they find themselves alone and in charge of their family, many recognize for the first time the harsh reality of being a single parent in the United States today.

The dramatic change in American family structure over the past half century has been well documented. The percentage of women with children under 18 not living with a husband rose from 10 percent in 1940 to 24 percent in 2000. The sharpest increase occurred between 1960 and 1990; since then the percentage has remained stable. Not only the statistics but the causes of the increase in single-parent families have changed significantly. During the first half of the twentieth century the primary cause of single parenthood was parental death; by the end of the century most absent parents were living, but they were living elsewhere. Moreover, while single-parent families have become more common in all demographic groups, the greatest increases have been among less-educated women and among African American families.[9] In 2002, 16 percent of white, non-Hispanic children were living only with their mother, one-quarter (25 percent) of Hispanic children were living in mother-only families, and among black families 48 percent of children were living in mother-only families. Thus, as the twenty-first century begins, one-quarter of all children—and nearly half of black children—are living in mother-only families.[10]

If we examine the data on U.S. mothers by educational level, we find that the percentage of mothers in the bottom third of educational attainment who were not living with a husband rose sharply during the second half of the twentieth century, as did the percentage of mothers in the middle third of educational attainment. In contrast, the percentage of those mothers in the highest third of educational attainment not living with a husband has remained stable since 1980.[11] Those women least prepared by their education to manage economically on their own are most likely to have to do so.

Why worry about the significant increase in mother-only families in the United States? Many observers, of course, are concerned about the psychosocial aspects of child rearing. They feel that children do better with two parents, when more than one adult is intimately concerned with and responsible for a child's well-being, and they also believe that young people of both sexes benefit from having a male role model in the home. A two-parent family, moreover, can provide a buffer for both parents and children—offering someone else to go to in times of conflict, someone else with whom one can discuss problems, options, decision making. Others—an uncle, a grandfather, an older sibling, a male friend of the family—can, and often do, play these roles, but they may be viewed by all involved as a substitute, lacking real authority and in all likelihood not as fully committed as a parent.

A key problem that the majority of single mothers face is economic. Because they must all too often manage on one income rather than two, because many fathers do not or cannot pay child support, because women who work full-time, full year still earn only 80 percent of what men who work full-time, full year earn, because single mothers are frequently forced to work part-time either because they need to be home to care for their children or because the jobs available at their skill level are part-time—for all of these reasons, mother-only families are often disadvantaged economically.[12] And economic disadvantage leads to a host of other problems, including inadequate housing, inferior educational opportunities, increased health problems, and a lack of health insurance. In 2002, for example, the median family income for all mother-only families was $22,637, approximately one-third the median income of two-parent families, $65,399. Even among white, non-Hispanic, mother-only families, in 2002 the median income was only $26,337, one-third the income of comparable married-couple families, $72,133. The gap between black married and mother-only families is similar: married-couple black families earn nearly three times the income of black mother-only families— $56,863 versus $19,189. Hispanic two-parent families have a median income of $39,617, essentially double that of mother-only Hispanic families ($19,455).[13]

Poverty data for mother-only families corroborate these income figures. In 2002, nearly 40 percent (39.6 percent) of female-headed families with children under 18 officially lived in poverty. This rate was nearly five times that of married-couple families (8.5 percent). Almost half of all black, non-Hispanic families and Hispanic female-headed families with children under 18 live in poverty (45.5 percent and 47.8 percent, respectively). Children under 6 live in the harshest economic conditions: more than half of all black, non-Hispanic, female-headed families with children under 6 live below the federal poverty line.[14]

Economic inequality translates into very different patterns of socialization of children, very different social skills and attitudes toward adults, toward social institutions, and toward their own entitlement. As Annette

Lareau points out in her ethnographic study of the impact of social class on children's lives, *Unequal Childhoods: Class, Race, and Family Life*, "inequality permeates the fabric of . . . [American] culture." She describes how the different child-rearing philosophies of middle-class parents, on the one hand, and working-class and poor families, on the other, lead to *"the transmission of differential advantages* to children" (emphasis hers). Both white and black middle-class children exhibit a greater "sense of entitlement"; in contrast, working-class and poor children are more likely to exhibit a "sense of constraint" in institutional settings.[15] The importance of class differences in American society is widely dismissed and even denied, and the dominant ideology stresses the existence of equal opportunity, of "a level playing field"; yet Lareau's study vividly demonstrates once again that economic inequities not only matter but are subtly and often not so subtly transmitted from one generation to the next in the socialization process.

Concern about single motherhood has also been fueled by the extraordinarily high number of teenage girls who become pregnant in the United States. While the phrase *children having children* has been widely used to dramatize and deplore the U.S. teen pregnancy rate, in reality the vast majority of teens giving birth are between the ages of 15 and 19. The other common myth about teen pregnancy is that a large percentage of teenage girls intend to become pregnant: on the contrary, nearly all studies indicate that the vast majority of teen pregnancies are unintended. Moreover, while the U.S. rate has been considerably higher than that of comparable developed countries, in recent years it has declined significantly. At its peak in 1991, the birth rate for all adolescent mothers ages 15 to 19 was 62.1 births per 1,000 females; a decade later, in 2001, that rate had fallen to 43.6. This decline is apparent in all racial and ethnic groups. For example, among non-Hispanic whites the rate peaked in 1991 at 43.4 and fell to 32.5 in 2000. For non-Hispanic blacks the rate, significantly higher than that of all other groups, declined from a high of 118.9 in 1991 to 81.9 in 2000;

among Hispanic teens the rate fell from 107.7 in 1994 to 94.4 in 2000.[16]

This study is a realistic, detailed examination of the lives of single mothers from their perspectives, intended to correct the harsh, hostile, often erroneous, sometimes venomous stereotypes about single mothers endlessly reiterated by pundits, politicians, and members of the media. Bizarre examples of highly unusual behavior are all too often put forth and deplored as though they were the norm and then are taken as typical of all single mothers. Moreover, these often outlandish examples are presented as the true experiences of the entire group, used to reinforce the prevailing stereotypes and to formulate social policy. This book examines the real lives of a variety of single mothers: how they grew up, how they became the sole or primary caregivers of their children, how becoming a single parent disrupted their lives and affected them, and how they subsequently rebuilt their social, emotional, and economic world. Its focus is on the impact of single motherhood on the women themselves—not the impact of single motherhood on the institution of marriage or the effect on children of growing up in a single-parent household. When people are able to tell their own stories, they can place themselves at the center of the narrative, becoming the actors rather than the portrayed. As Carolyn Heilbrun has observed, "Power is the ability to take one's place in whatever discourse is essential to action and the right to have one's part matter. This is true in the Pentagon, in marriage, in friendship, and in politics."[17] This book is written to provide single mothers the opportunity to take their place in the discourse about the nature of single motherhood, its complex causes, and its equally complex consequences, and to aid them in having their part matter.

The broader questions of how we perceive our lives, how we construct the causes and effects of events, and how we present ourselves—both to ourselves and to others—are also complex. In *The Triumph of Narrative:*

Storytelling in the Age of Mass Culture, Robert Fulford declares, "Most of us feel the need to describe how we came to be what we are. We want to make our stories known, and we want to believe those stories carry value." Fulford stresses that one of the goals of stories, or narrative, is to try to come to terms with and "at least partly *contain* the terrifyingly haphazard quality of life," to feel some sense of control over the course of our lives. We are, in some sense, "organizing the past so that it makes acceptable sense . . . *bearable, endurable* sense" (emphasis his).[18] Through narrative or stories or recollections about our lives, we explain our lives to ourselves and to others. Through narrative we come to know one another, to understand the principles by which we and others live. As Pirandello stated, "I construct myself continually and I construct you, and you do the same."[19] Our stories and anecdotes are often symbolic, illustrating a larger point that may not even be articulated—communicating our values, our belief system, who we feel we are, who we want to be, how we want to be seen. Joyce Carol Oates has underscored the importance of these stories to who we are, asking "For what is 'identity' but our power to control others' definition of us?"[20] The power to control our narrative is intimately connected to the way others perceive us, which in turn is a key determinant of the way we perceive ourselves. This book therefore presents these women's narratives of their lives largely in their own words. Single mothers are entitled to define themselves, to present themselves as they choose rather than being seen and put forward as a category—and a generally denigrated one at that.

The heart of the study draws on interviews with fifty women who have been single mothers at some time in their lives. The interviews were done over a three-year period, from July 2001 through June 2004. While the women vary in ethnic, racial, and class background and in age, all of them met one key criterion: each became a single mother without intending to do so. Women who planned to give birth or adopt children without a partner have been excluded from this study—not because their stories are not important and instructive but because I believe their experiences are very different. The women who are included took many different paths to becoming a single mother. Some have been separated from their husbands, divorced, or widowed; others were single at the time of conception but assumed that their male partner would be available for some level of support—emotional, social, financial—as well as at least sporadic fathering. Some of the women have since married or re-married, but all had sole or primary responsibility for the care of their child or children for a significant span of time.

Some might question the appropriateness of examining such a wide range of women in a single study. Why include both unmarried women who became single mothers and those who have been separated, divorced, and widowed? After all, women who become pregnant outside of marriage may well have very different experiences, with qualitatively different relationships with their partners, than women who took the step of marrying but whose marriages faltered. Similarly, why include widows, whose marriages ended through no doing of theirs or their husbands, and who therefore have had significantly different experiences, possibly leading to different feelings about themselves and their status as well as to different perceptions about them by others? It is my view that mothers from this wide variety of backgrounds have more shared experiences than experiences that separate or differentiate them, and that to de-stigmatize and move toward greater understanding of their lives and their experiences we must surmount the usual barriers of marital status, class, race, ethnicity, and age in order to study these commonalities. Virtually all the women interviewed for this study experienced a severe and often abrupt disturbance in their lives. They married expecting to stay married or even to live happily ever after. They did not anticipate separation or divorce, and surely not widowhood. The single women assumed they would not become pregnant and, if they did, that their male friend or lover would be around in some capacity; their plans for their future lives were based on these assumptions. Once their lives were profoundly disrupted, the women experienced genuine loss. The nature of the loss differed, depending on the circumstances of their lives, but all experienced it—including the women who themselves chose to end relationships they felt were dysfunctional and those who eventually created far more positive and rewarding lives for themselves and their children.

Many of these mothers also showed a powerful and often courageous resilience as well as the strength and ability to find new ways out of their exceedingly difficult and often wrenching situations. After they entered the world of single motherhood, the women all had to face putting their lives back together—making new living arrangements, dealing with financial issues, balancing work and nurturing, finding adequate child care and after-school care, figuring out the role of extended family and friends, exploring the often delicate problem of having a social life, and sometimes dealing with their own self-doubt, feelings of inadequacy, and sadness. They all were forced to grapple with these issues regardless of how they became single mothers. To be sure, more affluent women have considerably more choice in solving these fundamental problems, but they too usually agonized about how to handle it all, about what was the "right" path for them. I felt that in the long run, we had more to learn by including women who became single mothers through many different routes than by considering each group in isolation from the others.

The women in this study all live in New York City or in the New York metropolitan area. They are racially and ethnically diverse. They include non-Hispanic whites, African Americans, Latinas, women of Caribbean heritage, Asians, and one woman of mixed black and white parentage. At the time of the interviews, they were separated, divorced, widowed, and never married. Several married for the first time or remarried after they became single mothers. In economic status, they range from poor to upper middle class. Using the standard sociological measures of education, occupation, and income, approximately one-third of the women are poor, near poor, or working class; another third middle class; and the final third upper middle class. Nearly half of all the women work in jobs that provide human services—some with a professional degree, most without. Several of the women work in nonprofit institutions; a number of them originally trained as or over the years have become trained as academics, physicians, and lawyers.

At the time of the interviews the women ranged in age from 23 to 89. The majority were in their 30s and 40s, a slightly smaller number in their 20s and in their 50s, and another group was over age 60. The older women could reflect on their backgrounds, their early assumptions and expectations, their lives over the decades, the factors and events that led them to become single mothers, and how their lives evolved as they matured and their children grew up. The interviews with the younger women, by contrast, focused far more tightly on their backgrounds, how they became single mothers, and their current lives. Clearly, we do not know at this time what directions the lives of the younger women will take. While a growing literature has been developing on lesbian parenting, none of these women identified herself as lesbian. Because all women who planned to become single mothers were excluded from the study, no single gay women who chose to adopt or bear a child were interviewed.

Most of the interviews were conducted face-to-face at a location convenient for the interviewees. Many took place in the women's homes, some in their place of work, a few in my office at Hunter College, and still others in a (relatively) quiet corner of a restaurant over a long breakfast, lunch, or dinner. These women are extraordinarily busy people, and I tried to inconvenience them as little as possible. Because of their hectic schedules, a few of the interviews were conducted over the telephone. In general, the telephone interviews worked very well; the women seemed engaged and eager to talk. Many people are so comfortable communicating by phone—even about very personal matters—that the telephone interviews seemed to flow as well as, and sometimes even better than, some of the face-to-face interviews, though of course eye contact and the observation of body language were missing from our interaction.

All of the women I interviewed were told of my previous writing about poverty among women and children and of my concern about the stereotyping and stigmatizing of single mothers. The cutbacks of social supports to those who had the least and the increase in poverty among women and children during the Reagan years, particularly during the early 1980s, led to my book *Women and Children Last: The Plight of Poor*

Women in Affluent America; the harsh debate about the growth and impact of mother-only families that took place prior to the historic welfare legislation of 1996 prompted a sequel, *Keeping Women and Children Last: America's War on the Poor.* I explained to the interviewees that this book was intended to portray single mothers primarily through their own words rather than through the perceptions of others. None of the women was paid for the interview, though obviously I did pick up the check if we were talking over a meal in a restaurant. The sample was found through word of mouth. I began by telling colleagues what I was working on and asking them for referrals to single mothers who fit the criteria of the study. The women who were interviewed then referred others, and so on. Out of all the people I called to request an interview, only two changed their minds after agreeing to talk with me; both of them were in the throes of breaking up with their partners and felt they simply were too emotionally distraught to discuss their experiences at that time. I did not call them back to reschedule. Almost all of the other women I approached readily agreed to be interviewed. In the initial telephone contact I explained my policy of confidentiality—that I would change all of their names in order to protect their privacy; I stressed this policy again during the interviews themselves.

The format was an open-ended interview that included several general themes. Using a conversational format, I asked each of the women to tell me something about her family background, about her childhood and her educational experiences, and then to describe what happened subsequently in her life. Once we got past their early lives, the women usually took control of the narrative. I asked relevant questions, but how to tell their stories—what to include, what to omit—was fundamentally their decision. Since I knew very little about them except that they unintentionally became single mothers and lived in the New York City area, they had the power to present their lives as they experienced and perceived them. It has been said that "narrative is always political because people choose which narrative to tell,"[21] and that is exactly what I wanted—these women's versions of what happened to them, how their lives evolved, and how they coped with events, conflicts, feelings, disappointments, struggles, and accomplishments.

The interviews generally lasted from one to two hours. They were not taped. Using my early training in listening and note taking as a psychiatric social worker as well as my extensive experience interviewing for previous studies, including work done in China and other countries, I took as complete notes as possible, filled them in immediately afterward, and then transcribed them, usually within twenty-four hours. Each woman is describing her own specific experience; as in my previous work, none of the narratives is a composite. While the fifty interviews form the basis of the study's overall analysis, more than half the women are profiled in depth in this book. They were selected both because they most clearly and vividly illustrate the central themes that emerged during the analysis and because they represent the diversity of age, race, ethnicity, and life experience of the entire group of women. It must be stressed that these women were at different points in their lives. Many were living through single motherhood at the time of the interviews and were describing ongoing events, conflicts, and problems. Others had been single heads of their families fairly recently, but had since remarried or their children had become adults; therefore their status changed as they moved on to the next stage of life. Still others were older women who were looking back at their lives as single mothers from a distance of many years. Many interviews present a snapshot, a moment in time; others give us the panorama of a lifetime.

With the exception of its introduction and first and final chapters, this book is largely organized around the narratives of single mothers. Chapter 1 discusses the intense criticism, particularly in recent years, of single parenthood and its presumed effects on the children and on the larger society. Chapter 2 describes the diversity and complexity both in the causes of single motherhood and in the lives of single mothers; it suggests that rather than being a negative force in American society, millions of single mothers actually embody the finest American values. The simplistic stereotypes that shape how single mothers tend to be perceived by the wider society clearly have little or no relevance to the women portrayed in this chapter and indeed to most of the women interviewed for this study. The many different permutations of loss—loss of a partner, loss of income, loss of self-esteem, loss of emotional and social support, loss of youth prematurely—which are all-too-common characteristics of single motherhood, are detailed through the lives of several women in chapter 3. Chapter 4 discusses the remarkable resilience and strength of many of these single mothers, who overcome extraordinarily difficult circumstances and go on to transform their lives. In chapter 5 several of the women describe and analyze the individuals, social institutions, and belief systems that have been essential to their survival over the years. But while many of the women have been truly heroic in creating and sustaining meaningful lives for themselves and their children, others have undergone such severe trauma or live in such trying material and personal conditions that they are having and may continue to have significant difficulty in putting their lives together in a positive, meaningful way. These derailed lives are discussed in chapter 6. Chapter 7 attempts to describe the disconnect between male and female socialization, expectations, and behavior and to analyze why men and women respond so differently to intimate heterosexual relationships and to the enormous responsibility of caring for children. And finally, chapter 8 utilizes the experiences of these women as well as comparative international data and policies to illuminate alternative ways of thinking and programs that would strengthen the well-being of all families.

It is important to keep in mind that life happens bit by bit, event after event. We may fantasize or plan our lives in large sweeps of time, but when we are living them one thing leads to another, gradually, sometimes almost without our realizing what is happening. Many have taken the status of single mother and then attributed to the individuals so labeled a set of personal characteristics that we have come to associate with that status—a set of negative attitudes and behaviors that seem to explain the status and that are summed up in a stereotype. But what these narratives demonstrate is that the negative, stigmatizing characteristics that so many people associate with single mothers do not apply to these women. Although some women do choose single motherhood, none of the women interviewed for this study did; many of them (including *all* of the unmarried women) did not intend to become pregnant at the time they actually conceived. When faced with an unintended or accidental pregnancy, they needed to decide whether to terminate the pregnancy or to have the baby. In making this crucial decision, they were strongly influenced by family members, by their partners, by their feelings about their future lives, by religious and moral values, by the debates in the wider culture, and sometimes by fear. After each event or decision they needed to move ahead and cope with the consequences as best they could. Some of these women entered into marriages or relationships that were simply mistakes; others became aware of severe problems in their relationships as the years went by. Still others were struck by tragedy. None of these women frivolously became a single mother.

The women who speak out in this book are younger, older, black, white, Latina. They have become single mothers by many routes. Among the separated and divorced, some have been left by their husbands and others have themselves left the relationship. Some have been physically or emotionally abused; others have not. Some are struggling financially; for others money is not their primary concern. But they have all experienced significant disruption in their lives, and this book examines how these women have dealt and continue to deal with wrenching changes in their hopes, dreams, and expectations and how they are rebuilding their lives in an exceedingly hostile social, economic, and political environment. This is also a study of strength, of resilience, of courage, and of support. Some of the women have heroically refashioned their lives and are clearly walking down a path uncharted by anyone in their immediate environment; for others their lives are still a work in progress. Whatever their experiences, they cannot be reduced to a simplistic stereotype, an "idée fixe," or a "controlling image." These women, their children, and their complex relationships cannot be neatly summed up, characterized by some preexisting formula; the rote predictions of their futures (often ominous) are rarely accurate. What is clear is that in all instances these women are committed to nurturing and raising their children—no matter how difficult their circumstances, no matter how bleak their futures may seem. These are serious, caring women trying to do their best for their children, trying to balance work and nurturing, trying to make ends meet despite resources that are often seriously inadequate, and ultimately trying to create meaningful, rewarding lives. This book attempts to move beyond facile, formulaic thinking and to present a textured picture of these single mothers largely through their words, through their own view of their lives. These are their stories.

1

Moving Beyond Stigma

By definition, of course, we believe the person with a stigma is not quite human. On this assumption we exercise varieties of discrimination, through which we effectively, if often unthinkingly, reduce his life chances. **Erving Goffman**, *Stigma*

Single motherhood is synonymous with deviant motherhood.
Martha Fineman, *The Neutered Mother, the Sexual Family and Other Twentieth Century Tragedies*

I was raised by a single parent. My mother died after a long illness when I was 5. My father was left with two sons, ages 19 and 21, and a very young daughter. Born in the United States, the youngest son of immigrant parents, he had climbed from the poverty of his childhood to comfortable middle-class status by working indefatigably since he was a boy (yes, he did shine shoes and sell newspapers from a very young age on the streets of East Boston), eventually starting and building his own business. In the years following my mother's death at the beginning of World War II, my brothers both left home, one to go into the army and the other to get married. Shortly afterward my father and I moved from the large apartment we had all shared in a nearby suburb to a smaller one in downtown Boston. Except for my four years at college just outside of Boston, he and I lived together there until I got married at age 22—in the bay window of the living room overlooking Beacon Street and the Public Garden.

We were fortunate to be able to have a housekeeper who arrived weekdays around 11 in the morning and stayed until after dinner. She was a friend and an ally, but there was no doubt that my father was in charge. He made the decisions; he set the tone. He gave a great deal and he expected a great deal. He expected a certain seriousness of purpose, good sense, and grown-up behavior. He expected chores and errands to be done right and done in good time. He was home nearly every evening, and when he had other plans he told me where he was going and what time he would be back. He had female friends, particularly one much younger woman who also became a good friend of mine. But he was my only parent; he had all the power. He was generous, loving, caring, irreverent, and funny but often unpredictable. He would become enraged when you least expected it and remain calm when you dreaded the angry outburst. What was perhaps most difficult was that there was really no one else—no one to go to, no one to intercede, no one to calm him down, no one to reassure me.

But I was fortunate. My two older brothers always remained a presence in my life. One took me to night games to see the Red Sox and has been my political mentor since I was barely a teenager and a true friend all these years; the other, something of a disciplinarian, was concerned and loving, the person you could really count on, not just when I was growing up but since I have been an adult as well. We have always been a real family.

What is most fascinating is that my father was never vilified, never criticized for being a single parent. In fact, my father was widely admired and praised. Because he was raising a daughter alone, he was seen as caring, self-sacrificing, truly committed to his family. No one ever suggested (I don't think they would have dared) that he should either work or not work outside the home, relinquish any social life (quite the contrary!), or not leave me in the care of others to go on vacation. Moreover, there was never a suggestion that I might behave in ways attributed by some to the children of single parents—that I might become pregnant as a teenager, that I might fail in school or engage in "aggressive, acting-out behavior" or in "screaming outbursts in class."[1] The perception of my father differed dramatically from that of millions of single mothers largely because of his gender: he was a man and therefore given respect, particularly for raising a child and for dealing with all the domestic details connected with maintaining a household. But other differences also contributed to his positive—some might say heroic—image in the larger community; most obviously, he became a single parent through the tragic death of his relatively young wife. Perhaps even more important, he was white and affluent and therefore exempt from many of the negative stereotypes that have defined single mothers over the decades.

The contrast between the admiration my father received because of his role as a single parent and the way millions of single mothers are perceived and treated is both stark and telling. Precisely the same role that won him praise and commendation earns single mothers hostility and condemnation. Not only do single mothers have the sole or primary responsibility for feeding, clothing, housing, and nurturing their children, often with grossly inadequate social and economic resources, but they must function in an environment in which they are constantly being judged and criticized—a social and political context in which they are systematically stereotyped, stigmatized, and even despised.

Critics tell us again and again what is wrong with single mothers, how pathological their behavior is, how they deviate from the norm. They are often portrayed as "dependent" rather than "independent," as lazy rather than hardworking, as unworthy and undeserving.[2] The culture is rife with denigrating descriptions of women raising children on their own. Single mothers are stigmatized on multiple grounds—for their race, their ethnicity, and their class as well as for raising children without a husband. Dichotomous narratives divide many women, particularly black women, into the "good" and the "bad," those who are lax with their children or those who are too strict, those who are perceived as overtly and excessively sexual or those who are perceived as hostile and even castrating toward men.

John Ashcroft, then a senator and later, during the first term of President George W. Bush, attorney general of the United States, wrote in the *St. Louis Post Dispatch* in the mid-1990s that the inner city is the site of "rampant illegitimacy" and a "space devoid of discipline." According to the social scientist Charles Murray, poor women are "lazy due to years of government programming" and "crazed trying to meet their own selfish needs."[3] The syndicated radio talk show host Michael Savage stated in June 2004 that "people on welfare should not have the right to vote, while they are on welfare. Period. End of story."[4] Former U.S. representative Jim DeMint, from South Carolina, a month before his election to the U.S. Senate in 2004, declared that unwed pregnant women and single women who are pregnant and living with their boyfriends should be barred from working or teaching in public schools.[5] Journalists have referred to adolescent motherhood as a "cancer" and have described teenage mothers as "breed[ing] criminals faster than society can jail them."[6] According to David Blankenhorn, the author of *Fatherless America: Confronting Our Most Urgent Social Problem*, "Father absence is the engine driving our biggest social problems." And Wade Horn, president of the National Fatherhood Initiative, told the *Washington Post* that "Growing up without a father is like being in a car with a drunk driver."[7]

Adam Walinsky, a lawyer concerned about violent crime in American culture, predicts that "black youths" born in the mid-1980s will become violent criminals because "three-fifths of them were born to single mothers, many of whom were drug-addicted." Claiming further that "unprecedented numbers will have been subjected to beatings and other abuse; and most will have grown up amid the utter chaos prevailing in black city neighborhoods," he warns that these conditions "have already assured the creation of more very violent young men than any reasonable society can tolerate and their numbers will grow inexorably for every one of the next twenty years."[8] Yet contrary to Walinsky's dire forecasts, which rest ultimately on his denigration of single mothers, crime has declined significantly in the United States over the past two decades; the fall has been particularly dramatic in New York City.[9]

Single mothers are thus often defined as deviants who are dangerous to their children, to the well-being of their family and of *the* family, and to the wider society as well. Proclaiming some people deviant has a dual function: while making explicit the norms of the culture and pressuring members of the society to conform to those norms, it also draws others in the population closer together. As the writer Rachel Brownstein says of herself and her college friends, "We laughed at joiners; it kept us joined."[10] But clearly not all single parents are viewed as deviants. Single fathers are often seen as exemplary citizens, acting in ways that far exceed society's expectations of them and thereby meriting honor and respect in the community. Moreover, to label individuals as deviant lifts one of their characteristics above all others: as their most important or significant quality, it makes them known as living beyond the boundaries of the community. The sociologist Kai Erikson notes, "When the community nominates someone to the deviant class, it is sifting a few important details out of the stream of behavior he has emitted and is in effect declaring that those details reflect the kind of person he 'really' is."[11] Thus, the single mother may be honest, kind, hardworking, devoted to her children, and even God-fearing; but if she has had a child outside of marriage, perhaps as a teenager, she is likely to be labeled deviant.

In the widespread and often vitriolic discussion of single motherhood, little mention is made of heroic single parents like the mother of the writer and musician James McBride, a white woman who raised twelve mixed-race children and sent them all to college, many to graduate school, to become doctors, teachers, scientists, and professors. As McBride writes, "She was the commander in chief of my house . . . the chief surgeon for bruises . . . war secretary . . . religious consultant ('Put God first'), chief psychologist . . . and financial adviser ('What's money if your mind is empty!')."[12] Or like the mother of Barack Obama, elected senator from Illinois in 2004, who describes the parent who raised him as "the single constant in my life." In his 1995 memoir *Dreams from My Father: A Story of Race and Inheritance*, Obama searches both for the father who left him to return to Kenya when he was 2 years old, a "boy's search for his father," and for "a workable meaning for his life as a black man." But while the central focus is on his absent father, Obama stresses in the preface to the 2004 edition—issued after his electrifying keynote speech before the Democratic National Convention that year catapulted him onto the national stage—that it was his mother who was central to the person he has become: "I know that she was the kindest, most generous spirit I have ever known, and that what is best in me I owe to her."[13] Similarly, Vivyan Adair, a professor of sociology at Hamilton College, recalls being raised by a poor mother who "even in the depths of poverty loved, nurtured, and somehow provided for her children with energy and panache." She points out that the omnipresent "dichotomous and hierarchical" narratives "orchestrate my story as one of chaos, pathology, promiscuity, illogic, and sloth. . . . They write the official story of who I am, but they are not and will never be, me."[14] "Energy and panache," the words with which Adair captures her mother's way of parenting, are almost never used to describe single mothers and certainly not poor ones.

Narratives that combine the ascribed characteristics of race, class, and ethnicity with the immediate causes of single motherhood have constructed a presumed hierarchy of single mothers—rising from poor women receiving public assistance who are often labeled "welfare mothers" and usually thought of as black, to working-class and middle-class mothers who are often assumed to be separated and divorced, to upper-middle-class widows usually thought of as white. Women seen as victims of particularly loutish or brutal behavior—spousal abuse, infidelity, abandonment, or lack of economic support—may be viewed with greater sympathy, but single mothers nevertheless are clearly assigned different ranks. This hierarchy of stigma segregates single mothers ideologically from the rest of the population by stereotyping and denigrating them as deviant at the same time as it separates them from one another. Thus, while single mothers are frequently perceived as an inferior group who harm their children and even pose a danger to the wider society, the various groups of single mothers often share little or no sense of solidarity. The barriers of class, race, ethnicity, and personal circumstance that divide us all keep them apart as well. Divorced, middle-class mothers struggling to find after-school care for their children may feel they have little in common with poor, inner-city women also struggling to find after-school care for their children. Widows trying to cope with unexpected tragedy generally do not perceive never-married young mothers who accidentally became pregnant as part of their reference group, though in all likelihood they similarly have experienced wrenching changes and profound sorrow in their lives. Moreover, because of the cultural propensity in the United States to see virtually all human behavior in individualistic terms, the economic, social, and cultural causes of single motherhood are frequently overlooked—both by the wider society and by single mothers themselves. The attitude in many quarters is that they have no one to blame but themselves.

It is ironic and particularly poignant that single mothers are being denigrated for what could be cited as their greatest strength: staying and caring for their children under almost all circumstances, frequently at great cost to themselves. While men all too often walk away—not only young, undereducated, underemployed husbands and fathers but employed solid citizens as well—the women stay and nurture, commonly while providing the family's sole support. Many are women who reject the alternative of abortion and instead commit themselves to twenty or more years of caregiving. Conditions may be nearly impossible, sadness may be inescapable, their dreams of higher education and professional work may need to be postponed or permanently discarded, but the women stay and cope as best they can. And yet they are criticized, castigated, and derided—for being responsible and devoted caregivers.

What does it do to people to be defined so negatively by the wider society? What does it mean to be defined by others very differently than one perceives oneself? Do the labeled, the stigmatized, internalize the negative version of themselves set out over and over again in the wider culture, or do they try to hold on to a more balanced, more accurate view of their lives? Does the relentless denigration cause individuals to become alienated from themselves, or does it cause them to become alienated from the larger society that mocks and derides them? One is reminded of the "double consciousness" experienced by blacks living in white America, as movingly described by W. E. B. Du Bois in *The Souls of Black Folk:* "the Negro is . . . gifted with second sight in this American world,—a world which yields him no true self-consciousness, but only lets him see himself through the revelation of the other world. It is a peculiar sensation, this double-consciousness, this sense of always looking at one's self through the eyes of others, of measuring one's soul by the tape of a world that looks on in amused contempt and pity. One ever feels his twoness."[15] According to Susan Stanford Friedman, a professor of English and women's studies at the University of Wisconsin–Madison, women are in the same situation: "Not recognizing themselves in the reflections of cultural representation, women develop a dual consciousness—the self as culturally defined and the self as different from cultural prescription."[16]

Single mothers are criticized not only because of their status but also because of how they arrived at that status. Most fundamentally, any family that does not include a man is faulted as deficient, defective, disrupted, broken. As one single mother of two, a widow, told me, "You're not seen as complete; you're not seen as a family unit. You're missing one of the points on a geometric figure and that makes you open and vulnerable." Mothers who become single through divorce are criticized for harming their children by divorcing and for supposedly acting on frivolous, shallow motives, selfishly putting their desires above their children's needs and well-being. Another theme in the litany against single mothers blames pregnancy outside of marriage on their unbridled sexuality. At the core of that accusation is the characterization of single mothers as irresponsible—for conceiving as teenagers or at inappropriate times in their lives, or for becoming involved with unreliable men who will not be stable husbands and fathers. In short, they should have known better, should have behaved differently. This view implies that these women have genuine choices—that they, for example, could have chosen a "responsible" man rather than an "irresponsible" one, one with a decent job rather than one with no job and few future prospects. The critics presume that young women should be able to figure out which men are "marriageable" and which are not good marriage material, to use the terms of the sociologist William Julius Wilson,[17] and that they can act on that knowledge. Impoverished women, particularly poor women of color, are castigated on multiple grounds—for not controlling their sexuality, for not choosing men more wisely, and for having children when they cannot afford to provide for them adequately.

But the poor and the near poor are not alone in being stereotyped and stigmatized. Single mothers in general have been blamed for many of the social problems afflicting American families. In her well-known article "Dan Quayle Was Right," Barbara Dafoe Whitehead claims that children who grow up in single-parent families are at greater risk for a wide range of emotional and behavioral difficulties than are those from two-parent families. Like many other critics of single-parent families, Whitehead uses the terms *stable* and *intact* to describe two-parent families and *disrupted* and *broken* to refer to single-parent families.[18] The sociologist David Popenoe echoes her when he declares that "because children from *broken* homes have a higher chance than those from *intact* families of forming *unstable* marriages of their own, the risks of family disruption are likely to accelerate" (emphasis added).[19] The language indicates which model is normative and which is outside the norm, which model is "right" and which is "wrong."

Popenoe's book *Life without Father* is subtitled *Compelling New Evidence That Fatherhood and Marriage Are Indispensable for the Good of Children and Society*. Indispensable? What about mother-only families when there is essentially no choice? What about families in which the father dies? What about families with a father who walks away, or is incarcerated, or is abusive to the mother or the children? What about gay women who wish to mother, to nurture, to raise children? While many social scientists may argue that children—and society—do better when couples are married and fathers are present, doesn't there need to be room for a variety of family structures that are not denigrated and stigmatized? What of the young woman who becomes pregnant and does not want to terminate the pregnancy, even though her boyfriend is not interested in playing a paternal role? What is she to do? Must she put her child up for adoption? What about the "mistake marriages," the name given by one of my interviewees to marriages that at least one partner knows is wrong almost from the start? An ideology that defines any family without a live-in biological father as inferior, unstable, and even harmful will make single mothers feel like outsiders and indeed encourage others to perceive them as beyond the pale. Though poor mothers of color are the group most denigrated by society at large, single mothers in virtually all categories are made to feel incomplete and inadequate, viewed in some instances as dangerous influences on their children and on society generally. The comparison of single mothers to drunk drivers quoted above makes clear exactly how potentially lethal some believe single mothers to be.

Many of the problems blamed on single mothers arise, in reality, from social and economic conditions beyond their control: low-wage jobs, inadequate education and job training, the effects of continuing racism and sexism, lack of affordable housing and accessible health care, and a social policy that blames individuals rather than attempting to equalize opportunity for our most disadvantaged citizens. Stigmatizing single mothers in ways that hold them responsible for widespread changes in the social fabric reinforces the view that the society does not need to examine its priorities or its social policy. This perspective suggests instead that individuals simply must change their values and their behavior. As Patricia Hill Collins points out, blaming poor women, particularly poor black women, for the underachievement of black children (and also for the problems that so many black men face) diverts attention from the political, economic, and social inequality they experience and is a classic example of "blaming the victim."[20] This narrative upholds the status quo by faulting those who have the least for not succeeding in American society. When the stigmatized group becomes the scapegoat for nearly every problem within a culture, society feels no imperative to examine its role in creating adverse outcomes or to improve social conditions: to raise the minimum wage, to develop more high-quality day care and after-school care, to create meaningful jobs at a living wage, or to encourage fathers to participate more actively in domestic life. The conventional wisdom is that those who step beyond the accepted boundaries of family life must be castigated and encouraged to return to the norms of earlier times; it is assumed that to make the lives of all families more workable, we must change the values and behavior of the "deviants" rather than modify elements of the social and economic structure.

Many who blame the problems of society on the rise in single-parent families compare female-headed families unfavorably to idealized images of two-parent families. According to the sociologists Sara McLanahan and Gary Sandefur, "When two biological parents share the same household, they can monitor the children and maintain parental control. . . . Having another parent around who cares about the child increases the likelihood that each parent will 'do the right thing' even when otherwise inclined." Moreover, "the two-parent family structure creates a system of checks and balances that both promotes parental responsibility and protects the child from parental neglect and, sometimes, abuse."[21] This kind of responsible and responsive parenting certainly occurs in many families, and the presence of two parents undoubtedly takes some of the burden off each parent and gives the child more than one caregiver and role model. But what about the family in which the father is rarely there—because he spends hours at work, or often travels out of town, or plays golf, or believes that parenting is best left to the mother? What about the family in which one or both parents are alcoholic or are emotionally unavailable because of depression or disinterest? What about the family in which a parent is physically or emotionally abusive? Comparing the average single-parent family with an attentive, caring, wise, near-perfect two-parent family only serves to emphasize the presumed gap between the "flawed" and the "ideal."

High divorce rates—they have remained around 50 percent for first marriages for several decades—have been used as another battering ram against single mothers. Several social scientists have alleged that divorce itself inflicts long-term trauma on children. In *The Unexpected Legacy of Divorce*, Judith Wallerstein, Julia Lewis, and Sandra Blakeslee claim that children never recover from the unfortunate consequences of divorce and that in fact the true impact may not become clear until they themselves reach adulthood. Others argue that while "divorce usually is brutally painful to a child . . . its negative long-term effects have been exaggerated to the point where we now have created a self-fulfilling prophecy."[22] But since divorce is widely believed to have particularly deleterious effects on children, many analysts directly criticize parents who divorce. Some blame the ease with which marriages dissolve at least in part on the current belief that marriage is a private matter between two people who, if they feel their relationship is not working, can simply decide to end it with little concern about their divorce's impact on anyone else or on society. As the sociologist Demie Kurz has observed, "those who write of 'family breakdown' believe that marriages are ending because men and women have forgone commitment to family life in order to pursue their own individual goals. To promote more happiness and well-being for family members, these analysts would like to strengthen commitments to the family as it is traditionally conceived."[23]

In their book *The Case for Marriage: Why Married People Are Happier, Healthier, and Better Off Financially*, Linda J. Waite and Maggie Gallagher suggest that in the current permissive and individualistic climate, many couples have relatively superficial reasons for divorcing. Fifty years ago couples were likely to stay together "for the sake of the children," but today, they claim, some choose to divorce simply because their marriage is "ho-hum" or "struggling." They add, "Adults may prefer to be joyously in love, but children don't much care whether parents zoom to heights of romantic ecstasy or not."[24] By resorting to overstatement and ridicule, Waite and Gallagher suggest that couples who decide to end their marriages are all too often shallow, immature, and self-absorbed. Among the women I interviewed, no one suggested that she did, should, or even might get a divorce because her relationship had become "ho-hum" or because she and her husband weren't "zoom[ing] to heights of romantic ecstasy." Reducing another's point of view to absurdity is a well-known and effective debater's device—as its frequent use in political discourse demonstrates—but perhaps one little suited to analyzing complex and often wrenching life decisions.

A lack of child-centeredness is also blamed for the high rates at which marriages dissolve. Looking back to eras when marriage was primarily an institution for procreation and for raising children, critics of divorce deplore what they see as children being "pushed from center stage."[25] But rather than pushing children from center stage, I believe, most parents today are being forced to deal with an enormously expanded stage. Perhaps what some analysts interpret as a shift away from a predominant focus on child rearing is more accurately viewed as obligatory multitasking. The mid-twentieth-century model of the traditional nuclear family—the mother who stayed at home and played the expressive role, nurturing the children, doing the domestic chores, and creating a haven in a heartless world; the father who played the instrumental role, earning the family's income outside the home—is, for the most part, a thing of the past. Almost all parents today have multiple responsibilities—child rearing, work, nurturing their relationship with one another, perhaps caring for other family members (particularly older parents), and, for some, community commitments as well. As they focus on the well-being of their child or children, parents, like all others in this complex society, must often play a number of other demanding roles.

One mother whom I interviewed describes the difficulties and dilemmas that attend being a single mother in the United States today. She talks about the different "vulnerabilities" that single mothers experience—lack of time, loss of income, the need to stay healthy and have health insurance, the fear of getting laid off. She emphasizes emotional vulnerability—"the loneliness, the sadness, the memories, the thoughts of lost youth, lost love, lost dreams"—and she speaks of social vulnerability, of "always being on the out, of always being judged, of being on the front line, like being in a foxhole 24–7." The sociologist Arlie Hochschild points out that while women's lives have changed dramatically in recent decades because of their massive entrance into the labor market, they "have undergone this change in a culture that has neither rewired its notion of manhood to facilitate male work-sharing at home, nor restructured the workplace so as to allow more control over and flexibility at work." Nor has society provided the kind of benefits and services that working families desperately need. Hochschild also notes that while more women are engaged in paid work, those belonging to the support system they might once have turned to for help with caregiving—grandmothers, aunts and neighbors—are themselves likely to be in the labor force. Thus, as the family shrinks in size, it is essentially "condensed and consolidated into the wife/mother, and increasingly now into the mother." Moreover, while divorce specifically and single parenthood generally create "a greater need for supportive community, it tends to reduce the size of that personal community."[26]

A number of factors influence how families establish their priorities. Many individuals and couples, concentrating on education, professional training, and career advancement, are postponing or eschewing childbearing. As women in particular have entered demanding professions in greater numbers, many decide to complete their education and training before they have children and perhaps to have fewer than was the norm in previous generations; in some instances, they choose to have no children. A physician I interviewed for a previous book told me about the difficulties of combining motherhood and work in a particularly competitive branch of academic medicine: "The male model *is* the working model. It never lets up. If you take time off, you'll get behind—in technical expertise, in publications, in climbing the academic ladder" (emphasis hers).[27] She and her husband, also a physician, have consequently decided not to have children.

Moreover, the recognition by men and women alike that most women must work so that families can pay their bills has made paid employment a central obligation in women's daily lives. As women work full-time, sometimes overtime or two jobs, their lives necessarily revolve around their jobs as well as around their family and home. In the mid-1990s it even became public policy to require poor women to leave their children in the care of others and find employment, often for wages that left them still mired in poverty.[28] Little discussion was heard at that time about the need for families to be child-centered. And once work becomes a necessity, women must also pursue continuing professional development. In order to provide their families with a decent standard of living and fulfill their desires to be professionals, several of the single mothers interviewed for this book felt compelled to complete their college degrees; some even went on to graduate education.

As researchers attempt to analyze the widespread breakdown of marriage, some level yet another criticism at young adults today, accusing them of looking for "a spouse who meets their needs for emotional closeness and intimacy" and for someone with whom they can have a "deep emotional and spiritual connection . . . for life" rather than someone who makes a good living or will be a suitable partner in parenting.[29] These critics suggest that young people's pursuit of an individualistic, romantic ideal may be fueling the high divorce rate, and they argue that putting the well-being of children first would provide firmer grounding for long-lasting relationships. But young people have many reasons to view marriage as a long-term relationship with someone with whom they feel a "deep emotional and spiritual connection" rather than as a partnership entered into primarily in order to create and raise children. The enormous emphasis on individualism in the United States; the media's relentless depiction of relationships based on romantic love, sex, and individual choice; and the increased disconnection of young adults from community life inevitably lead people to think in terms of their individual needs and wants rather than their larger responsibilities to society. In addition, with most people in the United States expected to live well into their 70s, couples who marry in their mid- to late 20s may have the good fortune to spend a half century or more together. If they have two children two or three years apart, couples are likely to spend perhaps twenty to twenty-five years in child rearing, including years when their children are young adults still in school and thus still dependent on them. While parents may remain close to their children throughout their lives, perhaps doting on grandchildren, this scenario can leave the couple an additional twenty-five years when children are no longer at the center of their lives. Choosing a partner who shares one's values, interests, and needs for "emotional closeness and intimacy" would seem to be very wise.

Although parents certainly need to devote their energies and commitment to rearing their children, to work, to caring for other family members, to participating in the larger society, and to nurturing their relationship with one another, attending to their own emotional, intellectual, and social needs is also crucial. The well-being of children is intimately connected to the well-being of parents. A mother who is not meeting at least some of her own needs will eventually, I believe, be unable to meet her children's needs—she simply will not have enough to give. Focusing on the well-being of children to the exclusion of the well-being of parents, particularly mothers, is both shortsighted and self-defeating. Much of our lives, it has been said, we strive to balance the conflict between the domestic ties that bind and the equally important duty to the self.

Except for relatively few households, the child-centered family is an anachronism, a throwback to the 1950s, when images of middle-class white women in aprons making tuna casseroles for dinner and giving their children milk and cookies after school were ubiquitous. These powerful images are kept alive by nostalgia, guilt, old movies, and television reruns of *Leave It to Beaver* and *Father Knows Best*. A more realistic picture of family life today—or at least upper-middle-class family life—is given in novels such as Allison Pearson's *I Don't Know How She Does It: The Life of Kate Reddy, Working Mother*. A London-based, 35-year-old hedge fund manager and mother of two, Kate juggles business trips to the United States and a 5-year-old daughter who asks plaintively, "Are you putting me to bed tonight? Is Mummy putting me to bed tonight? Are you? Who is putting me to bed tonight? Are you, Mum, are you?"

She needs to write "nine fund reports . . . by Friday" and bring mince pies that look homemade to a nativity play and Christmas party at her daughter's school. She learns she must make an emergency trip to Stockholm to hold a client's hand exactly when she was planning to finish her Christmas shopping, buy the tree, and prepare for Christmas dinner. Her list of New Year's resolutions includes "Adjust work-life balance for healthier, happier existence," "Spend more time with your children," "Call friends, hope they remember you," and "Sex?"[30]

And Kate Reddy is married—to a devoted, understanding, successful architect who is even able and willing to cook dinner with some frequency. Moreover, she has a relatively reliable, caring nanny whom the children like. Nonetheless, Kate's life is often a nightmare—too little time, too much to do, and the ever-present guilt that she is not doing all of it better, particularly the mothering. In the middle of the night, when she's pounding the store-bought mince pies with a rolling pin to make them look homemade only three hours after returning from the United States, her husband tells her that no one expects her to produce anything for the school event. She responds, "Well, I expect me to."[31] But imagine if Kate were a single mother trying to survive day-to-day on her own, with (in all likelihood) only one income, no partner with an equal sense of responsibility and commitment to the children, and almost surely no nanny. Where are the engaging, hilarious, and sophisticated novels or films or television programs about the single waitress, nurse's aide, hairdresser, or social worker working long, hard hours and taking care of her children? Why do we care when she's a married hedge fund manager— or a physician, lawyer, adviser to the president of the United States, or vice president of a Fortune 500 company—and not when she's a single mother struggling to do it all on a limited budget?

The impulse to stigmatize single mothers and blame them for almost all of the social problems faced by Americans today is driven by the belief that individuals have little influence on and are little influenced by the culture or society around them. This way of thinking minimizes or completely negates the impact of continuing inequalities based on race, gender, and class. It dismisses the effects of joblessness, inadequate education, and poverty on individual opportunity, on decision making, on feelings of optimism or despair, on hope for the future or feelings of entrapment. It holds the individual responsible for social trends and denies that such global phenomena as industrialization, urbanization, an economic downturn, and the technological revolution affect people's lives. It places the onus for changing society and correcting social problems on individuals and families while denying the need to create more humane social and economic conditions. Such an outlook dovetails perfectly with the ideology of the American dream, the insistence that any individual can be successful in the United States if only she or he works hard enough and lives an upright life.

Until we recognize that virtually all families—affluent, middle-class, working-class, and poor, two-parent as well as single-parent—similarly require adequate economic resources, opportunity, human services, and emotional support, we are unlikely to see their problems and needs clearly and address them effectively. And until we move beyond the stigma and the stereotypes and recognize the often incredible strengths of our family units, acknowledging that millions of them care for one another "with energy and panache," to use Vivyan Adair's words, we will not respect them enough to take their experiences and their perspectives seriously. Contrary to the omnipresent negative stereotypes, most of the women interviewed for this study have acted with uncommon courage, resilience, and strength when faced with the exceedingly difficult problems of single motherhood. They work long hours, nurture with little respite, and still manage not only to survive but to live creative lives and raise children who themselves contribute to the larger society.

Rachel Brownstein, the author of *Becoming a Heroine: Reading about Women in Novels*, points out that many nineteenth-century novels center on the "marriage plot," which focuses on "finding validation of one's uniqueness and importance by being singled out among all other women by a man. The man's love is proof of the girl's value. . . . Her quest is to be recognized in *all* her significance, to have her worth made real by being approved. When . . . this is done, she is transformed: her outward shape reflects her inner self, she is a bride, the very image of a heroine" (emphasis hers).[32] Many of the women depicted in this book may well have thought, as women for centuries have been taught to think, that their uniqueness, their importance, would be validated or confirmed by a man's love, that their value was dependent on his approval. Once they realized that this traditional plot was not going to be the story of their lives—that the men had abandoned them or died or that the relationship was too problematic to survive or that they themselves needed to walk away—these women had to find other ways of structuring their lives, of proving their value, of being recognized, of validating their importance, not just in the eyes of others but especially in their own eyes. They embarked on a new quest, one in which they were the central characters in their lives. In creating new paths for themselves, in taking genuine risks, and in combining, often under very difficult circumstances, doing and caring, many have been truly heroic.

In *Psyche as Hero: Female Heroism and Fictional Form*, Lee R. Edwards defines a hero as one who "possesses vision, daring and power: to . . . break with the past; endure hardship; risk death and survive—at least in spirit. The hero dances in the spotlight."[33] Many of these women indeed possess vision, daring, and power. They are willing to break with the past and certainly to endure hardship. They validate themselves through their own actions in both the private and the public spheres and have become the central characters, the heroines, of their lives. But the prevailing stereotypes about single mothers serve both to obscure their real stories and to isolate them from the wider society. Their narratives tell a very different tale and perhaps can help end that isolation. In order for the heroine truly to "dance in the spotlight," not only must she realize her centrality in her own life, thereby taking charge of it, but the wider society must also recognize the role she is playing. The following chapter illustrates both the diversity and the complexity of the lives of single mothers and also makes clear that rather than living at the margins of society, as some hostile depictions suggest, these women exemplify the finest American values: courage, determination, commitment to others, and independence of spirit. Despite their difficult and unexpected life circumstances, these mothers struggle and find ways, step by step, to create secure, loving, and meaningful lives for themselves and their children. Rather than being stigmatized, they should be celebrated and indeed applauded.

2

Genuine Family Values

————

I am a strong person. Even as a child I knew I was a strong person.
Soledad Martinez, 46-year-old mother of two

Soledad Martinez is a 46-year-old Latina woman. She begins by talking about her childhood:

I grew up in an "intact" family. I was one of seven children, the third from the youngest. My mother was a housewife; my father owned his own business. When I was 10, we lived in El Barrio [East Harlem] and I could look over to Columbia University across town and to me it looked like a church. I said to myself, "I'm going to go there some day." It seemed like heaven.

When I was 10, we moved to Puerto Rico but it didn't work so we returned to the same block, the same public school.

When I was 16, my father left. The store was burned out and he just disappeared. We never saw him again. There were rumors that he had fallen in love with a 25-year-old customer. My parents had been married for twenty-five years. When he left, it was overwhelming for my mother. But at the same time she learned a family secret—that my father had sexually abused my older sister, who was mentally retarded. When I saw my father touching my sister and told my mother, she smacked me. I think she was in denial but that somewhere she knew. The upside to his leaving was that he was not there to abuse the girls any longer.

My mother had never worked; after the fire in the store the Red Cross referred her to welfare. We received welfare for one year; then my mother worked as a home attendant. And I worked and helped her.

By now the older children were grown and the only ones left at home were the three youngest children and my retarded sister.

When Soledad was 23, she got married. She and her husband had a son, who is now 23, and a daughter, who is now 21. After that she went to college full-time, received her B.A., and then went for a graduate degree from that school that had once looked like heaven. She recalls that while she was in school she didn't sleep many nights, because she had to study. If she had a paper or a test, she could not count on her husband to help with the children. In fact, she says, "He would start with his nonsenses when I had a paper or exam but I said, I'm going to do it."

> I was the only one in my family going to college. Being poor when we were growing up, the kids made fun of me and my poor clothes; I vowed that when I get older, I'm going to college and I'm going to get a job and I'm going to buy beautiful clothes.
>
> I am a strong person. Even as a child I knew I was a strong person. I was the oldest of the youngest. There were the four older children and then the three of us. I knew I wanted to go to college and become something. None of my siblings went to college. My brother is a truck driver; my sister works in a bank. It has to be inside you.

Soledad describes her husband as an ex-marine who was "very controlling." She says that he was "abusive" toward their son. "My son had a high activity level and needed to be busy" but her husband felt that a child should be perfect and behave just as he thought appropriate. Not only was her son frightened of his father, but so was she. "He told me if I left he would kill me and would take away my kids. And he was emotionally abusive. He said I am a nobody, that I wasn't attractive, that I was flat-chested and had no butt, that I was the ugliest thing in the world."

According to Soledad, her husband was extremely and irrationally jealous. She spent most of her time in the house, leaving only to go directly to school and then back home. He would check the gas gauge when she went to her classes to see if she was going anywhere else, so she "just went directly back and forth to avoid problems and fights." She continues:

> When I told him I was going to leave, I didn't even think of the consequences. In May 1984, I graduated with my master's degree. By July I had my own apartment and a job working with children in a local hospital. I always wanted to save children—perhaps because of my own home life. That was my goal. Once I left my husband, I said, "Now what?" I moved to an empty apartment. I had to provide for myself and my kids. I was earning only $21,000 a year.
>
> When I left him, I didn't take anything. I only took clothing and toys. I would do it all myself. Sometimes I didn't have enough for myself but every Sunday after church we had breakfast at McDonald's. It was a treat. It cost $5.00 but the kids still remember it today.

Soledad and her husband were divorced within three months, but they fought for a year and a half over child support and custody of the children. She describes that very difficult period:

> He filed for divorce first and got temporary custody. The kids were 8 and 6. It was the toughest time of all and it was all due to the neglect of my lawyer. He didn't file some papers he was supposed to file and then he died and I had to get another lawyer. The kids were so confused. He was feeding them negative information about me. We had a real tug-of-war. So we went through family court and the psychiatrist said they must give custody to the mother and he was only to have supervised visitation rights.
>
> During this period I had anxiety attacks. I was even suicidal. All due to the neglect of a lawyer. Eventually, my husband told me, "I was just doing it to get you back. It [his taking custody of the children] was never going to happen." Eventually the judge gave his decision and the kids were escorted [to my] home by the police. After that, their father didn't see them for a year and a half.

For the next few years, Soledad spent all of her time either working or spending time with the children. There was "no time for me, no time for going out, dating, clubbing." Her mother helped by taking care of the children after school and during school vacations.

Soledad met her present husband at a Christmas party at the hospital where they both worked. The night of the Christmas party, she recalls, they went back to her apartment and played with the kids. Later she and he talked for hours and fell asleep "fully dressed" on the bed. The next morning, her daughter said, "Mommy, there's a man in your bed," and she responded, "Don't worry. I'm going to marry him." Five months later, they were married. As she says, "It just worked. Their father has next to no presence."
Soledad describes her children:

> My son went to college and got his degree; my daughter did the same and is now in graduate school. And I've instilled in my daughter to be a strong woman. She has a boyfriend but she's very strong with him.
>
> I have good kids. I never, ever, ever gave them freedom. I always needed to know where they were and who their friends were.

When people generalize about single mothers, are they talking about Soledad Martinez? Are they describing the young girl from El Barrio whose father deserted the family, whose mother was forced to go on welfare, who vowed that when she grew up she would make a different life and did? Are they describing an abused wife who achieves her dream of an education, becomes a professional, and makes a second, happy, successful marriage? No doubt their parents' conflict and divorce was difficult for her two children, but would their parents' staying together have been better? Should Soledad have stayed in an abusive, restrictive, and eventually loveless marriage to ensure that the children would continue to live with both parents? Soledad is one of the many faces of single motherhood: brave, smart, willing to take risks, devoted to her children, able to recognize a mistake and to take a chance on starting again.

Linda Powell, a 27-year-old African American woman, presents a very different picture of single motherhood. She speaks easily and fluently about her teenage years:

I grew up just outside of New York City. When I was 14, I got pregnant but my mother didn't know and we moved down South. I always said I'm never going to have kids; I was going to be a registered nurse. But I was going out with her father, had sex and got pregnant. I was scared out of my wits. I got good grades so I was not supposed to get pregnant.

My mom and dad were divorced. I was the middle child. The oldest was my brother and he's dead; my sister got her B.A. and is now getting a master's degree. She's been working two jobs to make all that happen.

My mother never talked to me about sex. We cut school to do it. I really didn't even know what sex was. My mother and father were strict. It was school and church but my friends and I were blossoming. The kids were flirting with us.

When I didn't get my period, I took myself to Planned Parenthood. I told the woman, "I'm going to have an abortion. My boyfriend is going to pay for it." She asked me, "Are you sure?" "I'm sure." So I told my boyfriend (he was 15 at the time), "I'm going to have an abortion" and that he had to pay for it. He said, "You're going to have the baby. You're not going to have an abortion." He told me his mother was opposed to abortion, that his sister had a baby and that they didn't believe in abortion. I never said anything to my mother.

I tried everything that summer. I tried falling downstairs. I tried dating men to get money. I was scared. It was the fear of telling my mother. And my father! They were always about school. I cried every day. I had no prenatal care until I told my mom. I was stressed out. I slept a lot. I didn't even show.

One day I had to tell my mother. I had made some friends down South so I asked a friend to come with me. First I packed my stuff because I thought she was going to kick me out. Instead, she hugged me. At first, she didn't believe it but then she said, "There were rumors you were pregnant. If you had told me, we could have worked things out."

Linda gave birth to a daughter in December; she stayed with her mother down South for six months and then decided to move back to the New York area to live with her godparents. She says that they could not register her for high school because they weren't her real parents but that

"God worked it out." She became an emancipated minor. But then the Health Department found very high levels of lead-based paint in the apartment in which they were living and her 11-month-old baby was found to have serious lead poisoning. The baby was hospitalized for a week to "get the lead out." After she was released from the hospital, they couldn't return to her godparents' apartment, so the baby's paternal grandmother offered to let them move in with her.

Linda continues:

> By then I hadn't gone to high school for a whole year. I went to an alternative high school. I got on social services. I stayed with her [the baby's grandmother] for about a year. The baby went to day care. Her father was in jail—I think for robbery—something stupid. So then I told her I didn't want to stay there anymore—teenage stuff.
>
> So I went to the Department of Social Services. They put us up in a shelter and it was horrible. And God just gave me a favor. We were in the shelter for three weeks. Usually you're there for six months to a year but I told them I'm basically trying to make it for me and my child. I don't smoke; I don't drink. I've never done drugs. So the social worker found me an apartment. It was transitional housing. I was going to school. My child went to day care. I graduated high school in 1993. God has blessed my life beyond measure.

After graduating from high school, Linda attended community college for a year while holding down a job. When she learned about a one-year licensed practical nurse program, she applied, took the entrance exam, and was admitted. She describes how she managed financially:

> All this was before welfare reform.[1] I was getting $218 a month, $100 worth of food stamps a month, and Medicaid. You really don't know what God can do for you. But it was hard! It was hard. [She becomes tearful.]
>
> Then I started going to the LPN program in a town not too far from here. Every day I put my child in day care and took the train. The program lasted from 8 to 3 every day. I did that program for a whole

year. Then I took the state boards, passed the first time, and got my license. At that point I started working in a nursing home. I was 19.

And I was going to church. I was truckin' at the church, too. Three days a week. Me and my daughter.

Currently, Linda works six days a week—five days at a school-based clinic and one day at the nursing home that first offered her a job after she received her license. At the school-based clinic she works with high school students who come in seeking treatment for "STDs [sexually transmitted diseases], pregnancy tests, everything." She frequently does classroom presentations in which she tells her story. She comments with real feeling, "I identify so much with them—not just the pregnancy. Some have already dropped out."

Linda explains what has helped her along the way:

Church is a most encouraging place. You know how people go into therapy? Church is therapy. God has blessed my child. My church has encouraged me so much—to trust God and have faith in God. That's what's keeping me through the storm. I read my Bible, read my scripture and he brings me through.

My pastors and how they encourage me! "You can make it! You get up!" My mom and my dad have also supported me. The foundation is from home. My mother kept food on the table. My father worked two jobs. He was a go-getter. They haven't been together since I was 11. My father moved to Alabama with his new wife.

When I was growing up, we couldn't watch TV, we couldn't go into the refrigerator until our homework was done. We grew up in the church but now we're more into it than our parents.

My daughter's [paternal] grandmother goes to this church. As a child I was reading my Bible. I got baptized and I've been in the church ever since. I love the life. If you're going to say you're a Christian, you have to trust in God in spite of how things look. We're close as a church. It's a love church. They open their arms. They would give me clothes. They have been so lovable to me and my kid. It's an apostolic church. I'm one of the nurses in church; I'm an assistant pastor, an usher, and at times I teach Sunday school. My daughter sings in the choir. She's been going since she was five months old.

Linda talks about her daughter and her daughter's father:

My daughter is now 12. Her father grew up. He doesn't give me any money per se but he calls her every day. But he does not give me any money; that's the part I cannot stand. His mother and I are like this. [She crosses her fingers.] And she has a host of aunts, a host of cousins; she has two grandmothers and a father but I'm so independent.

Relationship with her father? Oh, no, honey! We haven't been together since we were 14 and 15. I just deal with him because of her. Other men? Because I'm so independent, that's a big wall. I'm dating now but you can't tell me nothing. I can be stubborn. He's 40 and he works at a supermarket. He's worked there forever and a day. He makes good money. He comes with me to church. We don't have to get married. Me—I'm more goal-oriented. I think about what he could have done. He's so smart. He takes us out. He spends money on us. He's 40 and he hasn't gotten married yet. I'm so independent. Even when I need money, you'd never know. If it doesn't go my way, goodbye—see you later. He does better than me. He talks to me. You have to talk it out. I'd break up with you in five minutes if it doesn't go my way. I've been on my own since I was 15. I want to get my RN and then I'll figure it out. She's going to be a teenager so she'll need to have more. After that, someone will come along.

As a single mom, you can make it. You need to have faith. It can happen for you. Where there's a will, there's a way. You might have to have an '88 car like I do. You might have to take the bus, the train. You lay down and have sex and have a baby and you can make it. You can be somebody!

The life of Linda Powell vividly demonstrates the inaccuracy of judgments based on stereotypical thinking about single mothers. To those who see the world in dichotomous terms—black and white, good and bad, functional and dysfunctional—Linda Powell is an African American, working-class unmarried mother who got pregnant at 14 and whose daughter is all too likely to turn out badly, probably with an unmarried teenage pregnancy of her own. But in her church and at work Linda is, to quote Jesse Jackson, "somebody." At church, which is an extremely important social environment for her, she is a "nurse," an assistant pastor, an usher, and sometimes a teacher in the Sunday school. These are clearly high-status roles in a setting that Linda and those close to her respect. At her job, moreover, she is a medical professional, a teacher, a role model, a respected member of the staff doing work valued by the larger community. Linda is indeed an African American, working-class, unmarried mother who got pregnant at the age of 14, but she is not the stereotype that those labels conjure up. She is, rather, a courageous, resilient, highly intelligent young woman who is determined to contribute to society and to achieve her personal dreams while raising a healthy, productive daughter.

Carolyn Miller took a very different path to single motherhood. A 42-year-old white mother of two, Carolyn Miller lives in a upper-middle-class suburb of predominantly single-family homes within easy commuting distance of New York City. She begins by talking about her life:

> I grew up in a suburb outside of New York. I have one older sister who lives in the Midwest. She was divorced for ten years and then moved there with her new husband. My parents have been together forty-five years. They are sad that their daughters are not as fortunate.
>
> I went to public schools and then to Boston University, where I majored in English lit and anthropology. I spent my junior year at Oxford and it was wonderful! I couldn't decide between law school and advertising but since law school required three years, I thought I would try advertising for a couple of years. I still think about law school but the children perceive me as a full-time mother. I can work here at home and pick them up from school at three o'clock but I'm also an adult in the world. I can go to teacher conferences in the middle of the day. It works for me.

Carolyn met her husband five years after college. He also came from the New York area and also worked in advertising. She says of that period of her life, "We both loved living in New York City. It should have worked. We dated two years; we were engaged one year. I had a *great* apartment on the West Side so we lived there. I always thought he married me for my apartment!" After living in Manhattan for three or four years, Carolyn and her husband decided to "start getting pregnant" but to look for a house first. They found the house (the one she now lives in), the mortgage was approved, and in her words she "got pregnant—like—the next day. I was 30." She adds, "The years in New York were the best years of our marriage! No children. No mortgage. No car. No lawn to mow. We only moved here because of starting a family. We didn't want to raise children in the city. It was a trade-off."

Carolyn had planned to take a four-month maternity leave, get a nanny, and go back to work. Her husband's income alone could not support them. But after she had the baby she realized that "there is no way I could leave him but I'm enough of a feminist to know that's not a good thing to do—to ask them to hold my job and then not go back but I felt I owed my child more than I owed my job." Carolyn solved her dilemma by starting to work part-time at home. As she says, "I'm a very responsible person. I can't turn my back on a job. I was fulfilling a commitment but it had to be from home. It had to be on my terms." She continues:

> What led to the divorce? Three things happened. Everybody has a point at which they reach their capacity. He reached that point when we were a married couple living in the city. He didn't have a dependent wife, dependent children, a mortgage. People used to say he looks like he has the weight of the world on his shoulders but, in actuality, more and more adult responsibilities fell on me. I'm here [at home] and can supervise things. It's no big deal for me to work up a budget, pay bills, watch for when the car needs an oil change. Not a biggie.
>
> He would mow the lawn. He would clean up after I cooked. But I would have to assign the chores. I pieced together the child care. I felt like I was doing huge amounts. I was doing everything. I refinanced the mortgage; he showed up to sign the papers. I don't think he's lazy; he's not a lazy person.

Carolyn feels that the responsibilities of living in a house with a mortgage and having a family to support created the first set of stresses that led to the breakup of her marriage. The second thing that happened was the death of her mother-in-law soon after being diagnosed with ovarian cancer. According to Carolyn, her husband went into a "tailspin" after that. "He was not coping. He would scream around the house. I finally got him into therapy." She continues:

> I thought therapy would restore him to the person he was, but it didn't. It wasn't a horrible marriage but after that it wasn't a good marriage. There was a detachment. He retreated. He never was very engaged with the kids. He worked near their school but never went to teacher conferences. He never went to back-to-school night. When I would ask about it, he would say, "Don't tell me what to do. Don't pressure me."
>
> The thing I really resented was that he would come home fifteen minutes after their bedtime. If I put them to bed later, he would come home later. I felt he was avoiding the children. He could have been home; he worked so close. I felt he was deliberately avoiding them.

The third thing that happened involved a Little League game. On a day that both sons had sports events, she took one to kickball while her husband took the other to baseball. She describes what happened:

> There weren't enough kids at the Little League game so they were going to play informally. The coach said it was up to each family to decide if the child needed to wear a helmet. My husband said my son did not need to wear a helmet and he got hit on the head. Then my husband did bad things. He told my son not to tell me about what happened and he didn't say anything either. The next day my son felt dizzy and he still didn't say anything. He could have had a concussion or a real head injury. How could he not have taken him to the doctor or to the hospital?
>
> After that he totally retreated. It went on for months. He wouldn't eat with us. He wouldn't go on vacation with us. If we were upstairs, he would go downstairs. I was trying to find another therapist for him. [He had stopped going to the therapist he saw after his mother's death.] It was affecting his work. It was affecting his friendships.

When Carolyn found a therapist, she asked her husband if he would be willing to go; he responded, "I don't need anything." When she asked if he would be willing to go to a therapist with her, he at first agreed. The night before they were supposed to go, however, he told her that he was leaving, that she would get a letter from his lawyer the next day, and that she had better do what it said. She recalls,

> He left me. In April 2000. I wondered, what is he going to do? He has retreated to his bachelor life. Here in this town. He has no responsibilities. He's in his comfort zone of responsibility. It's not a marriage in which there was infidelity or anything. It was like he had an early midlife crisis.
>
> In two days he emptied the marital bank accounts, got an apartment, moved things over to the apartment, and redirected his paycheck from direct deposit into our account to his account. He left me the mortgage, the summer house lease, the bill for summer camp.
>
> He then became a deadbeat dad. He paid nothing. His lawyer said, "Don't you buy them so much as a quart of milk," so my lawyer sued him. He asked for custody 51 percent of the time. He was not set up to have custody of the children. It was a bad faith attempt of using the children [as a bargaining chip].
>
> The judge gave me sole custody, temporary sole custody, and also determined child support. And we are supposed to share medical expenses. Since then he has paid on time and to the penny accurate but he is not contributing to the medical expenses. There are so many fathers who are worse!

The court appointed a law guardian to conduct a forensic evaluation, which they needed in order to get the recommendation that the children should live with their mother and visit their father; it took eight months and cost $20,000. Although she works at home part-time, Carolyn says with a sense of outrage, "And I'm a stay-at-home mom!"

> They talked with and tested the kids. The kids were put in the middle; they were being asked to pick between their parents. If he had not been a deadbeat dad, none of this would have happened. He's not looking

out for the kids' needs. The judge asked him if he's going to sue for permanent custody and he responded, "I haven't decided yet." But that has to be decided before everything else. Money has to flow in the direction of the child. If he gets the children, he would get the house. It would be financial long-term revenge.

I never would have believed he would be this way. There is no need for it to have been like this. I've tried to be civilized. Until recently he had daytime-only visitation. He wouldn't let our older son shower. He wouldn't let him do his homework. He was into demanding his rights. Homework was using his time. But a parent has obligations to his children. He hasn't allowed them a play date. He never takes them to the barbershop. Parenting means looking to what the children need. It's a learning curve, and I've got to give him time to learn how to be a parent.

Carolyn describes how she has handled the separation within the community:

At first I wasn't public at all about what was going on. I was very, very quiet about it. Once he moved out and we were suing each other, there was no going back. I'm basically a very private person and this community has a very small-town-y feeling. You don't want to be bad-mouthing your spouse. A few very good friends and family know what's going on and they think he's a piece of shit. I don't want to pull people into the whirlpool, but everyone is taking my side! Everyone who knows is not speaking to him anymore. He is choosing to remain in this town. If he behaved differently, it would save his own face. It's not in his best interests to act like this. He is more revenge-bound than self-protective.

Although Carolyn says that she has "good friends, family, a book group, and a Boy Scout group," she has in the few weeks before her interview felt the separation more keenly:

Until recently, they were with me on Friday and Saturday nights but now he has them every other weekend and it's hitting me very hard. When the three of us were together, we didn't feel like a broken family. When they are with him for the weekend, I'm alone. It's a very hard transition. I didn't cry when he left; now I'm getting a delayed reaction. I had to be strong for the kids but this has broken our family. I can't depend too much on the kids. My older son especially needs to live his own life.

I am feeling isolated and lonely. I feel all alone. I'm working at home so I am alone a lot. But I'm a happy-spirited person. I'm not going to wallow in it. I'll give myself three weeks to feel bad. I can't be dependent on the kids for everything. They need for me to have fun.

Social life? Well, recently we were invited to a party as a family, so I show up with my kids and I'm assuming that everybody is part of a nuclear family. I'm talking to this guy and we're having a nice conversation and I assume his wife is talking to someone else and then he says that he wishes his children were there but they are with their mother this weekend. So he called me and we went out to dinner on Saturday night. It was my first date in seventeen years. He has two boys, too. It was so nice. He did the driving, picked the place (actually he gave me a choice of two places); he made it happen. It was a pleasant evening with a pleasant person. My friends have been offering to fix me up but I waited a year and a half. I didn't want to do anything wrong, but do I have to be a nun? It did a little bit toward restoring my confidence. He placed a good-night call to his kids and three-quarters of an hour later I placed a good-night call to my kids. I had checked him out with my hostess and with a friend who knows him. He is truly divorced and a good guy.

So many people have offered to fix me up. It was flattering but I was never ready. Now I think maybe my baggage won't keep people from being interested in me. After a while you feel invisible.

I am an overachiever and I feel I have failed at something. I thought I would be in this marriage forever. We feel betrayed by our expectations. I'm not a "This is my second husband" kind of person. I feel we are responsible for our own happiness. I did not *ever* expect to be divorced, but I had a very lonely year before we separated. After all this I realized how little partnering I had had.

I know I'm strong enough to do the single mother thing but I don't want to be alone. I'm trying to figure out how to not see myself only as a mother. I'm as good a mother as I know how to be. Now that I'm not a wife, I'm in transition. I don't want to get my identity only through other people.

Not only are all single mothers not alike, as the dominant images would have us believe, but the broad range of their individual circumstances reflects the wide variation within the society at large. Soledad Martinez left her abusive husband and set about making a different life for herself and her children, but Carolyn Miller's husband left her. After increasingly retreating from his roles of husband and father, he returned to near-bachelor status in the same community, leaving them to reconstruct their lives and identities without him. And they are still adjusting to their new status and to new rhythms of life. Even though their marriage existed almost in name only, Carolyn clearly viewed his departure as a profound rejection from which she is still recovering.

Rose Conti presents a very different history of becoming and being a single mother. A 64-year-old white woman, she lives in a medium-sized city in the New York metropolitan area and begins by talking about how much she loves her work for a nonprofit organization. Actually, when she was younger, she had thought she would be a teacher because she had majored in psychology at college and minored in education. But her life did not develop at all as she had expected. She describes her early years:

> I grew up in the Bronx. I had two older brothers, one ten years older and the other six years older. Along with my father, it was like having three fathers. They were an enormous influence on me. They were always there for me. They both went to college—one went into advertising, the other became an engineer. One of my brothers told his wife, "My sister is my best friend."
>
> We were an Italian American family. My father owned a gas station in Westchester County. He had come here from Italy when he was 27. When I think about it, I think what courage—to leave his entire family and come to a strange country. My mother was born here.
>
> I graduated from a small college in Westchester. My husband and I dated in high school. He went to the Naval Academy and became a naval officer. After we married, we moved to Newport, Rhode Island, and I became a service wife. I had taught after college but when I got to Newport I realized I couldn't do what I wanted to do. I couldn't

teach because we might be shipped out at any time, so I became a substitute teacher. I thought my career was over.

Meanwhile, I was pregnant. I was due October 19 and delivered October 24 but the ship had left days before. As I'm on the gurney, I think, what's wrong with this picture? In the movies, he's there with the roses but in reality he's 90 miles offshore and forgot to have the roses sent. He saw the baby for the first time in January.

After a difficult miscarriage while her husband was at sea, Rose had a second daughter, two years after the first. Her husband was hoping then to go to graduate school, but since he spoke Italian, he was offered a position at the Italian Naval Academy in Livorno. They discussed it; and "since the sun never set on an argument or a decision," they decided at 4 A.M. one morning that he should take the position in Italy and do graduate school later. Rose describes what happened next:

> A year and a half after we arrived in Livorno my husband was supposed to participate in a regatta. It was postponed a couple of times because of choppy seas but finally in March 1966 the regatta left. Two days later there was a knock on my door and naval men were standing outside. The boat had capsized and all the men were lost except for one who survived. The navy was all set to pack up our stuff and fly us home but I wanted them to find him. They searched and searched with boats and floodlights but found nothing. Finally, we were whisked off to Rome and then to New York.

Rose and her daughters, ages 4 and 2, stayed with her mother for a while, but she didn't feel she could stay there indefinitely. She had a good friend back in Norfolk, Virginia, who urged her to go there, and she did. It was "a way of standing on my own." She and her older daughter, who was having problems, went into therapy. She describes herself as "catatonic. It wasn't the way it was supposed to be." She continues:

> I looked to the church for help but didn't find it there. I went to a priest and talked to him about what had happened, and he told me to think of myself as Mary.

Finally, on Memorial Day I had a dream and in the dream my husband spoke to me and said he was coming home to me. Later that day the navy men showed up. They had found my husband. A fisherman near Livorno had set up his nets and they found the body. I called my therapist and said, "Son-of-a-bitch, my husband is dead!"

After that, Rose and her children moved back to the New York area. She says she realized there was no reason for her to be in Norfolk; she wasn't "one of them" any more. She became a teacher but after her second year became aware that the job left her with nothing at the end of the day for her own children. Then, the manager of a store that sold cooking utensils suggested she work there. When he asked her, "What do you know about copper?" she replied, "I'm teachable."

Following that job she worked for five years for the college she herself had attended; she moved into a house, using her husband's naval benefits as the down payment. Rose explains how they managed financially: "When my family was concerned about us financially, I would say, 'I'm not struggling. We're fine.' The girls knew we couldn't have everything. When I say we can't have it, we can't have it. They both worked as they got older. They knew if you want this, you do that." Even though her daughter could have attended the college without paying tuition if Rose had continued to work there, she left that job when she felt she had accomplished in it all that she could. She then began working in marketing with a business partner who later became her "companion." She says, "We never married. We really worked well together. We had ten ideas in ten minutes. We had a good thing going." He has since passed away.

Her husband has continued to occupy a central place in the lives of Rose her and her children. She recalls, "The day my daughter was getting married, my husband came to me in a dream. He was in his dress whites and said he would be with us. I told my daughter, 'Your father was at your wedding.' I made him very real to the children. I've been back to

Livorno several times. The Italians put up a memorial to the men who died in that regatta."

Both of Rose's daughters are professional women; both are married— according to Rose, "to men like their father—strong, silent." She talks about getting support from her friends and her family—her brothers, her sister-in-law, and her mother:

> My mother was a big support. She took care of the girls, cooked extra, told me to bring the laundry over and always had it done when I got back. I feel as though I've been blessed. This summer I'm going to Italy with my brother and sister-in-law. We're going to Livorno.
>
> People around me were always saying I have to get married—have to have someone to take care of me. But I had elements of strength even before my husband died. I belong wherever I want to be. I always had to be a winner. I gotta do what I gotta do.

When asked why she thinks people were there for her, Rose answers, "There's a vibration that pulsates, that responds to that need. They say it's all energy anyway." She continues:

> Why did that man know he had to get on that boat? And when he went, he wore his wedding ring—not his academy ring. He sometimes wore one or the other. And though he wasn't very organized with his papers, after his death I was looking in his drawer for papers I needed and I found something that said, "What to do at the time of death" and under that all the checks made out to pay the bills—all made out in advance.

Being widowed is, of course, yet another way of becoming a single mother. Widows are sometimes exempt from harsh criticism, because their single motherhood wasn't their fault—they are the victims of an obvious tragedy; but they must deal with many of the same problems that other single mothers experience. All find themselves coping with loss, but the way the loss occurs is clearly significant. Widows' partners have not chosen to leave them, nor have they chosen to end the relationship. They do not experience the feelings of rejection and failure likely to be suffered by women whose marriages or relationships come apart. And while they may feel anger at losing their partners, it is different than the anger women feel toward someone who has abused them, been unfaithful to them, disappointed them, or left them. Moreover, many widows, like Rose, keep their husband's memory alive both in their own minds and hearts and in the minds and hearts of their children. These children often sense that their father is somehow watching over them—in the case of Rose's husband, attending a wedding in his dress whites.

These four women illustrate the broad range of experiences encompassed by the term *single mother*. Despite coming from a poor family in which her father sexually abused one of her sisters and then abandoned his wife and children, Soledad Martinez clearly has an inner core of belief in herself and a recognition of her own strength. She had the determination to go to college and graduate school, even while her husband was denigrating her and spying on her. She had the courage to take her children and leave, though she was earning only $21,000 a year and still had to fight a custody battle. And she had the hopefulness and belief in relationships and in the future to fall in love again and create a successful marriage.

Linda Powell became a single mother because of a complex confluence of factors that are by no means unique to her: the social pressure to have sex accompanied by her ignorance about both the sex act and its consequences; the reluctance of her family to discuss sex, and her consequent fear of telling her mother about her pregnancy; the power of a 15-year-old boy to tell her she was going to have the baby rather than have an abortion; and her immaturity or ambivalence, which led her to accept his dictum. Since that fateful time, she has essentially been on her own.

Though she did have some support from family, from her church, and even from the welfare system, she is fundamentally that American ideal—a self-made woman. As a teenager, through rebellion, good sense, or a combination of both, she moved away from harmful situations, made the often destructive system of social services work for her, acquired the education she needed, worked indefatigably, and took good care of her daughter. She has even kept alive her dream of becoming a registered nurse.

Carolyn Miller's life has turned in a very different direction than she had expected when she was a young professional living in Manhattan, dating and then marrying another young professional with similar interests. She assumed they would move to the suburbs, have children, and live happily ever after. But Carolyn and her husband, as their lives played out, evolved in different directions, with different needs and expectations. Even though she realized that he wasn't the kind of husband and father she had imagined and wanted, her life was turned upside down when he walked out. She is still rebuilding both her life and her identity.

And Rose Conti, widowed at age 27 with two small children, lost not only the husband she loved in the choppy seas off the Italian coast but also the essential structure of her life. Showing great resilience and flexibility, Rose developed her work life as well as her social and emotional life as she raised her daughters. She didn't settle for the comfortable, easy route in any sphere; instead, she stretched her own limits and took on new challenges.

Each of these women expected a completely different life course than the reality she faced, which required her to make significant adjustments—both psychological and material. Responding to the crises in their lives, they acted with courage, creativity, and caring. Contrary to the negative stereotypes, these single mothers epitomize the finest American values—or, as some might say, family values. They work hard, care for their children, have an independent spirit, and live their lives wisely and thoughtfully. And they are able to move ahead despite suffering major disruptions and wrenching losses. The following chapter describes some of these disruptions and losses and the ways in which these and many other women have attempted to reconstruct their lives and the lives of their children.

3

Loss

It was really difficult. I had the worst depression. I almost lost myself. **Young Heoy Lee**, 43-year-old mother of two

Everything changed when Bob died. My world came tumbling down because he was no longer here. I cried all the time. The only time I didn't cry is when I was teaching. I felt lost.
Barbara Tucci, 60-year-old mother of three

A central theme in the lives of virtually all of the women interviewed for this study is loss—loss of a partner or a spouse; loss of emotional support, social support, financial support; loss of self-esteem; and loss of status within their immediate community, within the larger society, and, perhaps most important, in their own eyes. These women have also lost the sense that life is predictable, coherent, continuous, that we can plan and assume that our plans will come to fruition. Loss was not an issue that I specifically focused on during my interviews with single mothers; nevertheless, it was a recurring theme in the experiences of women of all ages, from every background, whatever their path to single motherhood.

Loss is intrinsic to all of our lives, but it is particularly salient in the narratives of women whose single motherhood was unplanned. Because a life course is structured by assumptions about the present and the future, often disrupted beyond recognition when a women becomes a single mother, these women inevitably suffer feelings of dislocation. Whether they are separated, divorced, widowed, or never married, the course of their lives is not what they had imagined, anticipated, or planned. After they experience an out-of-wedlock pregnancy, the dissolution of a marriage or long-term relationship, or abandonment by or the premature death of a lover or spouse, many people feel a sense of chaos, of uncertainty, of loss of their lives as they had envisioned them. This level of disruption can lead an individual to question her very essence, her identity and self-worth. In some fundamental sense, a woman can lose her sense of who she is or who she thought she was.

Although the women in the previous chapter differed in how they became single mothers, they all experienced feelings of loss: Soledad Martinez lost the economic and social security of marriage; with her pregnancy at age 14, Linda Powell lost her youth as well as her sense of who she was and who she was going to become; Carolyn Miller lost her image of her life as a wife, her status in the community, her presumed life course, and her sense of herself as a success; and Rose Conti lost the partner on whom she relied, a touchstone, the structure of her life, her sense of having abundant time. That the changes in these women's lives may in the long run be positive, that some may have been initiated by the women themselves, affords little protection. Soledad became a professional with a graduate degree and eventually made a loving, successful second marriage; nevertheless, when she walked away from her abusive first husband, she lost the financial security of his income and her specific place in the social structure. She had to manage on the low wages she was able to earn and found herself in a custody battle that might have deprived her of her children. She, like many women, suffered substantial loss before reaching a positive outcome.

Soo Hyun Park's self-description—"I used to be a very strong person but I became powerless"—captures one kind of loss. A 44-year-old mother of two, Soo Hyun grew up in South Korea. Her father was a doctor of traditional medicine; her mother was "at home." She has two sisters and two brothers and states that she was the "baby" of the family. Both of her sisters were married through what she calls "matched marriages." In Korea, she says, she had a business of her own: "I ran a gift shop and made my own money."

The man who became her husband worked and lived in the United States but returned to Korea to "find a wife." He had been divorced twice and was twelve years older than she; Soo Hyun met him through his cousin, who had been a schoolmate of hers in high school. She liked him, she says, because she knew his aunt, because he was well-educated, and because he counted a minister and a physician among his family members.

Because they had no time for a wedding, they just went to a government office and obtained a certificate. He promised they would have a real wedding in the United States but it never happened. He returned to the United States first; she followed later. When he picked her up at John F. Kennedy International Airport, he asked if she had brought the agreed-on dowry of $30,000. She told him that since it was only legal to bring $5,000 into the United States, she had brought only that much cash; but she had packed and sent all of her household goods, which, she told him, were worth more than $30,000. After she arrived, he refused to sponsor her either for citizenship or for a residency permit. When she asked him how she could get a job without papers, he told her to get a job for which she would be paid under the table. She never asked him about it again.

Two children of Soo Hyun's husband by his previous wife lived with them at the beginning of their marriage. She became pregnant right away and gave birth to twins. According to Soo Hyun, her husband refused to give her any money; she therefore had to call her parents in Korea and ask them to send her funds. Their house was situated on an acre of lawn that she had to mow. He wouldn't connect the dryer, forcing her to hang up the wet laundry for a family of six outside. All the unaccustomed physical labor began to damage her body. Soo Hyun describes her life:

> He used to beat the children, particularly the two older children. He beat the twins, too. He took out his anger on the children but he never beat me. He would beat them for no reason. When the older child was 7 and her brother was 3, he kicked the boy so badly that his sister called 911. The police came but I didn't want to tell on my husband so I

signed a statement saying everything was all right. I thought he would stop but he never did.

When the twins were old enough to travel, Soo Hyun sent them to Korea to live with her parents for the summer. During that period "there wasn't any rice in the home," as her husband refused to buy any food. According to Kim, throughout their marriage he never once bought anything for her or her children. He didn't buy groceries; he didn't buy the children schoolbooks, toys, or clothes. Her parents continued to send her money to enable her to purchase some of the essentials that she and the children needed. Although he didn't drink or "womanize," she says that "no money came out of his pocket." Moreover, he didn't want her to speak to anyone; and if she did, he would beat the children.

After the children went to Korea, Soo Hyun herself "escaped" and followed them, using money and plane tickets that her parents had sent her. While she was home, she received a letter from her neighbor telling her that her husband had declared her a missing person. Fearing that he would accuse her of kidnapping, she returned with her children to the United States. At that time, with the help of her neighbor, she went into a shelter for abused women and hired a lawyer.

It took three years for Soo Hyun to get a divorce. Because her husband felt she wanted the divorce in order to "get his money," he quit his job. Then he disappeared. During the long divorce proceedings, Soo Hyun's husband accused her of mental instability and she had to be tested by psychologists. Her stepchildren, who eventually went to live with their biological mother, wrote letters describing how he beat them, and her children told what had happened to them, but the psychologist said the letters were questionable and that the children "sounded rehearsed." During this period, Soo Hyun learned her husband had removed all the money from two bank accounts and from his insurance policy; there was almost nothing left. He also claimed he was unemployed and therefore had no income. Her lawyer urged her to just bring it to an end, telling her she would get neither alimony nor child support. Indeed, she says,

"He never gave me one dollar," though the court eventually ordered her ex-husband to pay child support of $169 weekly, which he has never paid. Currently there is a warrant out for his arrest. He has the right to visitation but has never exercised it. Asked about their father, the children respond, "He abandoned us."

Soo Hyun was left with no money, two young children, and medical problems that included a very painful back condition. Her family sent her money as long as they could, but finally Soo Hyun was advised to apply for public assistance. When I interviewed her, she was living in low-income housing, caring for her children and coping as best she can. When I asked her why she didn't take the children and return to Korea, she replied that divorced women there bear a great stigma. She therefore feels that she and probably the children are better off here. She is trying to improve her English so she can do more with her life; the children are now in the fifth grade and are doing well in school.

When Soo Hyun came to this country, she knew very little English and therefore had great difficulty communicating with anyone in her new environment. She moved into her husband's home in an upper-middle-class New Jersey suburb populated mainly by white professionals and consequently was wholly removed from the social and cultural milieu in which she was raised and in which she thrived. Entirely unfamiliar with the customs and expectations of American society, she didn't know her rights, she didn't know how to function within the community, and she didn't know how (and in any case was afraid) to ask for help. Within the span of less than one month, she had gone from earning her own income, running her own shop, being surrounded by friends and family, speaking her own language, and knowing the customs of her culture to an isolated existence in a strange land, totally dependent on a stranger who was physically abusing the children in the household and emotionally abusing her. At times, she says, she even felt she was losing her mind. Wrenched out of her own milieu, far away from her entire support system, and living with a hostile, withholding, abusive husband, for a time Soo Hyun genuinely lost the sense of who she was. She lost her identity.

The experience of 43-year-old Young Heoy Lee is almost the mirror image of Soo Hyun Park's. Born and brought up in Korea, Young Heoy moved to the United States with her family when she was 19. She attended college in New York City, paying for her tuition by working many hours a week. She met her future husband in New York when he was a foreign student. As "the first son of a first son," he was considered very special in Korean culture. Young Heoy explains, "It's like being the head of the family, having the most power. Like being king and inheriting the kingdom. He was always the first, the most important."

After they married, Young Heoy and her husband lived in New York City for four and a half years. He worked at the World Trade Center, and Young Heoy recounts a telling interaction at his job: "One day his boss asked him to order lunch for the team and he replied, 'I didn't come to work here to order lunch.' So he quit that job. He had been living here for ten years but he was a control freak and thought he was special because he was the first son of a first son." According to Young Heoy, he quit other jobs as well, and life became "difficult and harsh." He "maxed out his credit cards, took out loans, and even used my ID to get more credit cards. I was making good money in the field of finance and had twenty-five people working under me, but he was depressed. He was losing his confidence. So I said, 'Why don't we go back to Korea?'"

When they returned to Korea, Young Heoy and her husband had one child, a girl. As she puts it, "We had to yield a son to the family. It was one of our duties. If the family is strong and rooted in tradition, it is a social custom. A woman has seven sins she can commit against the family and one is not giving a son." Her husband's 90-year-old grandmother kept pressuring her, as did her father-in-law. In addition, Young Heoy's American citizenship made it illegal for her to work. She finally did find a job teaching English to children of "high society families." Earning about $3,500 a month, she totally supported herself and her children.

During this time she had another child—again a girl. When she gave birth the second time, her only visitors at the hospital were her brother-in-law and his wife. And, according to Young Heoy, "His family was still demanding a son."

Young Heoy was under other pressure as well, for she was expected to serve large numbers of relatives and other guests at the memorial ceremonies and birthday celebrations that the family organized. The older women did the cooking, and she had to set up the tables, serve, and clean up afterward. She frequently worked from 8 A.M. until 10:30 at night. According to Young Heoy, in Korea the men "don't do anything." In New York, her husband "was there for us. In Korea he got into Korean customs. He stayed out late. We never saw him." He was teaching at the time, and went to many events with his "teaching teams." She could not even call him at work—he never gave her his telephone number. And, she says, "He didn't give me any money for support," yet he was spending $1,200 for a suit and $200 for a shirt. Adding to her economic problems, a new president took office in Korea who cracked down on under-the-table employment and other lawbreaking. As part of the new, stricter policy, anyone found to be engaging in illegal activities was subject to an automatic tax audit; as a result, the families who had employed her were afraid to let her continue to teach their children. When Young Heoy found she was no longer able to work and asked her husband for money for the household, he handed her a $10 bill. According to her, this pattern went on for two and a half months. During this time, "It was really difficult. I had the worst depression. I almost lost myself. I had been going to church since I was born but he didn't want me to go to church or call my parents. He didn't want me to visit them even when we lived in New York. Sometimes my kids lived on a piece of bread. Even though I screamed with pain, his family protected him."

Because of her husband's status in Korean culture and the nature of their relationship, their interaction was always somewhat formal. She describes how she addressed her husband. She says there are three ways of speaking to people in Korean—with most respect, the next more familiar way, and the most familiar language. During their ten years together she always spoke to him in the most respectful language and tone. She finally felt, "I cannot live like this. I don't know what to do. Culturally I was not trained to ask for money from my family after marriage. They worked so hard. They came to the U.S. at 47 years old. My dad was a cook/helper and then a driver and my mom was a waitress. I couldn't even tell them what was happening, but I couldn't hold myself in any longer."

Eventually, Young Heoy's brother-in-law called her father-in-law and told him, "I don't think Sister-in-law can continue like this." Her father-in-law then deposited $10,000 in one of her husband's accounts, an inactive account for which she had the bank card. On the same day, Young Heoy went to the bank, withdrew exactly the sum of money she needed for three tickets to the United States, took a diaper bag for her younger child, picked up her older child at school with just her book bag, and flew to California, where her parents were living. Young Heoy recalls, "I had no hope. Even when my father-in-law gave me the money, he said, 'Why don't you yield a son for us?' My two girls are my most valuable treasures in the whole world. What am I doing here? I almost killed myself. I would think I am going crazy. And the way women are treated in Korea is another reason to bring my girls to America."

After staying in California with her parents for a few months, Young Heoy moved back to New York City. She is currently struggling to support her daughters though she has some serious medical problems. Her husband does not give them any child support. He called their older daughter on her birthday, but that is all he has done. Young Heoy says, "I have threatened him, begged him for some support but nothing happens." She indicates how much it costs her when she adds, "And I have so much pride." Moreover, she hides her worry and her upset feelings and anger both from her children and from her father, who is currently living with them in order to help her out. She doesn't want to "show any weakness" to them; she feels she must handle her worries and fears herself.

While Soo Hyun's sense of self, her very identity, was broken down after she moved to the United States and was subjected to emotional and economic abuse by her husband, Young Heoy experienced similar feelings and abuse after she moved back to Korea with her husband. An educated, highly intelligent, competent young woman when she was living in New York, Young Heoy became depressed, distraught, and full of self-doubt when she found herself living in a very different world where a son was demanded of her and she found herself actively discriminated against both because she was a woman and because she had not given her in-laws what they desired most in the world. As she says, she was brought up as a "princess" (though her parents were not by any means affluent) and then, when she and her husband moved to Korea, she was treated as though she were Cinderella, the daughter overworked and despised before she encountered the magic of the glass slipper.

Young Heoy is now working at a shelter for homeless women. She tells me, "I feel so much for homeless women and for women suffering under traditional customs. They are people neglected by Korean American society. I want to help them get proper help. They cannot even scream about their pain." She wants to send a message to women—that they "should believe in themselves. It is not always going to be pleasant but they need to believe in themselves." She admits that she sometimes feels guilty for leaving Korea and for leaving her husband but points out that he was sometimes violent toward their older child, yelling and hitting her. She continues, "Whenever I don't have enough money, I feel guilty. When families come together, I feel guilty. Then I think if I give them double love, they will be fine."

Tragic events and emotional abuse frequently combine to make the strongest people question who they are and lose their sense of self. Jennifer Soriano is a 25-year-old Latina college senior. She describes her early life:

> I grew up in Brooklyn and lived there all my life. I went to public school. My favorite was junior high school; it was a school for gifted and talented kids. I learned how to play the clarinet and I sang in the choir. In high school I wanted to be a nurse, but an internship at a hospital where I changed the diapers and bedclothes of elderly patients influenced me to decide not to go into health work.

My mom was 23 when she had me. She was a single mom and in an abusive relationship. They weren't married but they were together until I was six or seven. My dad was in and out of jail forever. For drug-related stuff. He still comes around to borrow money from me—to this very day. My mom's story is pretty sad. She went to college; she wanted to get an undergraduate degree in social work but she dropped out because of her relationship with my dad. He had a drug habit. She had to apply for welfare. He was abusive physically and emotionally but she was stuck on him. And then she got hooked on drugs—cocaine, speed, heroin. We had no money for food, for clothes. I would eat at a neighbor's. This was going on when I was from 7 to 11.

I would go to my grandmother's for weekends (my mother's mother). When I was 11, on the last day of school, I went to my grandmother's and never went back to my mom's. I lived with my grandmother, my grandfather, and my aunt until I got pregnant at 18 and my grandmother kicked me out. She is very traditional, religious, Pentecostal—so I had to leave.

I knew when I told them they would ask me to leave. My mom knew already but I didn't want to tell them until I had moved my things to my mom's. But my son's father told my grandparents. He announced to everyone that I was pregnant. He wanted me to have an abortion but I didn't want to. When I went to the doctor for my prenatal visit—I was almost four months pregnant—she showed me a picture of the baby at that stage and I couldn't do it. No, not religious reasons, moral reasons. I told my boyfriend I was not going to have an abortion and he called me names, was mean to me, and threatened to tell my grandmother. When he did and she asked me if it was true, I couldn't deny it. So she threw all my stuff in a shopping cart and told me to leave.

At that time Jennifer's boyfriend was 18, not working and not in school. All he did was "play basketball at the YMCA." They had been "boyfriend and girlfriend" since they were 16 and had talked about what would happen if she got pregnant. She says, "I really, really believed he would stick around." He did "stick around" until she was eight months pregnant, and then he didn't come by any longer. When the baby was two months old, he went to jail because he was "in a fight with a gay guy. They said it was a bias crime." Jennifer recalls,

> I didn't want to be pregnant. I felt I really, really loved him at the time. He was my first boyfriend and he said I was his first girlfriend. He came from a pretty good family with doctors and lawyers. His mom is a businesswoman, one uncle is a lawyer, another is a doctor.
>
> My son is 6 now and he looks just like him, too. No, he has never given me any child support—none. His problem is that he doesn't have a GED so he can't get and keep a good job. And he doesn't want to go to school. My son sees him often and I am worried that he sees him as a role model. I'm trying to stop his seeing him so often. My son loves him a whole lot; he talks all about him all the time. I'm angry at the fact that he doesn't help me so we end up arguing. And then he becomes verbally abusive, verbally and emotionally abusive, and he doesn't even care if my son hears it.

Jennifer currently lives with her son in the Bronx because she can't afford the rent in Brooklyn, but she's on the waiting list for public housing there. She says she doesn't know anyone in the Bronx. Every day she goes from the Bronx to Brooklyn to bring her son to school, then travels to Manhattan to work, back to Brooklyn to pick up her son, and then back to the Bronx at night. Her grandmother or her aunt usually picks up her son at school and brings him to their place. When she gets there, they generally have dinner before she and her son return to the Bronx. Jennifer recalls, "When my baby was born, I had no contact with my grandparents. I felt like I really hurt their feelings. They called me all those names—said I was dirty—and then when the baby was born, they came to the hospital, bought me a carriage, bought clothes for the baby. It all changed." According to Jennifer, her grandfather has Alzheimer's, her grandmother is 74 and says she doesn't think she'll live to see her graduate, and her aunt is manic-depressive. In addition, she says, "My mom is pretty bad now. She has AIDS and is pretty bad."

Jennifer's son was born the year after she finished high school. Everyone told her she should go to college but it seemed impossible to her:

"We had no food and no clothes. I wanted to work but I didn't want to affect my mom's [welfare] budget." She did begin college when she was 20; since that time, she has worked for an advocacy group that helps poor women. Extremely knowledgeable about recent welfare legislation, she has become experienced at public speaking and a true leader within the organization. What she would really like to do after she graduates is to go to law school.

I ask her about her social life, and she replies,

> No, I don't have any other men. Nobody likes me. I'm kind of nervous. My son's father says I'm ugly, that no one is going to look at me twice. He calls me names—ugly names. He's mean and evil—with me only. He tells me, "You've been in school all this time. You're never going to graduate." [crying]
>
> I'm going through the same thing my mom went through. I don't know why but when I was growing up, I felt angry toward my mother. My dad would come around once or twice a year and sometimes bring me a coat. I loved him so much. When we finally talked, she told me how he treated her and I finally understood. He has a job now. Something good will come of his life and I'm going to be down here. I'm going to turn out like my mom. [crying] I remember when things were so bad that I would have to go to a neighbor to ask for a can of ravioli.

Jennifer is a highly intelligent, stunningly attractive, extremely able young woman. Despite serious setbacks, she has managed on very little money to make her way to her senior year in college while working and caring for her son. And yet she struggles constantly with feelings of inadequacy, sometimes of hopelessness. She has been battered all her life by forces that she cannot control that threaten to drag her down—particularly her drug-addicted mother, her irresponsible father, and her self-absorbed and vengeful boyfriend, who uses her as an emotional punching bag. Despite the support her grandparents have given her (except during her pregnancy), she seems like a swimmer who is valiantly attempting to reach shore only to be beset by huge waves and a strong undertow that threatens to pull her under. On one level, she knows how able she is and realizes that she is living up to her promise; on another level, she doubts her competence and intelligence and feels overwhelmed by the circumstances she faces and the emotional abuse she endures. Jennifer's losses are multiple and ongoing: her childhood; her naive belief in her father; her once positive relationship with her boyfriend, who she thought would stand by her; her dreams for the future; and even, on bad days, her faith in herself.

The clearest and perhaps most wrenching form of loss may be the death of a spouse or partner. Barbara Tucci, a 60-year-old white woman who lives in a suburb outside of New York, talks about her life "before Bob and after Bob."

> I grew up in a small town in upstate New York. I have one older sister and one younger brother. My father owned his own business and my mother worked in the school cafeteria once the kids were in junior high school. I went to public schools and then commuted to a small college nearby. After college I taught for two years. I got married during my second year of teaching and right after that Bob, who was in the ROTC, was activated for Vietnam. While he was in Vietnam, I returned home and taught.

After moving to the town where she still lives, Bob and Barbara had their first child and then two more shortly afterward. She was a stay-at-home mother, active in the Brownies and the Cub Scouts, in the PTA, and in the children's religious education. As the children grew, Barbara gradually went back to teaching.

She describes the day her husband died:

> When Bob died the children were 16, 19 and 21. He was out jogging. I was talking on the phone to my mother. It was a beautiful, beautiful day. A policeman came to my door asking if I had a husband out jogging and what he was wearing. I told him what he was wearing and he said he was injured. I thought he meant like a sprained ankle. I went with him to where Bob had fallen on someone's front grass. They were working on him with paddles. I jumped into the ambulance with him. They said it wasn't allowed but I did it anyway. He was dead on arrival at the hospital. It was a massive heart attack. He was 50 years old.

He had no history of heart disease. He had physicals every three years, was a nonsmoker, tall, slim. He jogged, lifted weights. One son was in high school; the other two were at college. I had to call them. It was the hardest thing I ever had to do in my life. Each of them let out primal screams and then said, "I love you, Mom."

I felt responsible for the three kids, for their emotional well-being, for how they would handle the loss. Bob was a real hands-on father. He was close to them, with them a lot. But he didn't delve into personal issues very much. We ate dinner as a family at 6:30 and I cooked every night. And often we would have one or two of their friends, too. When the kids were young, Bob went to business school at night so he didn't see them as much then.

According to Barbara, "Everything changed when Bob died. My world came tumbling down because he was no longer here. I cried all the time. The only time I didn't cry is when I was teaching. I felt lost. We were such a good team." She adds,

I was the same person with my friends but I didn't feel like the same person in life. I insulated myself with friends. I still felt married for about five years. I left my wedding rings on my left hand for a long time and then moved them to my right hand. I really felt the kids got gypped. I got gypped, too. You get snatched out of your life. And he was gypped. He never got to see them grown up.

Barbara and her children had several other tragedies to cope with shortly after Bob's death. Two of the children's friends committed suicide, and Barbara's mother died the following year. She says, "Prayers helped me. Other people's prayers, my prayers helped me. And I finished up my master's degree but I cried over everything. I had chest pains; it was all those funerals we had to go to."

Though she has many good friends, Barbara on a fundamental level was alone:

Ultimately, everything was my decision. I had to fill out the financial aid forms for college. I had to juggle everything. The financial decisions were very difficult and I didn't want to burden people with my problems. I felt I had to deal with them by myself. Sometimes I had to rob Peter to pay Paul.

I felt like I was sinking into an abyss. The kids looked so sad. We all cried—especially around the holidays. He would have been such a fantastic grandfather! I thought I would grow old with him. And the loneliness of not having someone; the person you're with every day is gone. You miss the intimacy—physically and emotionally. In my dreams sometimes, he's right in bed with me, hugging and making love.

On one "beautiful, beautiful day," Barbara's life was torn apart. Her emotional world, her financial and social support, her intimate life were totally disrupted in a single moment as she was talking to her mother on the telephone. Her loss is immeasurable. Fortunately, she had family, friends, and work to help her through this time, but it took her several years to recuperate and find a new equilibrium in her life.

Often we think of loss as something that happens to us: the death of someone we love, a betrayal by a lover, a dismissal from a job, the withdrawal of a good friend, the alienation of our children. But people can experience painful feelings of loss as the result of actions for which they themselves are primarily responsible. Several women in this study walked away from relationships, and though they felt at the time that the decision was best for themselves and their children, they nonetheless suffered profound feelings of loss and grief.

Carolina Delgado is a 40-year-old Latina mother of three who is currently separated from her husband. She begins with her early life:

I was born in Puerto Rico into a middle-class family. I am the older of two. My mother was a secretary and my father worked for the government. They both had associate degrees. My parents still live there. My husband and I moved here in 1990 for professional training, for opportunities, for a better standard of living.

I met my husband in the first year of college. We were friends. I always wanted to be a doctor. After two years of college, I got pregnant and we decided to have the baby. We entered medical school together. We lived with my parents and they took care of our son, but we were the real parents. We were both 20 when he was born. Today he is a junior in college and we have two other children—one in the sixth grade and one in the second grade.

When we were in medical school, we were thought of as the perfect couple. We were so young and so in love. After medical school, we came to the U.S. for our residencies. We wanted to be together. When we had our second child, my mother-in-law came here for three months, but when our third child was born I took six months off. When I had to take time off, it wasn't a problem; the hospital was supportive. I was very involved with the kids; he was very involved with his job in the city. He was in a different world. He would say, "We need a new car. We need this; we need that." Before this, we used to have a life of no worries. We had many friends, went to many parties, many barbecues. Every birthday, every christening. When we moved [to a new house], we lost the group.

Carolina also feels her husband was not getting the attention he needed but that he could not or would not articulate what he wanted. And she felt the woman in the family had to do everything and do it well. She didn't ask him to help around the house because, as she told me, "If you're not going to offer, I'm not going to ask. And then I got angry at his not doing what I wanted him to do."

She describes what happened next:

After fourteen years of marriage, he entered into his crisis. He was unfaithful. I thought it was the end of the world. I blamed myself. We went into treatment and celebrated our fifteenth anniversary together. He thought we should move and get a better job. So we built our dream house. We stopped going to therapy because we had to put the money into the house. Before moving into our new home, we were drifting apart. We went to bed upset and I knew something was wrong. Little things were getting him upset. For example, he played in a softball game and I couldn't go because of a professional emergency. He really minded. He told me, "This wife was there; that wife was there."

I said we should go into therapy again but he said, "No way." He was unfaithful again and I said, "This is it. I want a separation." The first time I blamed myself. This time I knew I had done everything to change. I said, "You're out." We went into treatment but he was not going regularly. Now he is having another relationship—with one person. Not the same person he was unfaithful with before.

I've tried everything but I can't do it by myself. Some friends say you have to stick by it [marriage]; it will pass—it's a crisis. But I can't do that. I can't destroy myself. I don't deserve it. I won't take it. So we separated again. Now he's living on his own. It's been four and a half, five years. It seems like yesterday. A friend of mine just lost her husband. I told her that's how I felt—like a death.

Being alone is so different. Not having a loving, caring relationship—someone to call you to see how you're doing during the day. You need that.

I think we could work it out. I always think things could work out. It is difficult still. You feel like you've failed at the most important thing in life—marriage and family.

Somehow the perception exists in the wider society—particularly among critics of single mothers—that single motherhood is a "lifestyle choice," something that happens without a great deal of thought and is taken rather lightly; it appears almost to be the fashion of the time, like New Yorkers choosing to wear black. None of the women whom I interviewed viewed their circumstances as a lifestyle choice. If they were unmarried when they became pregnant, they thought seriously about the possibility of terminating the pregnancy and chose childbearing even though the road would be exceedingly difficult. Many of the women were abused and stayed in the relationship nonetheless—sometimes because they were too beaten down to leave. Others chose to leave marriages because the relationship became untenable. And, of course, still others lost their partners because of death.

No matter what their circumstances, all these women have suffered loss and have had to go through an extensive period of adjustment, figuring out how to live on their own with their children, how to support their newly reconstructed family, and how to develop a new way of thinking about their roles, their status in society, their very identity. As one woman wrote of her experience of becoming a single mother, "It all started eight years ago. The divorce overwhelmed each of us—parents and children—as we struggled to adjust to a completely new way of living. Trying to help my kids cope while nursing my own grief was the biggest challenge of my life."[1]

Because of the characteristics of my sample—women who had not planned to live their lives as single mothers—by definition all my interviewees had to cope with events they had not intended or expected. Their lives did not evolve as they had imagined, and at very least they experienced a sense of loss after realizing that their expectations, their hopes and dreams, were not coming true. Soo Hyun Park, for example, surely assumed or at the very least hoped she would live a happy, comfortable life in the United States with her new husband. Young Heoy Lee, a successful, educated woman who was raised "like a princess," doubtless assumed she would live a good life with her husband and children while engaging in work she enjoyed—as she had done prior to marriage. Jennifer Soriano, a highly intelligent, personable young woman, planned to go to college and certainly did not factor in an unplanned pregnancy, being ordered to leave home by grandparents whom she loved and respected and on whom she was dependent, emotional abuse by her boyfriend, and years of balancing child rearing, school, and work. Barbara Tucci assumed that she and her husband would live long lives and see their children grow up and have children of their own, and Carolina Delgado, part of a "perfect" couple, without question never anticipated separation or divorce.

As Gay Becker points out, the "contemporary Western conception of the life course" entails the "predictable, knowable, and continuous." When those expectations are not realized, people experience a "loss of the future"—as did all of these women. Becker adds, "Restoring order to life necessitates reworking understandings of the self and the world, redefining the disruption and life itself."[2] Mariane Pearl, the widow of Daniel Pearl, the *Wall Street Journal* reporter kidnapped in Pakistan and brutally murdered in January 2002, describes such reworking after that terrible event: "Right now I'm just functioning by task ahead. That's how I have been living. One day I was living with Danny, and now I'm living with Adam [their son, who was born after her husband's death] in New York. We've lost that sense of normalcy, of things having coherence. That highway I thought was my life doesn't exist anymore."[3]

Part of re-creating some semblance of continuity after a major disruption may be the telling of life stories, often structured by focusing on adversity and then on ways the individual has attempted to overcome adversity. In some sense, these interviews have been structured around the events leading up to adversity, exploring the nature of the adversity and how the women are coping or have coped with the unexpected, often tragic developments in their lives. Interestingly, the only women unwilling to be interviewed were those in the throes of disruption. Nearly everyone else who was approached readily agreed, and many even seemed eager to tell their stories.

Moreover, the very form of the interviews reflects the way many people, particularly in Western cultures, think about their lives. According to Becker, the "traditional Western paradigm" is one of "predictability and order in people's lives."[4] The standard American view of the life cycle—childhood, adolescence, young adulthood, education, work, serious relationship or marriage, children (most likely), middle age, old age, death—is often seen as the way things are supposed to be, the correct journey through life. Any serious aberration or interruption throws the entire plan into uncertainty, even chaos. No one plans that her husband will drown at sea or drop dead of a heart attack while jogging in the neighborhood. No one imagines that her "perfect" marriage will disintegrate, disrupting all preexisting plans and assumptions about the present and the future and raising questions about her own self-worth. And though it may be hard for some to believe, most teenage girls, even those having unprotected sex, do not seriously think that they will get pregnant and thereby fundamentally disrupt their lives for years to come—perhaps forever. Moreover, a cataclysmic interruption in our imagined life course removes the sense of invulnerability that envelopes many of us like a protective shield, keeping at bay the fear that any disaster could happen at any time.

After individuals experience such a disruption, one of their central tasks is finding a way to reestablish a sense of continuity, the feeling of having at least some control over their lives. Widowhood, divorce, a sudden and precipitous drop in economic status, the birth of a baby at an unfortunate time, or abandonment or repeated physical or emotion abuse by a trusted lover can make people lose their bearings, their feelings of belonging, their sense of identity. They are suddenly in a different place; relationships may become strained, skewed, unfamiliar, uncomfortable, strange.

But although disruption and loss can be extraordinarily painful, they can also be catalysts for change. Many of the women interviewed for this book turned their lives around in remarkable ways. I often found myself wondering where they found the strength, the courage, the resilience to become something totally different than they had ever imagined—and totally different from any other member of their family or their social network. Where did that risk taking come from? Where did they find that belief in themselves, that image of what they could become? In the next chapter we encounter single mothers who have moved away from disruption, anger, grief, and, all too often, profound self-doubt to create very different lives for themselves and their children.

4

Resilience, Strength, and Perseverance

There's always been something within me, a drive. Sometimes it was dormant; sometimes it comes out. . . . How other people perceived me gave me strength. If they think I can do it, maybe I can.
Eva Sanchez, 45-year-old mother of two

I made a completely new life. I followed things that had always been important to me.
Hannah Alexander, 66-year-old mother of one

Battered and bruised, emotionally and sometimes physically, many of these women have lived and are living their lives with uncommon courage, determination, and creativity. Soledad Martinez obtained the education she dreamed of, left an abusive marriage, and went on to fashion a rewarding career and form a loving, companionable second marriage; Linda Powell's pregnancy at 14 left her impoverished and virtually alone, but she nonetheless has made a rewarding life with her daughter and has managed somehow to hold on to her dreams for the future; Jennifer Soriano, bounced back and forth between relatives as a child, surrounded by family members who suffer from severe medical and emotional problems, pregnant by accident, deserted and then abused by the father of her child, has made it to her senior year in college, holds down a challenging job, and in her optimistic moments retains real faith in herself, despite ongoing distress. What gives these women the strength to persevere, to raise their children responsibly, and to care for themselves against all odds? How are they able to avoid repeating the traumas of their childhood?

Yet another example of uncommon strength and drive is Jeanne Gonzalez, a 27-year-old Latina mother of two. Jeanne talks about her life:

> I have two children—a son, 10, and a daughter, 4. I was a teen mom. I grew up in Brooklyn and have two younger siblings—*much* younger. My mom has been a single mom—always. I have always thought of my grandmother as really my mother. She was married but now she's widowed. She's 73 but she's still strong. She was from Puerto Rico; they migrated in the early '6os.
>
> In many ways I consider my grandmother a single mother. She worked and did most of the child rearing. My grandfather provided income and he was like "I'm in charge," but she did everything. I tell her, "You were a single mom."
>
> She is part of my everyday life. I don't have as much contact with my mom. My children are very close to my grandmother. She stayed in my life. I told her, "I'm going to college." We do everything together. She takes care of the children. I do her checkbook, go with her to doctor visits, help her with shopping.

Jeanne's son was born when she was 16. When she became pregnant, she was in the eleventh grade and comments, "I didn't get kicked out; I was lucky." She had her baby "during winter break" and then went right back to school, to an outreach program for teenage mothers. She had already been accepted at college but had no idea what to expect; only an aunt had even finished high school. Jeanne continues,

> I never planned to have a child as a teenager. I never pictured marriage, but I always wished my baby's father would be part of my son's life and would provide for him. But he was not part of his life. He grew up in a two-parent home. He was 17 or 18, also in high school. But he dropped out and was incarcerated for five or six years. I see him on and off. My son is aware of his surroundings and knows what's happening. His father blames everything on his incarceration but the truth never comes out of him.

I was too afraid to think of having an abortion. The first thing my mother said when I told her I was pregnant was, "Do you know what you've done to me?" She suggested an abortion but I was too afraid, not knowing what is going to happen to me. So I thought I would just have the baby.

According to Jeanne, her mother "kicked [her] out of the house," embarrassed by her pregnancy and worried about what people would say. Jeanne's grandmother told her that her mother had done the same thing—gotten pregnant as a teenager. At first, Jeanne went to live with friends and continued attending school. Later, she returned home and her mother added her to her welfare check. But, Jeanne says, "I needed my own [public assistance] case so I went to live with my grandmother. She has always been supportive—financially and every other way." She recalls her life at that time:

It's really rough being a teenage parent. I wanted to do teenagery things but I couldn't get welfare, I couldn't get housing. I had jobs in supermarkets. It was a constant struggle. It still is. And my mother was so angry she wouldn't help me down three flights of stairs with the carriage. I had a big carriage and had to bring it down and then up three flights of stairs. Physically it was too much. And emotionally I was still a teenager. I was trying to do my homework and trying to pay attention to the baby. And my friends, they have babies but they were not trying to go to school.

While Jeanne was in college full-time, her son developed a neurological illness and at age 4 had to have surgery. Her life after the operation was consumed by "running around to doctors, speech therapists, everywhere." She dropped out of college for one semester and then returned, taking one or two classes at a time. She had just become a full-time student again when she found she was pregnant with her daughter.

I was on the pill. I was really scared. I was in the middle of school and working. I was scared because I had to run around with my son's illness. I was scared to tell my grandparents I was going to have another baby.

I could not bring myself to tell them—especially my grandfather. I was too scared to have an abortion; I was too scared of the procedure. What was going to happen to me? If I had an abortion, I would have to live with that decision for the rest of my life. And I knew that others have five, six, seven children and survive. I could never come up with a solid reason why I should have an abortion.

The father of my daughter is in and out of my life. He's immature, younger than me. He gives me money now and then. He gives me money for both kids. He works and he's married. He married a few months after my daughter was born. He's deceitful. He has three children. I finally realized he's not the person for me. I went through the pregnancy by myself. He did not know [about the pregnancy] but I knew he would have a little more relationship with my daughter. I knew I would not be with him. I knew I would be a single mother.

By working and going to school part-time, Jeanne completed college: "I kept saying, 'I want to graduate; I want to graduate.' No one from my family came. Some people from my work came but I didn't get to celebrate and I need to celebrate. My son was operated on at the same time." Jeanne's son is now doing better but he has vision, speech, and language problems. He also has some memory deficit and some physical impairment of his leg. Her daughter, who is healthy, is in a pre-K program on the Lower East Side, but her son needs special education services, so Jeanne must take each child to a different school before starting off for work.

Jeanne would like to go on to graduate school but isn't sure "where to focus my energy. Journalism? Pediatric nursing? Speech pathology? When I went to the program in speech pathology [at college], the director discouraged me. She said, 'You're a mother; there's no way.' It was a horrible experience." As much as she would like to continue with her education, she knows that it would be a lot of work and she's not rushing into anything. Sometimes she wonders, "Am I able to do all this?" For now, she has decided to take some time off from school, to concentrate on work and on taking care of the children's school issues.

Some people tell her that she should have found a man who is a doctor or a lawyer and she responds, "In Bushwick? Where am I going to meet someone? Kids in my neighborhood are not kept busy so they hang around in the streets with the wrong people. I meet people like my father. He has been in and out of my life. I met him when I was 11. I had never in my life met him before that. He's a really smart person. The last I heard, he was in Florida."

Jeanne's mother has asthma and has moved from the welfare rolls to disability assistance. Her younger brother and sister also have asthma and receive disability. She applied for disability assistance for her son but he was rejected; she plans to reapply. She and her children live on a very limited budget, since her need to pick the children up from their schools at the end of the school day makes it impossible for her to work full-time. She is enrolled in Medicaid and WIC—the Special Supplemental Nutrition Program for Women, Infants and Children, a federal program to provide nutritious food for low-income families—but not food stamps; she was told she earns just over the limit and therefore doesn't qualify.

Why does Jeanne have such different aspirations than other members of her family? Why did she, despite the odds against her, go to college, graduate, and then look ahead to professional training? Almost no one in her immediate environment took the path she chose; indeed, only one relative even graduated from high school. Does her relationship with her grandmother give her the strength, the drive, the self-confidence to persevere? Was the catalyst her mother, who has been on welfare for years but who said to her, "You need to go to school. You need a career. You don't want to be like me." Or was it possibly the people at her workplace, who are very encouraging and strongly believe in greater opportunities for women exactly like Jeanne?

Eva Sanchez, a lively, 45-year-old Latina mother of two sons, came to this country from Mexico with her parents when she was 15. They all stayed in the New York area for two years and then returned to Mexico; but shortly thereafter, when she was 17, she came back to New York on her own. She explains,

I liked this country very much. I felt there was opportunity to grow as a person. I grew up on the outskirts of Mexico City. I grew up very poor but you didn't realize how poor you were. We never saw ourselves as different. Now I see a big difference between classes—the working class versus the upper middle class. The main recreational hobby of the working class, the working poor, in Mexico is watching soap operas and having parties in the streets.

When Eva was in the United States with her family, they lived in a suburb north of New York City. After finishing the eleventh grade back in Mexico, she went back to that same suburb. When she was here the first time, she says she "made connections." An elderly woman had offered to let Eva stay in her home, if necessary, when she returned. But, she says, if it hadn't worked out there, she had other people to turn to. She recalls, "I thought I'll get a job. I was determined. It was a matter of survival. I had seen a better world for me and I was eager to have that opportunity. I did not see my brother and my parents for seven years. That was the price I had to pay."

Eva describes the next period of her life:

I lived with this woman and finished high school. To pay my room and board I did some cleaning, some gardening, some shopping, whatever she needed. I won a [National] Merit Scholarship and went to college nearby. I went there one year and then got married and dropped out. He was someone from Central America. I think we were both somewhat lonely. Without thinking about a relationship, we formed one. I didn't realize forming a family would be so difficult. Neither one of us had any skills. We both dropped out of school. He became a short-order cook.

We lived in a one-room apartment overlooking trash cans and garbage. I got pregnant and after the baby was born, I immediately got pregnant again. After that I said to my gynecologist, I want to tie my tubes. He raised all kinds of questions—something could happen to your kids, you could get divorced and remarried and want to have more children—but I really wanted it. I could see clearly the relationship was not going to work. I was going into what I was trying to escape. I had a tubal ligation when I was 21.

When the children were small, they went to day care while Eva did part-time jobs like cleaning people's houses. Her work evolved over the next few years:

There's always been something within me, a drive. Sometimes it was dormant; sometimes it comes out. Also, I went to a support group at my son's pre-K where they talked about careers, dreams, what we wanted to be. They suggested volunteering so I went to my local public library to volunteer. You know, I was putting books back on the shelf. Then I became a volunteer Hispanic outreach worker. I met other mothers and they would sometimes babysit for my kids.

Then I got a paid job at the library. After that I was offered a part-time job with the town. It was a little better than minimum wage. I worked there two years. And then serendipitously someone asked if I would type a letter for her. Now I didn't know how to type so I looked at another letter to see the format and I copied the format picking out the keys. [She illustrates typing with two fingers.]

Eva was then offered a part-time job with another agency and "jumped at it." Her brother, who had come to New York from Mexico to go to school, helped with babysitting. Eva's relationship with her husband "was not good. He was not ambitious." When her children were in kindergarten and first grade, Eva's boss told her they would like her to work full-time. She says, "I was still typing with one finger. The director was very patient with me. First, I was a clerk, then a secretary, then an administrative assistant. Then I decided I should know how to type, so I took a course and got a diploma as an executive secretary."

When the children were in the fourth and fifth grades, Eva realized that her marriage was just not working. She says, "I was determined to end the relationship. He held me back. I tried to tell him, 'You do it [work hard to get ahead] instead of me.' I worked very hard." At that time Eva was working three jobs. When the director of her agency wanted to name her assistant director, she decided that she needed to go back to college, that without an education she "was not going to get anyplace." She took evening classes, two at a time, and she graduated eight years later with a degree in sociology.

Eva talks about the breakup of her marriage:

> Being together was doing more harm than good. It was not a good relationship. We triggered the worst in each other. It was very difficult for the two boys. They wanted him to be part of their lives but he was not attentive to their needs. They couldn't count on him.
>
> I went to work. I tutored people in English after work. I ran home to make dinner. I made sure they were doing their homework. Then I ran to school. I couldn't rely on him for anything. Once in a while he gave us $100 but he really wasn't there. And the boys started rebelling just like other kids. They were suffering from the breakup.

Since the divorce, Eva has taken a job with greater responsibility in city government and has gone on for a master's degree. She has also remarried. She describes her second husband as "very smart, very loving, very caring to my children. He would do anything for them. He would have been such a great father. Sometimes I regret tying my tubes."

Eva believes she is very lucky to have had positive role models in her life:

> In Mexico, I had an uncle who told me there's a better life out there. He would tell me not to watch the soap operas and instead get a book; for birthdays he gave me a book. My parents only went to the first grade of grammar school but my father was dreaming about my getting a diploma. How other people perceived me gave me strength. If they think I can do it, maybe I can. Like the director of the agency where I worked. I adopted many of her ways. She liked good food; I became very picky about food. She owned a Cross Country Volvo; I just bought a Cross Country Volvo. She told me, "I really want you to go to school." She is very well-to-do, very well educated. She saw ability in me.

Listening to Eva speak about her life, one has the feeling that she was special in the eyes of others from her childhood on. Particularly telling is her comment that "How other people perceived me gave me strength." Her uncle, her father, the elderly woman with whom she lived in New York, the people she worked for—they all saw a person with special qualities: intelligence, surely, but also perhaps drive, ability, the capacity to relate warmly to others, and a willingness to work very hard for her goals. Eva did not have these opportunities in mind as a young woman; but she constantly needed to be open to new possibilities and, on some level, to believe that she could achieve at ever higher levels as her goals evolved, step by step. Her willingness to leave her family in Mexico and to make her way alone in New York at the age of 17 at once exemplifies the incredible courage shown by innumerable immigrants over the past two hundred years and at the same time is an individual story of courage, faith in self, and willingness to take risks. But human beings are multifaceted, with multiple needs. Lonely in New York, isolated from her family and culture, Eva met and married a young man who she very quickly realized was wrong for her—at least wrong for the parts of her that yearned for a different life. Her experience reminds us that people are often made up of contradictory needs. Part of Eva needed and wanted the intimacy, companionship, and perhaps security that she thought marriage would provide; yet that same relationship would, in time, frustrate and impede her hopes and dreams for the future. It was a "mistake marriage" that clearly turned out to be a bad choice.

Eva decided at the extraordinarily young age of 21 that she needed to stop bearing a child a year and took the drastic step of having her tubes tied. As the years went on, her willingness to be open to new experiences was key to her development: going to the support group at her son's school, volunteering and then taking a paid job at the library, typing a letter when she knew neither how to type nor how to turn out a professional document, constantly being willing to take risks. At every stage, one opportunity led to the next; but what clearly underlies the narrative is Eva's capacity for hard work and her fundamental belief that if given the chance, she could live up to people's expectations and achieve her goals.

She came to realize that the marriage had been a false step. It was going to both hold her back and force her and her sons to live in a hostile, acrimonious environment. Going it alone was in some ways easier than living with constant conflict and colliding values. Like Linda Powell, Eva Sanchez represents an American ideal—the self-made person (Horatia Alger, if you will). She started with nothing, worked hard, acquired skills and education, leaped several social classes, overcame the impediment of English not being her first language, and made it in America, caring for her children all the while. In Eva's life, moreover, two powerful American values collided: the importance of staying married, particularly when children are involved, and the importance of achieving one's own dreams and potential. Whether her opportunities pertained to advanced education, higher status, upward mobility, or making significant contributions to the community, Eva viewed them as being in direct conflict with the norm of staying married to someone who neither shared her aspirations nor truly understood them. Eva is hardly alone in experiencing these contradictory imperatives.

Hannah Alexander, a 66-year-old white woman, illustrates the dual themes of falling into a youthful mistake marriage and dramatically remaking her life after becoming a single mother. She starts by talking about her childhood:

> I spent my early years living in Coney Island and the Bronx. My roots are in the Bronx. We moved to California when I was 8; we lived in what we called "the farm." It was in the boonies. We raised chickens and only had cold water in a bathroom that was outside the house.
>
> I went to a little country school. We were the only Jews for miles and miles. For high school I went to St. Gabriel's, where I got involved in debate. I won a debate contest and that got me to the national contest, which was in Philadelphia. After the debate I went to visit my grandmother, my aunt, and my cousins in New York and fell instantly in love.

He was in the navy and stationed in Cuba. We got engaged. I was 18 and had just started college. I left college and got a job to make some money.

We got married and went down to Guantánamo. Before I knew it, I was pregnant. The first year was a rocky start. We were both immature and didn't really know each other very well. There was a lot of tension in the relationship. He was assigned to shore patrol and they had a big red light district; he had an affair with one of the prostitutes. And I'm seven months pregnant with no supports, no friends, no family, no school. I was struggling to deal with the pregnancy and it was super, super hot.

My daughter was born there in July 1956. We came back in October of that year and lived with my in-laws. I was struggling to make the relationship work. His parents were very difficult and there was a lot of conflict in the house. I focused on my daughter.

When Hannah realized that something was really wrong, she went to a therapist, "someone I could talk to." He was very supportive of her returning to school; and when her daughter was "two to three-ish," she applied to a public college nearby. She recounts: "My husband hid my acceptance letter." When she found out she had been accepted, she started going to classes but needed her husband to babysit. He was also going to college—on the G.I. Bill. By then they had their own apartment in a low-income housing project. At one point he left and went back to his mother's. He returned to their apartment, but she got the flu and had to drop out of school. Later she threatened to leave unless he agreed that she could go to school. He did agree, she returned to classes at night, and they moved to a better place. Hannah started going to college full-time and placed her daughter first in a preschool program and then in a full-day kindergarten. She describes what happened next:

> My husband and I continued to have our difficulties. We moved to a middle-income project where he met our next-door neighbor who smoked pot and he got into that. I graduated summa cum laude and thought, "Why am I taking this shit?" I went on to graduate school in clinical psych and received a Woodrow Wilson grant. So the outside world was validating me as a person, as an intellect, and meanwhile, he's very self-centered. Finally, in January 1965 he left for good.

I was very upset. I felt abandoned. I wanted him but I wanted him to be different than the way he was. I thought I was going to fall apart. It turned out later that he had a girlfriend and he moved in with her. Eventually I felt as though a huge burden had been lifted off my shoulders. I felt like I could be me. I was relieved of the awful burden of this difficult man. My daughter was nine and a half when we split.

At first, Hannah says that her husband gave her money irregularly. She describes him as very angry but adds with some feeling, "You'd think *I'd* be angry!" Though he was seeing their daughter every other weekend, he would simply bring her to his parents and then leave. She describes the situation as "very horrible" for her daughter. "I would send the kid off OK and she would come home a basket case."

Hannah and her daughter moved from the Bronx to Greenwich Village, closer to her graduate school. She describes this period as a "difficult time." In the Bronx, she had a very helpful neighbor and friends; in the Village, "it was just me and her." Her daughter became depressed and Hannah got her into therapy. Hannah and her husband divorced, and he stopped giving money. To get child support, she says, "I had to go to family court so I said, 'Screw it. I can manage. I can make it.' " To make matters worse, one day her mother-in-law came to visit without phoning first. Since they might not have been home, Hannah told her, "In the future, just call me first." According to Hannah, "She took that excuse to cut off all relationship with my daughter. Not a birthday card. Not a present. No child support. And I didn't want to spend my days in court so I just let it go. And she wasn't seeing her father at all. Not a phone call. I never forgave him for that."

Hannah became very active in the struggles against the Vietnam War and for women's liberation, and she worked professionally in the field of community psychology in a hospital in the Bronx. She describes herself at that time as "a political person waiting for a movement to happen." As she says, "I made a completely new life. I followed things that had always been important to me." But even as Hannah was actively discovering who she was and participating with energy and enthusiasm in the movements of the late 1960s and 1970s, she was also in conflict with her teenage daughter, who did not share many of her interests. Hannah had been raised to be "active and competent"—even as a child she was expected to shop, cook, and take care of her brother—but she describes her daughter as "more depressive." While Hannah was immersed in trying to change the world, her daughter wanted a more conventional life, "like experimenting with makeup and hanging out with her friends."

After her daughter was grown, Hannah returned to school and received her master's in social work. She also remarried. Her husband, who had been a psychology professor, is someone with whom she has much in common. As she says, "His values are my values." Her daughter is also married, is a teacher, and has one son, to whom Hannah is very close.

When discussing how she survived the difficult times in her life—enduring the end of her marriage, raising her daughter alone—Hannah credits friends and neighbors. She states forcefully, "They got me through. It would have been impossible without them." But then she continues: "It was really important that I was doing something I really loved. I *loved* what I was doing. I *loved* living in the Village. It was safe and decent. My life was so full of meaning. I *loved* working in the South Bronx. I loved it! I just loved it!"

Hannah, like Eva Sanchez, married the wrong man. Perhaps she was just too young to know who she really was, who she might become. Or was she one person at 18, becoming another—an intellectual and political activist—only after she experienced an extremely difficult marriage and divorce and found herself totally on her own and responsible for her own daughter? And, of course, this major turning point in her life occurred during a momentous and, for many, thrilling period in American culture and politics. The belief that people working together could really bring about significant social and political change was in the air. The civil rights movement of the early 1960s had demonstrated what could be accomplished through collective action and commitment, and the antiwar and women's movements learned from the sit-ins, the marches, and the other organized efforts of thousands of people. Hannah's evolution must also be seen within this historical context, an empowering time that surely affected Hannah both personally and politically.

Jeri Miller, a 54-year-old white mother of a biracial son, also talks about how she dramatically changed her life after her son was born. She begins with how she got pregnant: "What did George Carlin say? Sex, drugs, and rock and roll. Didn't he say without drugs and alcohol, we'd never procreate? Most of us don't say, 'Let's go upstairs and conceive Johnny.' And it was the '70s and prior to AIDS. And I was sexually active—no, I mean *sexually active*. I was 29 when I got pregnant. I say he was my thirtieth birthday present."

The oldest of four children, Jeri grew up in a small town in Massachusetts. Her grandmother was a single parent, her mother was a single parent for a short period of time, and her sister is a divorced single parent. Jeri's son's father left at the end of her seventh month. He has never shown any interest in his son or provided any child support.

When her son was a baby, Jeri worked part-time as a bookkeeper. When he was eighteen months old, the ceiling in her apartment fell in. She recalls, "There had been a fire in the apartment above mine and no one had cleaned it up properly so it was raining in upstairs and eventually the ceiling fell in. I just got the baby out of his crib in time." While Jeri was trying to get the ceiling fixed, she became, in her words, "very, very depressed." So, she says,

> I went into therapy and first I was seeing a psychiatrist at Lenox Hill Hospital [on Manhattan's Upper East Side]. He was a nice boy but he really didn't get it. We talked about my being suicidal but I told him I'm not suicidal—if anything, I'm a homicidal type. I got very aggressive. I flipped out on him. I told him, "I want a woman therapist *now*." He finally got it and arranged a meeting with the female social worker who had done the intake interview.
>
> She was wonderful, absolutely wonderful. She really helped me. She changed my life. I could not have done it without her. She was very directive. She said to me once, "If there was anything you could

do, what would it be?" I said, "Go to college." And she asked me again, "If there was *anything* you could do, what would it be?" and I said again, in a small, hesitant voice, "Go to college," and she said, "But Jeri, you can go to college." But I didn't think I was smart enough. If I was good at a job, I thought it was easy or I was lucky. My therapist had me tested and then I started college. Psychologically, I took it two weeks at a time. I took five courses each semester and I loved it!

Jeri describes how she managed to attend college full-time with a toddler to care for:

I went on aid. I don't call it welfare because it has nothing to do with the real meaning of the word *welfare*. My therapist put my son in day care. It's the only way anyone can make it—if you're single or whatever. At the day care center a group of mothers met, and it seemed to me the single mothers had it easier. If I fucked up, I had no one else to blame. I wasn't angry with anyone. In a way I was lucky he left before my son was born. He never abandoned my child. I didn't have to be angry. It was one less thing to deal with.

According to Jeri, becoming a single mother changed her: "When you're a single mother, you start to feel like you're in charge. You're the bottom line. Everything hangs on you. But you can't do it without good friends. I have wonderful, long-term friends from work, from college, from that day care group, through thick and thin. They are a support group, a support system. No one can do it without friends."

At college, Jeri was in the honors program and had two majors and two minors. But it was her women's studies courses, she says, that gave her a "whole new paradigm. There were so many ways of looking at everything—from this angle or that perspective. It changed everything. Then I went to law school and it was a wonderful, wonderful experience! They were trying to teach us how to think and how to learn because in law it is new every day."

When asked how she took care of herself while raising her son, Jeri responds that going to college and law school *was* taking care of herself. She continues, "And therapy. Fifty minutes once a week all about me!" She credits her therapist with helping her to sort through how to be a good mother and achieve something for herself. It wasn't until the ceiling fell in, literally, that Jeri became depressed enough to seek help, to insist on a female therapist, to begin to see herself differently—at first through her therapist's eyes—and then to make the fundamental change in her life of going to college. Once she entered an academic setting, she experienced the joy of learning and came to recognize and get pleasure from her own intelligence and ability. She has since raised her son while working as a lawyer—something she would never have dreamed of doing when she was "rocking and rolling" in her mid-20s.

Judith Berman, a 62-year-old white mother of six, also made profound changes in her life after her marriage ended. She was born and raised in New Jersey; but at 20, she says, after a year and a half of college, she went to Texas to visit a cousin and "While I was there, I met a young man, fell in love, got pregnant and got married. It was a summer romance that went on."

Judith and her husband had six children in seven years. A few years later, their marriage ended: "We were together for ten years. He walked out. That had happened before but this time I wasn't going to take him back. There had been problems in the marriage. He had several affairs. He had temper tantrums. He had a spotty work history and he didn't always put us first." When Judith and her husband separated, the children ranged in age from 9 to 2. Since she and the children had "no means of support," she applied for welfare; eventually they received Aid to Families with Dependent Children (AFDC), food stamps, and Medicaid. Judith describes her husband as a "noninvolved, nonresponsible parent." She elaborates:

> He wouldn't come for the children when he said he would; he wouldn't bring them back when he said he would. The woman he was living with after we separated jumped off a building. That could have been me.

He was no help; he was an impediment. When my son got married—he had gone to medical school—someone said to his father, "You must be very proud." He responded, "No, I didn't raise them."

Judith went back to school part-time; after she finished her B.A., she went on to graduate school. She describes that period of her life:

I finished my graduate degree in 1974. It was one of the worst periods of my life. It was the time of the gas shortage. I had no money. I had crazy babysitters. For a time I lived on Pathmark waffles. I was still receiving AFDC. One day I remember I had an oral presentation in class. My oldest daughter was 13; my youngest was 5. They were both sick. I left them home alone. I had to do it; I had no option. It was the first time I had ever left her alone with a younger child. After the presentation I came home and took them to the pediatrician. They didn't even have the same illness. He didn't usually accept Medicaid but he did with me. I was just another white, Jewish girl who had made a bad marriage. I fit in. I was just like the previous patient. I was one of them.

And all this was when there was no school lunch program. The kids had to come home for lunch. Neighbors helped, friends helped, other women helped. And it was the early 1970s. Legal Services was on your side.

After her husband left, how did Judith have the strength, the courage, the faith in herself to return to school, obtain the welfare benefits and health coverage they needed, and eventually earn a master's degree despite having six children to care for? She literally remade her life—and in doing so remade her children's lives as well. Judith remarried six years after her first husband walked out. Her present husband, a highly educated leader in the community, shares many of her interests and values and gets along well with her children. Judith too has become a professional who is well respected in the community.

Perhaps Lourdes Garcia most vividly illustrates the profound changes that have taken place in the lives of some of the single mothers I interviewed. Lourdes, a 60-year-old Latina woman, grew up in the South Bronx. She was the oldest of three children but in effect was an only child, since one brother was ten and the other brother twenty years her junior. She begins by saying, "I never thought I had the brains to do anything. I thought I was either stupid or crazy." Lourdes went to a community college when she was 40 and had to take remedial English. Because she felt it was "shameful" that she didn't know how to write, a friend of hers encouraged her to practice. She wrote a story that she tried to find to show me. When she couldn't find it easily, she said, "Oh, I know it. I'll tell it to you."

I grew up in an Irish neighborhood. When I was 12 years old, my friend and I were invited to Tommy Daly's birthday party. My friend had one party dress; I had fifteen Sunday dresses, party dresses. My father was a French chef so he was middle class and my mother's father was a judge in Puerto Rico. I was named after my mother's two sisters—one who got her doctorate at NYU and was the intelligent sister and the other who was the socialite, the femme fatale.

I was the only Puerto Rican on the block and going to the party I was worried that my hair was going to frizz. That would show I had black blood, that I was a spic. I had a gorgeous dress. Tommy was one of twelve brothers—all gorgeous. I already had an attitude. I really felt like an insect but my attitude covered that. My friend was in seventh heaven.

At the party everyone was eating, dancing and playing spin the bottle. On the way over, my friend said, "I'm in love with Tommy." I was in love with Tommy too but she said it first so that meant I was hands off. When we played spin the bottle, the bottle turned toward Tommy and then it turned toward me so we had to go into the other room for him to kiss me. He shut the door and turned to me and said, "I can't kiss you. You're a spic." I collected every fiber of my being and said, "How could I kiss you? You have a green line on your gum" and he did. We went out of the room and nobody knew but he was fiddling with his mouth trying to wipe off the green on his gum the rest of the evening and I was glad. Then I cried for two weeks. I cried because I wasn't white. I cried because I didn't have a long neck. I cried because my eyes weren't blue. I cried because I was Puerto Rican.

Lourdes describes her family as "very Catholic" and calls herself the "parental child," meaning the child who took care of others, including at times her parents. Her mother was "always babied; she was afraid of the world. My mother drowns in a cup of water." She feels she had a "wonderful" childhood until she was a teenager. She had a lot of friends, "a group of girls." But when she became a teenager, her father's attitude toward her changed. He told her, "You're a woman now and you can't do this, you can't do that. You can't talk to men; you can't sit on your uncle's lap."

> When I was 15, I had my first boyfriend—he was Irish. So we petted and tongue-kissed and because I thought it was a sin, I confessed it and the priest told me to say so many Hail Marys at the fifteen stations of the cross that my friends asked me what I had done that was so bad. But I couldn't tell them I had tongue-kissed so I made something up and said I had taken something from a store.
>
> My father always said, "You don't have to be the best; you just have to go up one rung" so that eventually the family as a whole would rise. My mother said I had to be like my intellectual aunt so I had problems with my sexuality—with being a good girl or a bad girl. I thought it had to be one or the other. I had a tough time with boys. I didn't want a Puerto Rican boy. And then I met the father of my children. I liked and chose poor rejects; I was going to fix him.

Lourdes studied art in high school and was exposed to "another world"—the art world in Greenwich Village. Married at age 20, she had her first child at 21. Her husband was from an Irish family, fourth oldest of twelve children. According to Lourdes, he "belonged to a gang, was a hoody kind of guy." Her father disapproved of him and thought he was "lower class." Lourdes thought, "I'm lucky I got him."

After their marriage, her husband started drinking. Lourdes recalls those early days:

> During the pregnancy, I was very depressed. I wanted to die. It was like a moth to light—me to death. My first child was a terrible delivery. It was very long and he suffered minimal brain damage. He was so beautiful, so perfect. It was the only thing I made that was perfect. He validated me. I was so proud of him. In two years I was pregnant again. My second son was a joy, dynamite, special. He was very alive, agile. He was me. The apple of my eye.

I was doing the rhythm [method]. Everybody around me was doing the same thing. A year and a half later I had my third child but I was very unhappily married. I contemplated suicide. My husband was drinking and fighting and he used to beat me, but my kids looked like John-John Kennedy. They were dressed perfectly. After my third child, I went into therapy. I knew I had to get out of the relationship. I lost weight and got rid of my husband.

After they separated, Lourdes started working in a law firm as a receptionist, made decent money, and met interesting people; she stayed there for eleven years. Some weeks her husband gave her $200; other weeks he didn't. When the children were small, she put them in the nursery downstairs in her building:

It was during that time when there were nurseries like that. The kids learned so much there and it was affordable. I couldn't have done it without that nursery. But it was tough. I had to get up in the morning, get ready, get the kids dressed, get them to the nursery, and then take the bus to the train to get to work on time and at the end of the day do it all in reverse, get home, get supper, and so forth. Without the day care I would have been on welfare.

In fact, at one time I changed jobs and got fired and had to go on welfare. It was terrible. They gave you so little and one time they gave me a can of Spam. Spam! I thought it was like dog food.

During this period, according to Lourdes, she used to "exploit men. I learned to use my femininity. It got me money. I learned from my girlfriends—don't put out. If you do put out, they better pay. I was like a femme fatale—a pro with men. Men were pawns to be used. Either use or get used. Better take than be taken." At one point, prior to the legalization of abortion, Lourdes became pregnant and had an abortion; when she got home, she could not stop the bleeding. Her girlfriends saw her through the incident, and in fact were very important to her throughout these difficult years. She remarried, but her second husband was abusive to her and to her sons so she "threw him out." But not before she became pregnant with her fourth son. She had to leave her job, went on welfare for the next two years, and was very depressed. In time she went back to work at the law firm—now with four boys to care for.

One day Lourdes arrived home from work and learned that her youngest son had been hit by a car. She describes that terrible time:

> I started screaming. He died fourteen hours later. He even had blond hair. Though it was curly, it was blond. He was my pride—we're not all that dark. And I was older, more mature. I enjoyed him more. What happened was that he crossed the street to get an ice cream and a drunk driver hit him. My oldest son saw it and called his father. My friends kept me afloat. They were there day and night—for a month.

Lourdes and her sons moved to Manhattan shortly after her son's death, and she went to therapy every night. Then she met a young woman at the law firm where she worked who encouraged her to go to school. She started community college and found she was an excellent student. As she says, "My whole world changed 180 degrees. After two years I transferred to the Columbia School of General Studies and it was the most exciting thing I have done. I got As and graduated on the dean's list."

Lourdes went on to graduate school and currently works as a professional social worker. She feels what really helped her was "women helping women," her friends who encouraged her and helped her through the exceedingly difficult times, as well as the day care center where her children were cared for and the welfare system that occasionally stepped in to provide emergency rent so they would not be evicted. Toward the end of the interview, Lourdes said, "My life is wonderful now." Two months later, on September 11, 2001, Lourdes's middle son, a paramedic whom she described as a "joy, dynamite, special . . . the apple of my eye," was killed trying to save people following the attack on the World Trade Center.

Lourdes's experience illustrates many of the issues and dilemmas that many women in the United States continue to face and that are even more pressing for single mothers, because of their precarious social, economic, and sometimes emotional situation. Her personal encounters with racial and ethnic prejudice and her consequent internalization of these attitudes; society's dichotomous view of women—either sexy or smart, or in Lourdes's words, "intellectual" or "femme fatale"; her constant struggles to balance work and care for children; and her precarious economic position, which led her to move on and off welfare and to form relationships with men for financial gain, all reflect fundamental conflicts in American culture. What is perhaps most remarkable about Lourdes's experience is that at the age of 40 she was able to overcome her self-doubt, class, ethnicity, and gender, the omnipresent impediments to achieving an education, and the constraints of her role of mother of four young sons to reach out to the educational system, totally engage in the learning process, finish her college degree, go on to graduate school, and become a professional. It is truly an incredible feat.

Several of these women have transformed their lives through higher education, obtaining a college diploma or, in some cases, graduate or professional degrees. Except for detailing some of their financial difficulties or describing the problems of simultaneously caring for children and running a household while taking on taxing academic responsibilities, these women say little about their struggles in these schools. But academic institutions are not always welcoming to women who do not fit the standard pattern of college or graduate students. Jeanne Gonzalez alludes to this problem when she repeats the dismissive comment of the graduate advisor in the speech pathology program at her college: "You're a mother; there's no way."

In their article "Can Education Eliminate Race, Class, and Gender Inequality?" Roslyn Mickelson and Stephen Smith state, "The dominant ideology assumes that American society is open and competitive, a place where an individual's status depends on talent and motivation, not inherited position, connections or privileges linked to ascriptive characteristics like gender or race."[1] But as Vivyan Adair and Sandra Dahlberg point out, many in academia view the normative student as "rational, ordered, stable and mobile"; those who do not meet these expectations may well be perceived as deviant, as the other. They add, "Women and people of color may enter and gain the credentials of the academy only when their values, language, and presence mesh with privileged academic codes. The same is true, of course, of working-class and poor students. A chosen few may enter, but only if they are willing to transform themselves."[2]

To illustrate the difficulties of poor, single mothers attempting to obtain an education, Adair and Dahlberg recount the experience of a woman they call Campbell. The process of moving from poverty to the professional class was, for Campbell, "full of twists and turns[,] . . . rejection and loss, oppression and resistance." Campbell recalls that when she entered graduate school, her program chair warned her that she would have to make some "tough choices," as the chair herself had done. She would need to find "superior care" for her child and make sure her husband was willing "to let her make graduate school and teaching her only priorities."[3] Campbell had to tell the professor that she had no husband and could not possibly afford the kind of child care suggested. According to Campbell, the chair refused to advise her after that exchange.

Campbell describes her typical day as a single mother/graduate student:

> Rising at 3:00 AM to correct student papers and make lesson plans; taking busses from home, to childcare, to the university and then back again every day; using public transportation with my daughter every evening to do my laundry, go to food banks, try to collect food stamps, access assistance in paying energy bills, or to visit free health clinics; arriving home at 7:00 or 8:00 in the evening so that I could care for my exhausted and often ill daughter, and then cook, clean and study until midnight; trying to get three hours of sleep so that I could start all over again in the morning.[4]

What makes it possible for these women—and many others—to overcome difficult childhood experiences, dysfunctional marriages or relationships, unplanned pregnancies, a profound shortage of resources—both financial and support services—and the often overwhelming responsibilities of caring for the children and maintaining the family? Where do they get the courage, the resilience, the ability to focus on positive goals rather than getting bogged down in the negatives that often surround them? How do they move from positions of relative powerlessness within their personal spheres and often the larger society as well to assume positions of greater authority both personally and in the public sphere, taking control of their lives? Power is conventionally conceived as power over others. Several of the women interviewed for this study have lived subservient to others for significant portions of their lives. Soledad Martinez's husband monitored her comings and goings daily and threatened to take the children if she left him. The husbands of both Soo Hyun Park and Young Heoy Lee withheld financial support, including money for food and other essentials, and terrorized their wives emotionally. Jennifer Soriano's male friend abused her verbally; several young women were thrown out of their homes by their families when they became pregnant. In addition, many of these women are also members of minority groups and suffer from discrimination and greater degrees of powerlessness because of their skin color, their ethnicity, or their economic status. The hurt thereby inflicted is perhaps voiced most poignantly and vividly by Lourdes Garcia in speaking of her feelings about being Puerto Rican. Yet, despite significant personal and structural barriers, many of them have managed to empower themselves to move toward greater control of their own and their children's lives.

The law professors Lani Guinier and Gerald Torres, authors of *The Miner's Canary: Enlisting Race, Resisting Power, Transforming Democracy*, suggest alternatives to the "power-over" model. They point out that acting with greater autonomy and dignity is a way of acting with greater power, stressing that "power is generative, it involves . . . becoming something. . . . It expands in its exercise."[5] Soledad's going to college and graduate school may have been her first moves toward self-realization and greater autonomy and essential steps in her decision to leave her husband. Education has played a major role in several of these women's lives, enabling them to act with greater personal agency. Jeri's and Hannah's therapists were central to their beginning to perceive themselves as women with real intellectual capacity and ability, but their college experiences opened up new worlds in which they began to believe they could play significant roles. Despite caring for four children with very limited resources, Lourdes managed to graduate from college and go on for a professional degree. Perhaps along the way she was also able to resolve her feelings of having to choose between being either a femme fatale or an intellectual.

Guinier and Torres argue that "power-over" can be replaced by "power-with," which they describe as "relational and interactive," requiring participation. In fact, they claim that participation leads to increased power regardless of the results.[6] This formulation brings to mind the thousands of participants in the civil rights movement—those who participated in the struggle to desegregate lunch counters in the South though faced with physical harm or jail, those who marched and demonstrated notwithstanding attack dogs and water cannon, those who worked to register blacks to vote despite the threat and reality of death. As Guinier and Torres articulate, it is through doing, through participating in the world around us, that we learn who we are, what we can do, who we can be. Eva Sanchez, for example, saw glimmers of how her life might change and felt more empowered to make those changes with every step she took. And those realizations, for better or for worse, took her farther and farther from a life with her husband.

Some might say that these women have an intrinsic toughness, an ability to adjust to new circumstances that most of us lack. Such admirable strength of character is seen as unique to certain people because of their genetic heritage, a particularly propitious upbringing, or sheer determination. Others suggest that this quality of resilience is not an innate characteristic of the special few but is rather, in the phrase of the psychologist Linda Hartling, "all about relationships." According to Hartling, resilience is generally described too narrowly both as "the ability to achieve good outcomes in one's life after experiencing significant hardships or adversities, such as poverty, family discord, divorce, lack of access to educational opportunities, racism, etc." and also as "the ability to recover from traumatic experiences, such as physical or sexual abuse, assault, severe neglect, and many other forms of trauma." Such a view focuses on individual strengths and qualities—intelligence, high self-esteem, temperament, internal strength, and the like—and promotes the belief that "the lucky few, *those endowed with these special strengths*, will succeed, will be resilient, and will become independent and self-sufficient despite encounters with significant obstacles" (emphasis hers).[7]

Other researchers have developed the concept of *hardiness* to explain the individual characteristics associated with resilience to stress. Those deemed *hardy* are thought to exhibit three characteristics: they can easily commit to the task at hand, they believe that events are generally within their own control, and they perceive change as a challenge rather than a threat. Hartling argues that this formulation of hardiness was based on studies of "white male middle-to-upper-level business executives" and suggests that while it might be useful in analyzing that group's response to stress and hardship, these characteristics are far less applicable to other groups, particularly women. She points out, moreover, that the relevant studies were done in the 1970s, when "business executives were the beneficiaries of invisible systems of relational support comprised of secretaries, wives, mothers, and undervalued services providers . . . who likely made it possible for these privileged professionals to be 'hardy.' "[8]

Many researchers investigating the nature of resilience suggest that contrary to widespread beliefs, its characteristic strengths are not entirely innate and developed in isolation from other people. Hartling and her colleagues at the Wellesley Centers for Women have set forth what they call the Relational-Cultural Theory (RCT) of psychological development. RCT postulates that the sources of resilience and strength in the face of hardship, tragedy, or personal trauma are relationships—not that certain individuals somehow have those qualities within them but that they have been and are continually developed, nourished, and strengthened by "growth-fostering (or resilience-strengthening) relationships throughout [the individuals'] lives." If we think along these lines, we might more appropriately define resilience as the *"ability to connect, reconnect, and resist disconnection in response to hardships, adversities, trauma, and alienating social/cultural practices"* (emphasis hers).[9] This approach moves beyond the belief that some individuals inherently have the characteristics to survive and overcome difficult life circumstances to focus instead on what strengthens the relationships that in turn encourage and build resilience. What indeed are the traits that strengthen resilience and how do we acquire them? What is the role of self-esteem? Do we gain self-esteem through individual achievement that enables us to build a sense of competence, through interactions with people who are significant to us and think well of us, or through some combination of both? What is the relationship between resilience and empowerment? What role does anger play in motivating these women to transform their lives despite their extraordinarily difficult circumstances? Anger propelled Jeri Miller to demand a female therapist who was key to her future development. Did anger similarly inspire Judith Berman to fashion a very different life for herself after her husband walked out? In some of these instances, does anger at their unexpected, unplanned circumstances or at their partners give these women the necessary impetus and confidence to overcome obstacles that they might once have thought were insurmountable?

And what role does opportunity play? How can individuals test what they can do, how well they can learn, what roles they might be able to play in the wider society without opportunities—in education, in employment, and in the life of the community? Finally, what is the relationship between social support and the strengthening of resilience? These issues will be explored in greater depth in the next chapter, when we examine the nature of the relationships and support systems that some of these single mothers have had or have developed.

5

"Everybody Knows My Grandma"

Extended Families and
Other Support Networks

My mom has been my savior. . . . She helps me in many ways. She helps me with his laundry; she also cooks for us and we bring it home. And she gives me emotional support. I speak to her every day. My mom is my everything. . . . That kind of emotional support allows you a chance to breathe, to rest, to get your center.

Cicely Franklin, 29-year-old mother of one

As single moms, we're always so independent, so self-reliant. But God is going to take you to the end of yourself so you will have to seek him. In that weakness, God can work. We have to leave that pride, that arrogance behind, live on a different plane to let him do what he needs to do. . . . I say, "Thank you, Jesus! Thank you for my kids. Thank you for my job."

Naomi Martin, 46-year-old mother of three

Karen Morrison is a 57-year-old African American woman who was born and raised in a small city north of New York City. After high school she attended community college at night but never finished. She worked and lived at home with her parents. She recalls,

I met Susan's father at a party at a mutual friend's house. We talked. He lived in Atlanta and constantly offered me a ticket to go there. He was twelve years my senior and worked in insurance. He was divorced and had two children from a previous marriage and one daughter from before he was married. He was highly educated, intelligent, a very nice person. I met him in the latter part of 1966 and became pregnant in 1967.

It was a devastating thing for me. He didn't use a condom and we didn't discuss anything in my family. My mother never discussed anything with me. It was thought to be sinful. I was raised in the church. My parents were good, loyal, strict. And unfortunately I listened to other people. They said if you urinate very hard that it passes so I did that and of course when you do that some passes but not all.

And it was all the more devastating when I thought, How do I tell my parents? How do I form my mouth to tell them? Actually, I went to Atlanta twice to have an abortion and didn't and then the third time I couldn't do it. [Even though abortion was not yet legal, Karen had found a doctor willing to perform one.]

I was helping my aunt to move around that time and I told her. I told her that I don't know how to tell my parents so my aunt told my mom. One day I was on my way to Long Island—to a friend's wedding, and my mother asked me, "Don't you have something to discuss with me?" I wasn't thinking of anything special so I said, "No." And then she said, "I have been your mother for twenty-two years and I have never deserted you and I won't do that now." And my dad knew but never said one word. After my daughter was born, I knew I had been beating myself up but there was no need to beat myself up anymore.

Karen describes her relationship with her daughter's father:

Susan's father only came up once during the pregnancy. My mother was incensed but I loved him. I wanted to marry him. Susan was born on his birthday. I called to tell him, but by the time he came to see her, she was one month old. When he did come up, my mother said that she had something to say and didn't want to be interrupted. She said, "I love my granddaughter and I would love you to be in her life but under no circumstances should you get married." He said he would marry me and I believed him because I wanted to believe him. He wanted me to come to live with him but I had already made one error and wasn't going to make another one.

Susan's father saw her at one month, ten months, and 10 years old. He would call periodically but would not come to visit. Eventually, he remarried and had another child and then moved to Birmingham, Alabama. Because Susan felt she really did not know him, Karen called him around her tenth birthday and he came to visit. After that, Susan started visiting him on holidays and during the summer. He sent her tickets to visit him and paid her expenses while she was with him. Otherwise he gave no child support. Karen felt she was not going to "chase him from state to state" and says that Susan was "well taken care of." Karen describes how they lived:

> I managed very well. I lived at home with my parents. I wanted to move into our own apartment, but my parents thought you should live at home until you get married. I did not have to listen to my parents but I did. I had great respect for them.
>
> Susan and I had the master bedroom. My father served as her father. My siblings were close to her. My friends were like aunts and uncles and were a lot of help. Susan had wonderful godparents who bought her things. I had no burden. When I went back to work, my mother took care of Susan. Then I sent her to nursery school. When she was 3, I started a new job which was a huge jump in salary at that time. So I took it and put it in the bank. And she did very well in school. She has a good head on her shoulders. She was number one in her class and when she went to Howard [University] she graduated magna cum laude.

Although she had the help of many people around her, Karen emphasizes that her parents were her primary support.

> Dad was an extremely awesome individual. He worked three jobs. He was an extremely proud man. He refused to go on welfare. He would work as many jobs as it would take. But he was always home for dinner at the dinner table. He also did a lot of housework, made lunch, made sure we changed our clothes after school. You know, then you had school clothes and play clothes. And everybody had to eat together at 5:30. Dad was the first black in our town to work in city hall, the first black auxiliary policeman.

But Mom was the driving force as far as God was concerned. We all prayed together. We had to attend church—always. And it carried down to the next generation. Susan is actively involved in Sunday school and in the town.

According to Karen, her personal experience has become her ministry:

I can speak to young girls and tell them that even if something happens in their life, they can still go on. I have three older sisters and they all got married without children out of wedlock. I didn't do it the way it was supposed to be done but I didn't dwell on that because Mom and Dad didn't dwell on it and neither did my siblings. Even my girlfriends' parents were supportive. It's a small community and they made it clear they would be right there for me. I've had the exact same girlfriends since kindergarten.

But all credit for anything I've done goes to my parents and to God. My father influences me more now than ever. He was such a wonderful grandfather. He died a few years ago but we pass the history down to the grandchildren. Mom is alive and well. She's 89 and lives in the same house with Susan, Susan's husband, and their 11-year-old daughter. We have five generations in my family.

Karen met the man she would later marry when her daughter was 1 year old. They married and moved into their own apartment when Susan was 8. After they married, Karen says, "There was a little jealousy" between her daughter and her new husband, but they all worked it out. Karen and her husband had another daughter one year after they married.

The picture Karen paints is of a strong and devoted family unit imbedded within a cohesive community. It is clearly not easy for highly respected, devout parents to welcome into their family the baby of an unmarried 22-year-old daughter, housing and caring for the mother and child without either showing anger or totally taking over the parental role. Karen's trepidation about informing her parents about the pregnancy is obvious—she calls the pregnancy "devastating," and says that she didn't even know how she could "form" her "mouth" to articulate the words that would tell them. Karen's respect for her parents and their authority within the family are also clear. As Karen points out, though she wanted to move with her daughter to their own apartment she acceded to their wishes that a daughter live at home until marriage. They all cooperated; Karen kept her life going, worked, dated, and eventually married and had another child.

But all supportive families do not necessarily let go when the young mother is mature enough to make the key decisions for her child. Keisha Johnson, a 33-year-old woman who migrated to the United States from the Caribbean, tells a somewhat different story:

> I was born in Jamaica and came here at the age of 6. I grew up on Long Island. I had a great childhood. We lived in a predominately white neighborhood. I did OK in school. I had a younger brother, five years younger. My mother never married my father. She got pregnant at 17 or 18 in Jamaica and they broke up. Then she came here and I was left in the care of my grandmother. After she was living here, she met my brother's father and they became the typical American family.
>
> After high school I went to college and got pregnant during my first year around the same age as my mother. I moved out of my house. West Indian families are very strict. When my mother found out, she wanted me to have an abortion. I was four months pregnant and my mother told me it was all right to have an abortion but I couldn't do it. It was not the right thing to do. My grandmother agreed with me. I went to live with her.

The father of Keisha's child was in college and "didn't want to have anything to do with a child." Keisha says that initially she wanted to be with him, but his treatment of her changed her mind. Eventually, she went to court to force him to pay child support, which he has since provided. She adds, "Now we're friends. He cares about the best interests of his daughter."

Members of Keisha's family have actively helped her raise her daughter—first her grandmother, until she died of pancreatic cancer, then an aunt who lives nearby. Before her long commute to work, Keisha drops her daughter, who is now 12, at her aunt's house, where her daughter catches the school bus. At the end of the school day her daughter goes to an after-school program, after which her uncle brings her back to the house. Keisha then picks her up when she returns from work. But, as Keisha points out, relying on family, while often essential, can breed problems. She has had some conflicts with her aunt and uncle:

> Sometimes they forget that I'm 33 and entitled to a life. I have recently found someone. They didn't know him and are not acting very nice. But I am her mother and there needs to be a line drawn now. There's a lot of conflict.
>
> My aunt is obsessed with my daughter. She couldn't have any children of her own and always wants her there. Sometimes she would make plans for me but I work late and I need my own time, my own space. Recently, she got upset because I cut my daughter's hair. She felt I should have informed her beforehand. But now I've gotten the point across. It was something I had to do.
>
> I am thankful for my family, especially for my grandmother. My very extended family has been both a help and a problem. At first, my daughter didn't even call me "Mom" so I said, "Who's the mother here?" If we disagree, I'm the mom. I feel the need to find my own space.

Depending on family can clearly be problematic for single mothers but often they have little choice. Because of her long commute, Keisha really needs the help of her aunt and uncle. She is extremely reluctant to look for work closer to home because of the benefits she receives at her current job, because from time to time her hours can be somewhat flexible, and because she is attached to both her work and her co-workers. Therefore, until her daughter is a bit older, she will have to grapple with the conflict between her dependency on her relatives and her desire for greater control and autonomy.

Generalizations about the lives of single mothers rarely examine or analyze the intricacies of their lives, the complexities of their affective relationships. Cicely Franklin, a 29-year-old woman, is extremely articulate as she talks about her background:

I came from a small island in the West Indies. I grew up in a tiny village. My sister and I along with our cousins were raised together. My mother and dad married very young and went to the United States to make a better life. So our grandparents were really our parents. I really had a chance to be a child—to run around in the backyard. People grew crops in the backyard. My grandmother took care of the crops; my grandfather went fishing [to earn a living].

They always told us, "Your parents are in the United States to make a better life. They love you." My grandparents took care of everything. Every month we got a barrel of food and clothing from my parents. School was very important. I had a very carefree childhood. I was taught respect for one's elders and the church was important as well. My grandma had eight children. She kept us all connected. Everyone knows my grandma—even today. My passion for social issues and for family come from her. She was the head of the household; she made the rules.

The family was essentially middle class. They had their own property. They were Anglican but I went to Catholic school. My mom took care of everything—money, food supplies. Even coming to the U.S. you had to be connected in order to get a visa and my grandmother knew everyone.

Cicely describes coming to the United States:

My sister and I came here when I was 15. We knew that my mom and my dad were sending for us but I had never lived with my parents so it wasn't easy. Also, my parents had gone through a divorce and my father had moved to England. Everything was joint—the bank accounts and everything—and Dad took pretty much everything and left. He sold the house and took that money, too. It was very difficult for Mom. And we were coming here at the same time. But she took care of everything. She always said if you don't have money, you make your brain work for you.

Just before Cicely left, her grandfather died. "I felt really badly leaving my grandmother. Honestly, I didn't want to leave. Living there was all I ever knew."

After Cicely arrived in New York, she entered the eleventh grade and then went on to her senior year in high school. As she says, "It was a new environment. I was in a co-ed school for the first time. American society was new, American teenage life." Then she went to a private college in Pennsylvania. She was the only black person in every class, but she wasn't really aware then of "racial dynamics and class issues." There were few black students in the college, and "we were all spread out."

Cicely spent her junior year studying at Oxford, and she used that opportunity to get "somewhat reacquainted" with her father, who was still in England. After college she went on to obtain a master's degree and then got a job with an advocacy group working with poor women.

Cicely describes how she got pregnant and the decisions she has subsequently made:

> I was raised with the belief that you're not supposed to have sex before marriage. I had my first relationship at 25. At 26, I met my son's dad. We dated a couple of years and then it got more serious. We were so comfortable with each other that the relationship just moved on. Mom didn't even know and we were not married so it impacted who I told. I had a lot of guilt. I suddenly became a bad girl because I was pregnant before marriage. It was really stressful to tell my mom. Of my generation, I was the first to be pregnant before marriage. Finally, she said, "I trust you. I trust the decision you're making. I'm behind you 100 percent." But I was very stressed out. I was disappointing my mom and my grandma.

Cicely discusses her complex feelings about getting married: "I didn't want to get married just because I was pregnant. I didn't want the fact that I was pregnant make me make a decision about my life. I always loved children and I always loved family. I grew up in an extended family. Also, I was really, really sick during the pregnancy. I couldn't even have a conversation about it all."

When I ask Cicely about birth control, she says that she had gone on the pill for a week but stopped using it because it made her "really, really sick." Her friend used condoms but not all the time, and sometimes "he would—ah—withdraw but that clearly did not work perfectly." When asked about abortion, Cicely responds that she believes every woman should have a choice but that it was not an option for her—not for religious reasons but because she "could not go through the procedure."

Cicely continues to explain her decision-making process:

> I'm the type of person who plans out everything. I used to think—by the time I'm 30, I'll be married. But sometimes things change. I'm very happy with my son. I am living in the present moment, in the context of my world. I am not going to make decisions because of other people's angst. I am not going to be the container for other people's ideas. My son is a gift. To do anything different would be not being true to myself.

Cicely describes the support system that works together to care for her son: "Now his dad and I live together with Sean. We are his parents. We share the cost of child care and other costs. We do not have an intimate relationship. The pregnancy was so difficult it turned me off of sex. Also, it takes a lot to keep a romantic relationship going and right now it's all going to Sean." Sean's paternal grandmother takes care of him during the day while both of his parents work. They bring the baby to her. Cicely says that it was difficult in the beginning because "she acted as though she knew what was best for Sean, as though she was his mom. She's very authoritative in her parenting style. I would tell her about Sean's routine and she said, 'We have developed our own routine.' I would like to put him in a child care setting by 2 if he is potty trained."

Cicely and Sean's father frequently meet at his mother's after work and have dinner there. She feels his mother goes "above and beyond" in ways that often seem "suffocating." They pay her $200 a week for caring for Sean. Cicely says, "It seems expensive to me but it works for her. My family would never take any money to take care of Sean but—never mind."

The help of her own mother has been crucial:

My mom has been my savior. I'd gladly share co-parenting with her. She helps me in many ways. She helps me with his laundry; she also cooks for us and we bring it home. And she gives me emotional support. I speak to her every day. My mom is my everything.

When Sean was a baby, he would cry, cry, cry. The doctor said he didn't have colic but he would cry for no reason. He wasn't hungry; he wasn't wet. There was no real reason. But my mom would hold him and he would stop crying. Having my mom there is more important than having Sean's father. That kind of emotional support allows you a chance to breathe, to rest, to get your center.

Having my mom and my mom's sisters is so important to me—their advice and their belief in me. They say, "What a wonderful mother you are," and you need to hear that. My mom got her center from my grandmother. Everyone could be in conflict and my grandma would walk in a room and calm everyone. She is a calming presence. If I'm half the mother she is . . .

Cicely analyzes the role of women in the village in which she was raised in the West Indies:

The women were very important in the village. Most people who were in control were women. Women did the child rearing. My grandmother worked in the home and outside the home. She grew the crops in the backyard and brought them to market. Reverence was given to women. The church was run by women. The prayer groups were led by women. I have a deep respect for women. They have made men irrelevant in my life. My grandfather played a passive role. The men of the village leave for months at a time to sail [in order to fish].

Summarizing her values, Cicely says that her grandmother raised her to "think individually and to respect tradition." She adds that she has a "collective sense of self, which is both good and not so good." She feels she denies too much of herself, that she makes sure everybody is OK and sometimes doesn't take enough care of herself, and concludes, "I'm becoming more and more aware of that."

Cicely is describing yet another model of single motherhood. While statistically she is a single mother, she and her baby's father live and care for their son together. Moreover, she is fortunate to have relatives on both sides of the family willing to help them and help with Sean's care. She has seemingly re-created the extended family in which she was raised. The dominance of women has also been replicated. It is women with whom she has the strongest relationship—her mother, her grandmother, her aunts, and Sean's paternal grandmother. Cicely says it best: "They have made men irrelevant in my life."

Moreover, Cicely exemplifies a fascinating duality, being simultaneously traditional and modern. She sees herself as part of a strong extended family, she respects the wisdom and experience of elders, and she hopes to carry on many of the traditions of her family and her culture. At the same time, she reserves the right to make fundamental decisions for herself, to break with tradition by having sex before marriage and, perhaps most surprisingly, by not marrying her child's father. As she puts it, "I am not going to make decisions because of other people's angst. I am not going to be the container for other people's ideas." While she sees herself as part of a larger group, her family, she also holds firmly to a view of herself as an individual with her own values and priorities. She indicates that she was too sick during her pregnancy to even seriously discuss marriage, but it had to have taken a great deal of strength and courage to make the decision not to marry—at least at that time. She knew she was profoundly disappointing her family and, of course, she was disappointing herself. She had very different expectations for herself and for her life, but she was not going to be stampeded into the knee-jerk decision to marry simply because others thought it the "right" thing to do. Cicely and her family are reproducing cultural norms that characterized their world in the West Indies. Sean is undoubtedly receiving an enormous amount of love and care and he will, in all likelihood, be the future beneficiary of considerable educational and material opportunities as well.

Other women demonstrate alternative models of survival. Joanne Calabrese, a white woman in her 40s, describes how she survived an extremely difficult marriage and a long, exceedingly acrimonious divorce. Born and raised in Ohio, the second oldest of five children, Joanne states, "We had no money but all of us went to college." She came to New York City with $50 in her pocket, hoping to sing in opera or musical theater. After several years of singing in off-Broadway productions, she found herself drawn to cooking as a career. This was during the early seventies, when she saw the food business as dominated by men. After taking night courses to learn to bake professionally, she was sent on a job interview to a major New York hotel. When she was told that they couldn't hire her because there were no women in the kitchen, she offered to work for free. After six months, she says, "They figured that this girl can do something so they hired me." At work she met and married a fellow cook but soon discovered that they were incompatible, because "he had made a firm commitment not to have children." After their divorce, Joanne remarried and she and her lawyer husband subsequently had two children.

> This marriage was a terribly abusive marriage. Mostly emotional abuse but the threat of physical abuse too. I was thrown down a time or two.
>
> I became somebody else. I could make no decisions of my own. I was constantly criticized. I gave him any money I made; I was told I was too stupid to manage it myself. Sometimes I can't even relate now to that person who inhabited my body. I was afraid the children would grow up thinking this is the way a woman should be and this is the way a man should act. When we split up, my daughter was 6 and my son was 3.

The divorce, Joanne recalls, "was a long process. He kept me in litigation and completely broke for nine years. He refused to leave the apartment but stopped paying the bills. He sued for custody and lost. He went the whole nine yards. He vowed to keep me penniless. He comes from lots of money—millions! He put his assets in his mother's name so I couldn't get at them. He uses money as a power tool." According to Joanne, "The children love their dad and I'm thrilled they do." She has sole legal custody but they share residential custody—one week with him, one week with her. They share all holidays. It's all spelled out in the custody agreement.

Joanne currently owns her own catering business in New York City. How did she make the transition from the insecure, frightened person she became during her marriage to the competent and quite confident person she seems to be today? She credits going back to her therapist, having close friends who had also been through divorce, and having "great family support." She elaborates:

> I learned I had to take care of myself before I can take care of my children. Also, I had to earn money. It was a long process letting go of feelings of being a victim and anger and hatred before I could take care of myself and my children.
>
> In 1992 I needed to start working again. I needed money so I hocked my engagement ring and diamond earrings to set up the catering company. I later got them back. I also borrowed $5,000 from my father; he wouldn't let me pay it back. My baby brother also helped me financially and emotionally. My other brother didn't help financially but was generous with time and support. My sisters gave money when I needed it, and I would do the same for them.

When asked why people, particularly her family, were so supportive in so many ways, Joanne starts to cry and struggles to regain her composure. She continues:

> My brother is a substitute father to the kids. He takes them to ball games. He taught them how to throw a baseball. He really played the role. They adore their uncle.
>
> Moving from married life to single life is difficult financially. I signed everything away to my husband. Interest in the co-op—everything. I got together with my brothers, discussed the situation, and decided to let it go. For a while, I couldn't pay rent; I was getting evicted. My brother paid the rent. I just got finished paying everyone back—my therapist, my gynecologist. They treated me for nothing. My gynecologist called me asking why I wasn't coming in for my checkup and I told him I couldn't pay him. He told me to come in right away anyway. A lot of people took care of me.

Joanne indicates some concern about her business: "My business does well but it's not recession-proof. But if I keep the prices down . . . . I'm very blessed to like what I do. Work is instant validation. It has helped to keep me sane." Joanne's business is located in downtown New York City, not far from the World Trade Center. The attacks of September 11, 2001, occurred five days after we spoke.

An intelligent, multitalented, middle-class woman was nearly destroyed—both emotionally and financially—by a marriage that went very wrong. She married someone far more powerful, more affluent, and more confident than she and watched as her confidence, her sense of self, and her good sense evaporated. As she says, "Sometimes I can't even relate to that person who inhabited my body." And yet, over time, she has been able, with the help of many people, to rebuild her life, her sense of self, her feelings of competence. The key people, aside from her therapist, were members of her family—particularly her brothers, who helped her financially and emotionally and who were there for her children. Moreover, in a society that reveres independence, Joanne had the strength and self-awareness to know she needed help and to accept it. The power of the myth of "rugged individualism" can compel many to feel they must recover from trauma and survive virtually on their own. Though Joanne felt she was beaten down until she almost could not recognize herself, she had the wisdom to let others help her up.

The story of Nancy Mendez, a 52-year-old Latina woman, is different again. One of seven siblings whose parents originally came to New York from Puerto Rico, Nancy describes her relationship with her husband, whom she met in high school, as "difficult." She states, "We were young and inexperienced. I must say I got married for sexual freedom. At that time I couldn't practice sex freely outside of marriage. I was a virgin. When I wore that white dress, it had to mean you were a virgin."

Nancy recalls that they "had problems right away. He wanted to change me as a person. He couldn't accept me." Furthermore, she had problems with birth control. At first she was taking birth control pills because "I knew the marriage wasn't very good, so I wanted to wait and see what happened." Then in 1969 doctors discovered she had a cyst on her uterus that needed to be removed. After the surgery, she asked the doctor if it was a good idea for her to be on the pill; when he told her that he didn't know, she switched to the diaphragm. But she "found it difficult to control—inserting it with the jelly—it would go all over the place so I gave that up." She started using foam; and even though she used a "double dose," she became pregnant.

Nancy's husband didn't want to have children yet. He wanted her to have an abortion, and though she had made an appointment she decided at the last minute not to go through with it. When her husband returned home that night and found out that she had not had the abortion, Nancy reports that he said, "Oh yeah? Well, that's going to be your baby," and he walked out. During her pregnancy, her husband was not around at all. After the baby was born, he saw his son a couple of times and, according to Nancy, "started treating me like a girlfriend. He would come over, have sex, and leave. So I told him, 'I'm not your girlfriend; I'm your wife. You can't come here, not provide anything, have sex, and leave.' " After the baby was a year old, he didn't come around any more.

Nancy then went to family court. She describes that period as the "most terrible time in my life—that I had to take him to court. And the judges were very lenient! If he said he didn't have the money—he said he wasn't working—they said he didn't have to pay." During this time Nancy and her son were living on their own, and sometimes she held two jobs. She worked as a gas station attendant; she sold Tupperware. Even during the ten years that she worked for Avon, she had to supplement her salary.

Nancy says she and her husband felt so much hostility that they didn't speak to each other. She acknowledges that she had a lot of anger, that she felt rejected by him, but she also recalls that his family was "very good to me. They lived on fixed incomes so they couldn't do much financially, but his mother and his sisters were very supportive." And her own mother was there for her "every step of the way. Emotionally. She was my babysitter until he went into pre-K and I didn't have to pay. We lived near each other and for a couple of years we lived in the same building.

She gave me moral support, financial support. I have to thank her from the bottom of my heart. Without her it would not have been possible."

After seeking redress in family court for years, Nancy finally began receiving money from her ex-husband. He had to make good all the arrears, which amounted to $10,000. He paid it gradually, and although the child support stopped at age 18, the back money put her son through trade school. Nancy states, "When all this happened, all that anger dissolved. I forgave him. My life has lightened up."

When her son was 16 and she was 38, Nancy was diagnosed with breast cancer. At the time she was living in Florida and working for a bank. She had left New York "because I was saving my son." He was having problems and she felt he could have gotten into trouble if he had stayed in the city. She gave up her job, which she says she loved, and moved with her mother, her brother, her son, and their dog and cat to Florida. They stayed only one year, but Nancy feels it changed her son's life. He told her, " 'I hate you for moving me to Florida' but he rose to the occasion." And she feels her ex-husband also rose to the occasion after her diagnosis. She recalls that he "felt very bad. He said, 'I know I haven't helped you. Maybe I can finish raising him.' " So their son lived with his father from the time he was 17 to when he was 19. Nancy recalls, "It worked fine. It was a miracle. They have a wonderful relationship now. And I forgave him. It was just what my son needed and he came to the rescue. I forgave him for everything he put me through—all those years of being a single parent. He said, 'Let me help you.' " At the same time, her son showed unexpected maturity. She recalls how painful it was for her to tell her son about her cancer: "I just kept crying and crying. I just couldn't do it. I didn't want him to see me become vulnerable. But it was something he handled very well. He was there for me. He went with me to chemotherapy. I had a real support system. It has been very positive."

Nancy's support system over the years included her ex-husband's family, her mother, and eventually, when she became ill, her son and her ex-husband. After years of anger and acrimony, when she was faced with a potentially life-threatening illness, her ex-husband came forward and behaved responsibly, even lovingly.

Today her son is in his early 30s, is married, and has a daughter of his own. He has a warm relationship with his father and his father's female friend. And Nancy has a "great relationship" with her granddaughter. Nancy feels that one of the reasons their relationships turned out relatively well is that she never spoke to her son against his father. When she was angry, she told her girlfriends but not her son. "I did the best I could. I did it out of love for my child. I tried to give him the things he would have had if he had two parents. I tried to be there for school and I tried to help with his friends. Maybe sometimes I overcompensated."

While many of the women acknowledge the invaluable help of their mothers, other family members, friends, neighbors, and babysitters with playing crucial roles in their coping with single motherhood, others also acknowledge the help of God in their survival. As Barbara Tucci, the widow whose husband died suddenly while jogging, recalled, "I knew God was going to take care of me. I had to rely on him. I think about what God gave me in this life. I've been in the depths of despair but I know that God will take care of me. I had bad luck. I don't think God only gives you what you can handle. That's a crock. He helps you handle what happens to you—God, he or she."

This idea of a personal god giving an individual strength or looking after her was not uncommon among the interviewees. Naomi Martin, a 46-year-old African American lawyer and mother of three children ranging in age from 14 to 9, went through a wrenching separation and divorce. Her husband got involved with a woman twenty years younger than he. Though she first says, "It doesn't matter," she quickly amends her statement: "Yet it does. It hurts." She describes her husband as "mentally abusive." It was "character derogation," she feels. "I was too fat, too thin, my breasts were too small. I didn't know how to make money. And I was an enabler. I kept trying to make it work. The harder you try, the angrier he gets. My sister said, 'It's like you plant a garden and he tramples on it.' "

Naomi knew the divorce was coming. Her husband was staying out until one in the morning, spending down his assets and accumulating debts. Around the time of the separation, she also lost her job, and because of back trouble she couldn't walk for a month. She recalls, "The first year [after the separation] I woke up every morning with fear. The marriage I knew about, but this was fear of the unknown."

Naomi says that she has always been searching for religious meaning. She recounts a transformative experience from seven years before our conversation:

> One day I brought the kids to a concert. At the time my life was pretty messy. There was too much sin. As we were leaving, someone said to me, "Hey, we meet here every week." I forgot the phone number but remembered the time and place. I went and the sermon was, "Who's Impressed?" It was about conspicuous consumption and I thought, he's talking to me.
>
> He talked about how Jesus was a carpenter. He carried fishing nets. Hey, he was a *man* but he had no sin. And when he was crucified, he went through all that for me so that I can have a personal relationship with God. God is my father. If you don't have a husband, God is my husband. And all he asks of me is to obey. Obey "love your neighbor as yourself." And I said, "OK. This is true." I knew this was true. There is nothing in my life that I can't let my children see. I have no secrets. I've been going to church for seven years and my kids have always gone with me.

Naomi talks about how her husband "hated my church. He used to persecute me about it every day. Then he tapered off and only persecuted me once or twice a week." She feels he hated it because it meant a loss of control over her. In particular, she wasn't willing to cover things up anymore, wasn't willing to "cover up sin anymore."

Naomi continues:

Jesus gave me a lot of strength. He enabled me to see flaws in my own character. I stopped drinking. The church doesn't require it but it stands for moderation in everything. I am a compulsive addictive person. If I take one drink, I don't make good choices. It really affects me.

As single moms, we're always so independent, so self-reliant. But God is going to take you to the end of yourself so you will have to seek him. In that weakness, God can work. We have to leave that pride, that arrogance behind, live on a different plane to let him do what he needs to do. Life always reminds you, you're in the way again. You have to ask, "Where are you really?" I say, "Thank you, Jesus! Thank you for my kids. Thank you for my job."

We get our strength from God, from his word—through prayer. He puts people in our lives but he doesn't do it all. You still have to make wise decisions. Figure out, really, where are you?

Naomi's religious beliefs have influenced her relationships and her day-to-day life. She feels she used to run away from relationships but she has learned to "live in the moment," to "speak the truth with love." And she has learned to "be humble with my children, to apologize to them." She tells them, "I'm so sorry I hurt your feelings." She feels she needs to pay attention to their character, to work on their hearts and character. "At this point in their lives, I can only influence them."

Her spiritual beliefs have influenced her social life as well: "Yes, I date, but it's Christian dating. Becoming friends, getting to know each other. Without sex or even a kiss. If we hug, it's to one side—not a full chest hug. And I love to entertain. I had a singles party recently and invited lots of people. Eventually I'd like to meet somebody, but not now. I have too much work to do on myself."

Cathy Morgan also discusses her religious beliefs. A 45-year-old woman who came to New York from Barbados when she was 24, she is the oldest of six children. Having worked in banking in Barbados, Cathy attended a public college after she arrived in New York. She married a man with a job in the financial district three years later, and feels she married "too soon." She and her husband soon discovered that they were simply incompatible, with differing views and values. Cathy became pregnant after their first year of marriage, and the couple split up two months before their daughter was born. Her husband's company closed and he moved out of state. At first, he sent her no child support, but when the divorce was finalized he was required to pay $400 a month. By then he owed $20,000 to $25,000 in back child support, which he recently started paying regularly.

Cathy graduated from college two years after her daughter was born. When asked how she managed, Cathy replies, "I depended on my family a lot and God placed certain people there for me." One was a young woman living in the apartment under hers, who babysat for her daughter. "She was a lovely, lovely woman—very supportive. She had children of her own and took care of three other children. Also, my friends and family made sure I had whatever I needed." Cathy continues,

> How did I manage? Through anger and determination. I used anger to push me to this point. Also, I had great support—both financial and emotional. My daughter would go to stay with my family on weekends. My sister was there to help. My mother and two sisters are part of my daughter's extended family. Also, the woman next door was a caterer and was wonderful to us. It was divine intervention. Some might say it could be coincidental. Things were so bad that I prayed, "God, please help me," and the caterer next door wrote me a check. I should have been homeless. We had a strange, angry landlord, but he was kind for once and it didn't happen.
>
> I was very angry at two things: that I could have had that kind of father for my child and that he didn't understand that he had to do right by his daughter. Much more than he had to do right by me.

After Cathy earned her undergraduate degree, she went to graduate school for her master's in social work. She says that she was "worn down, very tired, but if I didn't do it then, I knew I would never do it." Cathy had calculated that with her B.A. she could earn between $18,000 and $20,000, and she "knew that wasn't going to work." Her ex-husband paid child support only sporadically. She would call him and ask him,

" 'When are you sending some money? How much are you sending?' It was humiliating. I didn't want to do it anymore." Her graduate degree made it possible for her to get a job in addiction services, but she soon decided to go to law school. Since graduating from law school, she has worked in the field of children's services, combining her legal and social work expertise.

Now, Cathy says, she is very active in her church and has many friends. She describes her daughter as "very secure," involved in basketball and dance, and in touch with her father and his family. She summarizes: "I really like my life the way it is. I just love my life." Then she adds, "But I wouldn't want my daughter to be a single parent. I wouldn't want her to repeat." Cathy names family and neighbors as key supports for her and her daughter but also God for looking after her and intervening in her life. She clearly knows she must do her part—obtain the skills needed to participate in meaningful work and be able to support herself and her daughter—but without doubt, she believes that God was there for her, perhaps encouraging her caterer neighbor to help at a crucial moment or leading her usually difficult landlord to behave compassionately.

Linda Powell, an outreach worker to teenagers and a single mother of a 12-year-old girl, makes clear the importance of her church in her life as she describes how the pastors and other parishioners have given her sustenance, love, confidence, and self-esteem. To Linda, her church is not simply a place to worship on Sunday; it is a community, and it embraces her and her daughter and encourages them to be caring, capable, giving people highly respected by the larger community as well as by themselves.

Sandra Mason, a 33-year-old African American mother of a 4-year-old son, elaborates on the role of the church in her life. A college graduate currently enrolled in a doctoral program in public health, in her twenties she was living with a young man whom she was considering marrying when she became pregnant. She says she was ready to have a child but never intended to have one outside of marriage. When she realized she was pregnant, she said to herself, "Oh my goodness, what have

I done?" Sandra and her child's father stayed together for the first four-teen months of their son's life. They talked about getting married, but finally she felt that "he needed to do a lot of growing up. I couldn't do it anymore. He left everything up to me. I was doing it all. He went from his mom's house to my house. Splitting up was the right thing to do. It wasn't about fighting, anger, and all that." Single motherhood, she finds, is both challenging and gratifying:

> Being a single mother is the hardest and most rewarding thing I have ever done. Even what I'm doing now—looking for a good school for Jonathan that I can afford. I had no idea what it would be like. Just the daily stuff. The self-sacrifice. Getting up in the morning early. I like to run and Jonathan is a very early riser so I have to get up really early to get in a run or some quiet time before he gets up. And when I get home at night, I can't get on the phone and chitchat. And reading the story before bed—I might be totally sick of *The Cat in the Hat* but I'll read it anyway.
>
> I'm always on the move. I'm getting him someplace. There's no time to do anything—even to just sit and watch TV. I'm on a very tight schedule. And I want as much time with him as possible. Luckily most of my girlfriends are single moms.
>
> I never would have chosen to be a single mom but now that I am, it's just what I am. At times I get overwhelmed. Sometimes I need a break. The problem is giving of yourself all the time, always being "on." When I come home from work, I would love to plop down in front of the TV. But I push through coming home from work, I push through dinner time, I push through bath time and then I get him to bed. Then I have time for myself.

Sandra grew up going to church with her mother, but since her son's birth, she feels as though it has become more personal and she is an active member of the congregation. Services are held at a college in the Bronx, and during the week many of the parishioners meet in small groups in someone's home for Bible study. The others in her group are all single mothers and "everyone brings their kids"; in addition to studying the Bible together, these women have become both genuine friends and a support group.

Sandra speaks of her concerns about her son and the kind of a person she would like him to be:

> I do worry about Jonathan growing up as a young black male in New York City. Society doesn't nurture young black men. I want to raise him to be respectful, to love women, but that is not what the culture is saying. And it is hard to protect him from the influences of the culture.
>
> A neighbor of mine is a good friend and is white. I want him to have both—black and white—in his life. And there are many fewer educated black males than females, and there are lots of women for them.
>
> But I'm getting myself together spiritually. I have the support of friends and family, but it's going to be hard. There are always going to be things that would be less difficult if I had a man, but I understand what having a relationship with God means to me—to Sandra as an adult.
>
> I teach Jonathan about being kind. We read the Bible together. We pray together. It is the center of our lives. What I try to teach him is not just because it is a nice thing to do. We are created by God. Our lives are not given to us to live willy-nilly. Especially with the pressures here in New York. But I don't know if I could do it with Jonathan without spiritual reasons. There are toys upon toys upon toys. I don't know if I could say no—except for financial reasons. There is no bigger purpose. I teach him—you are accountable to God for what you do.

Naomi, Cathy, and Sandra all stress the importance to them and to their child rearing of belonging to a community of like-minded worshippers. They are sustained not just by the presence of God and the Bible in their lives but by the friendships, the support, and the strength they gain from sharing their perspectives and their lives with other believers. And being actively involved in these communities helps many of these women to clarify their own thinking, to develop their leadership skills and, in turn, to increase their self-confidence. Furthermore, in a culture that all too often seems relentlessly materialistic, individualistic, and violent, their religious communities reinforce the spiritual and humane values they are trying to teach their children—values frequently negated by the larger society. Those values are further reinforced by the ultimate authorities—God and the Bible. Sandra feels strongly that a woman raising children, especially black male children, in a culture that so often disparages them, stereotypes them, and teaches them false and frequently harmful values needs the added clout of religion and a community of believers to support her efforts.

Hannah Alexander also talks about being part of a community and associating with people who shared her values, but her feelings of connection were made through her antiwar activity, through her work in the South Bronx, through her desire to change the world by participation in social movements. As she says, "I made a completely new life," one that she loved, that made her feel alive and truly felt right for her.

But while Hannah's work and community activism connected her to her deeply held beliefs and to others who shared them, to some degree the very activities that meant so much to her alienated her from her far more conventional daughter. For some single mothers, figuring out who they are and connecting with others who share their beliefs may offer little direct help to them in raising their children. The child may ultimately benefit from the mother having a better sense of her own identity, priorities, and values, but at least in the short run, what is important to the mother may sometimes seem contrary to the best interests of the child.

After Judith Berman's husband walked out, she and the children were forced to turn to public assistance, food stamps, and Medicaid. Surviving while she went back to school became her primary task, and she accomplished it by utilizing skills she had learned in her political activism. Judith points out that she didn't "start out savvy" but "got savvy very quickly." She explains,

> I had been part of the antiwar movement and the women's movement. I used to say I stopped the Vietnam War myself! So I very quickly learned and shared what I learned with friends and they would share with me. It was a very supportive atmosphere.
>
> We all helped each other. The blind leading the blind. I took a friend's son to the pediatrician when she couldn't. Women leaving bad

marriages were helping each other. It stemmed from the women's movement. Women helping women.

Much of her social life, according to Judith, revolved around other women and their children:

We would take the kids to the Little League games and then go back to someone's house. It was difficult finding babysitters on New Year's Eve so we would often spend it with other friends and the children all there. Social life didn't necessarily mean going out with a man. If I got a sitter, I might go to school, go to a doctor, go to therapy. I knew it was more important to get my head together than to go out on a date.

Judith survived as well as she did by drawing on her social and political skills and networks for her own and her children's well-being. She quickly learned what services she was entitled to and how to obtain them. She made common cause with other mothers in similar circumstances, and they not only helped each other day to day but also formed a social network and validated each other. Listening to her, one gets the sense that she both found the emotional and social support she needed and accessed intelligence and strength within herself.

These women have developed rewarding, successful lives despite profound disruptions and challenges. What supports have been particularly significant to their emotional, economic, and social survival? First, almost all credit their families with enormous ongoing help—emotional support, child care, financial support, food preparation, laundry—with simply being there for them. Most often they speak of their mothers, but they also frequently mention their grandmothers, siblings, aunts, and occasionally other family members. Grandmothers seem to play a very special role in the lives of many of these women. When the young women's mothers are incapacitated, unavailable, angry, punitive, or rejecting, many of the young women reach out to their grandmothers and enjoy close relationships with them. Jeanne Gonzalez and her grandmother are not just close relatives; they seem like close friends—a small mutual aid group, actively taking care of each other. Cicely Franklin was raised by her grandmother while her parents were in the United States. She reveres as well as loves her grandmother. Keisha Johnson also had a very special relationship with her grandmother, who died of pancreatic cancer.

Sometimes, as in Karen Morrison's experience, the family seems to function as a unit, weaving the single mother and her child into the fabric of collective life. Karen and her daughter moved into the master bedroom; her father functioned as Susan's father; her siblings treated Susan as another member of the family. Cicely describes both of her son's grandmothers as an integral part of his care and of the well-being of the small, nuclear, nonmarried family. They provide child care, emotional support, food, and, above all, a haven in a very hectic and complex world for the young mother, the father, and their son. Could Joanne Calabrese have gotten back on her feet without the help of her brothers? Could Cathy Morgan have completed her education without her mother's support? But family can be at once a blessing and a problem. Keisha and others have had to assert their authority in order to make it clear that *they* are the mothers—not the relatives who are mother surrogates during part or all of the working day and who clearly become extremely attached to the children and to their role as caregivers. For a woman to lay claim to her rights as a mother is frequently very difficult when she is still relatively young herself, has at least in the past perceived her relatives as authority figures, and has been raised to treat them as such. Insisting on one's own role as parent can be a delicate and problematic matter, especially when the young mother desperately needs the relatives' help and support.

Several women credited support at work or the affirmation they received from their work as crucial aids in the process of creating a new life for themselves; many mentioned good friends or caring neighbors as essential to their survival. But second to the family, the institution most often credited with helping them emerge from the trauma of loss and the profound disruption of their life course is religion. Sometimes they cite religious beliefs; in other instances they speak about the embracing community of the church; and often the women point to God's intercession in their lives. Cathy Morgan, for example, believes God has directly intervened in her life, particularly when she was face-to-face with near disaster. Sandra Mason and Naomi Martin cite specific religious teachings as instrumental in their formulation of beliefs and rules for themselves to live by and to raise their children by. Sandra describes how difficult it is to raise a child, particularly an African American boy, in a materialistic, violent, often bigoted U.S. society; religious principles make it easier for her to say no to her son and to teach him the values of caring and kindness in an all-too-often uncaring and unkind world. When these women speak of the importance of religion in their lives, they are animated, eager to make themselves understood, and enormously involved in what they are describing in vivid and fluent language.

Moreover, they clearly recognize the communal or social aspects of their religious conviction and activities. The various roles they play in church; the social support they receive from other members of the congregation or from the pastor, assistant pastor, or other church leaders; the sense of belonging they gain from their attendance at Bible study groups; and the feelings of friendship and solidarity they experience with other single mothers in their church make them feel like insiders rather than outsiders—they feel needed, valued, respected.

Hannah Alexander had many similar experiences not in a church but in her work in the South Bronx and in her involvement in the social movements of the 1960s and 1970s. She felt she had found her niche; she was actively involved in issues in which she truly believed. In a sense, she seems to feel she found herself. Judith Berman, too, found in the struggle against the Vietnam War a group and an ideology to which she was committed. Through those activities, through graduate school, and through her close association with other single mothers she gained a renewed sense of self-respect, of competence, and of belonging that sustained her though economically and emotionally difficult times.

Many of these women seem to gain strength, sense of self, and an ability to develop very different identities and commitments after the profound disruptions in their lives forced them to take risks—to discover their own talents and abilities, to depend on others, and even to explore and expand their fundamental belief systems. Their resilience, their courage, their creativity in developing new ways of living their lives, and their willingness to take risks indeed are strengthened by their relationships with others, but many of these women also seem to have a layer of strength not readily visible in their family members or close friends. Moreover, some of the women speak of always knowing, even as children, that they were strong or of being told by significant people in their lives that they were special.

Thus Eva Sanchez as a child was told by her uncle and others that she had real ability and that therefore she could make a different life. Subsequently she was able to form relationships with others who had faith in her and who helped her to gain skills and belief in herself and to transform her life: she changed from a low-income, unskilled, struggling mother of two to a highly respected, educated, professional woman. She combined belief in self and a willingness to take risks with an ability to learn and relate warmly to others who in turn helped her—emotionally, socially, and professionally—to make what was essentially a new life.

But there are many women who are not so fortunate—who do not have family, friends, and neighbors to help them when their lives have been seriously disrupted by unexpected pregnancy, unsuccessful relationships, personal tragedy, poverty, ill health, and depression. In the next chapter, women whose hopes and dreams have been derailed talk about their lives.

6

"I Have to Do Something with My Life"

Derailed Dreams

I thought I was going to be a doctor but that's all changed. I changed my life. **Pamela Curtis,** 26-year-old mother of one

Then I met my daughter's father. I had sex with him and the third time I got pregnant. I went through the whole pregnancy myself. I made two appointments for an abortion but I couldn't go through with it. I should have done it. I love my daughter but I haven't accomplished anything.

Diana Suarez, 23-year-old mother of one

Many women have been able to cope remarkably effectively, even heroically, with the challenges of single motherhood, but others suffer more severe consequences from poverty, isolation, emotional burnout, and unfulfilled aspirations. Single mothers are, not surprisingly, frequently mired in the basic activities of daily life—working, caring for their children, putting food on the table, paying the rent. And low-income women bear a double burden as a profound shortage of resources is added to single motherhood. Long work hours, low pay, inadequate education and training, and insufficient, inaccessible, and costly day care and after-school care together create hurdles that are nearly insurmountable as these women attempt to make a decent, rewarding life for themselves and their children. When critics decry the negative impact of single motherhood on children, they generally overlook the courage and creativity, the resilience and risk taking needed by almost all single mothers to survive and by the indomitable to thrive. They also fail to discuss the myriad ways that a family-friendly social policy could ameliorate the extraordinarily difficult living conditions of many mothers and their children.

For some, single motherhood when combined with other serious problems can make life almost too difficult to bear. Gina Sacco, a 58-year-old white mother of two, describes her childhood years:

> I was born in 1942, the youngest of four girls. My parents were born in Italy. My father was a laborer; my mother a housewife. We lived in Brooklyn. We were a Catholic family. My father was nonpracticing; my mother was practicing.
>
> I really didn't have much of a childhood. My mother had crippling arthritis so I grew up having to be very responsible. My oldest sister married and moved out. I had to bathe my mother; I had to wash her hair.
>
> My father was a European type. There was a lot of sadness in the household. At 17 I graduated from high school and went to work as a secretary to help contribute to the family's income. Then I went into a convent. Nobody knew I had done that. I had read about altruism. I had gone to Catholic school and I got altruism from religiousness.
>
> Also, my mother was a very good person. She taught me—don't be disrespectful to adults. I wanted the missionary life. I wanted to bring Jesus and goodness to people who didn't have it. I wanted to go to South America and work in impoverished areas. I was in the convent for six years.

Then Gina's mother died suddenly of a heart attack. She says, "It was a major blow to me." After her mother's death, she left the convent but didn't feel she could return home to live. She finished her undergraduate degree and found a job in addiction services in the South Bronx.

Her future husband had been a priest at the same religious institution where Gina had been a nun. They lived together for a while and then married in 1974. After learning they could not have children, they adopted a newborn in 1978. Three years later they adopted another boy, one who had briefly been in foster care. Her sons are now 23 and 20.

Gina explains what happened to her marriage: "In April 1995 we separated. Some years later we divorced but I've been a single parent since 1995. I am spontaneous, vivacious, enthusiastic; Jim is passive, suffers from depression, and is sometimes immobilized. Jim told me we were getting divorced. I wasn't calling for a divorce. We are *so* angry with each other. He helps support us minimally; he gives $700 a month."

Gina's children have had serious problems for many years. Her older son was a "head banger" and perhaps "learning disabled" as a toddler. He was tested at the time and found to have little impulse control. As a young boy, she says, he was "a pariah. The teachers didn't like him. I had to always be there; I had to always be in the school yard. He could have a pretty violent temper and had to put other people down—especially his younger brother." Now he is, in her words, a "very engaging, smart young man," but her younger son has been having serious problems. As a small boy he was "a beautiful child, empathetic, a social being. But he suffered from hearing loss and wasn't paying attention or learning because he wasn't hearing. He was acting out. He went to a school for learning disabled children and finally got his GED." Recently, he has been "stealing, lying, doing drugs. He has been stealing from me, he's been arrested, bailed out. He goes with a horrible crowd of kids, real lowlifes."

Currently, Gina feels "stuck" with dealing with her younger son. He is "abusive" to her, calling her a "whore." She has to remember not to leave her pocketbook around because he will steal money from her. She has spent innumerable hours in courthouses and, when her son "overdoses," in hospitals. Moreover, she has to deal with him all by herself: while his father has promised help, telling him, "When you're ready, I'll be there," she says, "I've never left his side. I'll always be there." As Gina describes it, her situation with her younger son is like a nightmare. She deals with it by compartmentalizing, by engaging in denial. As she puts it, "I keep getting pulled down but consciously do things that lift me up. I try not to get immersed." During their marriage she and her husband had shared all the household chores. After they separated, she recalls, "It all came down on me."

Did Gina miscalculate when she married Jim? Was he not the kind of person she had thought or hoped he would be? Would the differences in their personalities have caused their marriage to fail under ordinary circumstances, or was the pressure, worry, and heartache of dealing with two children with serious problems a burden too heavy for their relationship to bear? Whatever the answers to these questions, Gina is left with the caregiving—just as when she was a child taking care of her disabled mother.

Susan Jackson, a 35-year-old mother of two, also discusses the impact of her son's illness on all their lives. She begins with her early years:

> I am originally from London. I came here with my mother when I was 13 and we moved to Brooklyn. She was a single mother, too. I went to public schools and went to some high school, but things were not going so great with my mother so I left at age 15. I did some housekeeping and cared for children.
>
> Then I moved to Rhode Island. It was very spontaneous. I wanted to see every state so I chose Rhode Island. I went to school and lived in while I took care of a young child. I lied about my age. During this time I got my GED and went to some college, but things were not going as I planned so I moved back to New York.

In New York, Susan took courses to become a nursing assistant while also caring for children. She met her children's father when she was 21. Fourteen years older than she, he had an administrative position at a private school. According to Susan, they first had a "friendship relationship" and then he asked her to come to live with him. She describes him as "older and very mature" and says, "I went for it." After graduating from her nursing assistant program, she was about to go to work at a hospital when she discovered she was pregnant: "I was very scared and didn't go for prenatal care. I was not married and I was very embarrassed at my situation. In April 1991 my first child was born but he was not there for me. We were fighting about financial matters and he was doing drugs—marijuana—and drinking beer and there were bills that needed to be paid so I had to go on welfare."

Susan recalls that she knew something was wrong with her older son when he was six months old. "He babbled and didn't make eye contact. By one year he couldn't say 'Mama' and he was very inappropriate with me. And I was pregnant again." Susan had two sons within two years and, as she said, "I didn't have anyone to support me—financially or emotionally."

The relationship between Susan and the father of her children deteriorated as time went on. She feels his priorities were drugs and alcohol—not the children. When she took a job as a counselor working the night shift and needed him to take care of the boys, he told her it wasn't going to work. He didn't want her to work; he didn't want to take care of the kids. Also, "there was infidelity," so she moved out in 1999. The boys were 7 and 8.

Susan became a counselor in a mental health agency where she is currently a supervisor; she is also taking college courses part-time. Managing it all has been hard:

> My older son is very difficult. I could only do everything because I have such good friends. They were very supportive. I currently work seven to three, so a neighbor puts my sons on the bus and I'm home to take them off.
>
> I do everything. Their father is not in their life. He has lost his job and he is not giving any child support, nothing. He has nothing to give me. For two years he gave no support. Eventually he was $5,000 in arrears and I was only requesting $200 a month. He could have seen them every other weekend but he's only been in touch twice.

According to Susan, her sons' father is "in denial" about her older son's autism. She says, "He felt sorry for himself. He was ashamed that he had a disabled child but he loves our younger son dearly." After a pause she adds, "He loves the older one, too.

Susan worries about her older son's future: "I think about that every day. He's good with computers. I'm not ready to put him into a group setting. This is my life now. He'll be with me. My other son is very, very good in school. He could be a lawyer or a doctor." When I ask Susan if she manages to get out, to do something for herself, she responds, "It's very rare that I go out." Then she says that sometimes her younger, 12-year-old son takes care of his 13-year-old brother. He helps him to shower and brush his teeth. She continues, "Sometimes I have to leave the kids at home alone—to go to a movie or go to the park to get that release. Many, many times I've done that. It's my secret. Sometimes I'm scared but there's no one around to help."

Susan inadvertently became a single mother. She formed a relationship with an older man who she felt was mature; but when she discovered she was pregnant, he was either unwilling or unable to participate in caring for a family. Because he was not there to help her financially or emotionally, she eventually felt she needed to move out and go it alone. Indeed, she was essentially going it alone even while she was living with him—but now she at least has greater control over her day-to-day life. Because her older son is autistic, she will need to continue to devote much of her life to caring for him. It is a burden without end, yet Susan feels considerable shame at occasionally leaving the boys alone so that she can have a little respite from caregiving—which, because of the nature of her job, she does day and night.

Becoming a single mother—no matter the cause or circumstances—inevitably has a significant impact on a woman's life. Some women find that they must make substantial adjustments in their aspirations and in their lives when they suddenly have sole responsibility for one or more children. Sometimes those changes are also sudden, but often they are made gradually. Pamela Curtis has a very different life today than she expected she would have. As she says, "I am a secretary at a hospital. I thought I was going to be a doctor, but that's all changed. I changed my life." Now a bright, personable, African American woman of 26, Pamela attended first-rate schools while growing up in New York City and then went to a private college just outside of Boston. When asked how she felt about her experience there, she replies, "I loved it!" But she got pregnant the summer before her sophomore year by a young man with whom she was having a long-term relationship. "The pregnancy was totally unplanned. When my daughter was born I was so sure we were going to get married. I was so naive. He said, 'Maybe one day.' He said that I should have an abortion but I didn't want to. I had visions of never being able to live with it."

At first Pamela expected she would return to college. Her daughter's father urged her to go back to school and leave the baby with his mother. She notes, "He always wanted me to go back to school. Lots of people think he's a bad person, but he's really supportive." But Pamela and her boyfriend had, in her words, "different ideas about raising children, about raising a family." She feels that "bringing up a child involves sacrifice, that it is my responsibility to support her, to be with her." Pamela believes her daughter's father is "negligent with his time." He both works for the telephone company and is a "DJ [disc jockey] on the side. That's his true love." When he was working as a DJ, according to Pamela, he would never be home. "He would go from his day job to his night job and feel he was doing the right thing—working two jobs and supporting us."

After Pamela had her daughter, they lived for a year with her mother before moving in with her daughter's father. When her daughter was 1 year old, she put together a combination of babysitters and day care and worked for a year. She then attended college in lower Manhattan, graduating with a degree in biology. She describes these college years: "I did internships, biology honors, the whole thing. Then I realized I couldn't live with the sacrifice of time and energy of being away from my daughter. I went from the mentality of 'Women should have a career' to 'I want to be with my kid.'"

Pamela's mother is an executive at a well-known brokerage firm; her father has an equally prestigious job at another firm. They are divorced and he has since remarried. Pamela describes her mother's attitudes toward marriage and education: "My mother used to say, 'You don't have to be married but you do need your education; you need to finish college.' When I told her I was pregnant, she was *very* disappointed. As it sank in, she became even more disappointed. She wanted it to be easy for me. Now that I have my own daughter, I understand. I don't want her to struggle."

Since her daughter was born, Pamela feels that she has matured significantly, that she really "stepped up to the plate." She has recently become much more interested in religion, in the Bible, and in finding out what she believes. She and her daughter's father were living together but not married, and as she was studying the Bible and "trying to learn what God thought," that arrangement suddenly did not seem right. When she discussed with him either ending the relationship or getting married, his response was "But why do we need to get married? It's just what society says we have to do." But she felt that society has "depreciated marriage—made it something you do not need to do." A few months later, she and her daughter moved to an apartment of their own.

Pamela's daughter attends a prestigious private school in Manhattan. At the end of the school day, she goes to an after-school program until 5:45. Pamela has been accepted by a school of education in a master's program but isn't sure how she can stay at her job, study for her graduate degree, and care for her daughter. It's a balancing act, and she is not at all certain she can work it out.

Her accidental pregnancy and decision not to have an abortion significantly changed Pamela's life. She had been living as a relatively privileged, middle- or upper-middle-class young woman, attending a New England college with the goal of becoming a doctor, but her choice to bring her pregnancy to term and to raise her daughter herself as much as possible, making the child her first priority, led her to dramatically alter her plans. Though she was able to complete her bachelor's degree, she changed her career goals from science and medicine to teaching. But Pamela is not sure if she can handle employment, graduate school, and motherhood. Can she work all day, go to school in the late afternoon and evening, and manage to spend sufficient time both on her studies and with her young child? Like many mothers, she is facing significant role and value conflict. On the one hand, she clearly would like to engage in challenging, rewarding work and be able to support herself and her daughter comfortably; to do so, she undoubtedly needs to go on to graduate school. On the other hand, she believes in raising her child herself, not in leaving her care to others. Moreover, Pamela's decision to move out of her boyfriend's apartment because of her newly developed religious beliefs makes her financial situation more precarious, even though he does contribute money to help support their child. Single motherhood has forced Pamela to grapple with fundamental conflicts; it has significantly changed her life, and, in all likelihood, her future as well.

Other women are also at risk for underachieving educationally and professionally, and thus may have their hopes and dreams derailed by single motherhood. Will Jennifer Soriano be able to fulfill her very real potential, care for her son, and preserve her self-esteem and sense of self in the face of her boyfriend's derision and hostility and despite her family's history, which continues to haunt her? Will Jeanne Gonzalez be able to move forward professionally and provide herself and her family with a decent life while caring for two young children, one of them a son with serious health problems? Will Soo Hyun Park regain her health, some measure of self-confidence, and the ability to support herself and her twin children in a strange culture, using a language she still does not know well, after a disastrous, abusive marriage that robbed her of both her emotional and her physical well-being? Will Young Heoy Lee be able to overcome her traumatic years in Korea to construct a meaningful, satisfying life and provide and care for her daughters? How will she manage when her father, who has been providing help by living with them, decides to return to California? Will she receive enough social, emotional, and financial support to enable her to attend graduate school and become a minister, as she hopes to do? The lives of these women have been derailed in some instances by accidental pregnancy and in other instances by decisions that may have seemed appropriate at the time they were made but that—together with motherhood and meager societal supports—have thrown their lives into turmoil, gravely and perhaps permanently disrupting their plans for the future. Getting themselves back on track will not be easy; for some it may not be possible.

The experience of Pat Clarke illustrates the problems that stem from combining unfortunate choices and single motherhood. A 37-year-old

African American mother of a 13-year-old son, Pat describes her family background and her childhood years:

> I grew up in Brooklyn, the youngest of six. My sister and I were nine years apart, so I was the baby. I grew up like an only child. My parents were older and I didn't ask for much. We came from a two-parent family. My father is from South Carolina. He was originally a long-shoreman, but he got injured so he became a custodian at a Catholic school. My mother worked for the transit system. She had gone to junior college.
>
> After high school I received a Regents Scholarship [offered by New York State] and went to college. I was a little lonely there. It was very big and I guess I hadn't realized how comfortable I had been in high school where I had known everyone. I met my husband the summer before my last year in high school. The lonelier I got at college the more I was taking his calls. He was a Nigerian with a great car who dressed very well—not that I cared about those things. It was really that someone was paying me a lot of attention. I knew he wasn't the right guy but it just sort of happened. He said, "You know, I can't stay in the country unless I get married," so I said, "OK."

Pat describes her husband as "very intelligent, a professional student." She says she helped him write all of his papers and that he has a "B.A., a master's, an M.P.A., and a law degree." When Pat got married at 20, she dropped out of college and got a job as a secretary. She feels she was "under too much stress." She describes going home one day to find the lights in their apartment turned off. She also found a package, which she opened by flashlight. It contained expensive clothes that her husband had bought for himself. Looking back, Pat exclaims, "Imagine. He hadn't paid the light bill but he had bought himself $200 pants!"

Realizing that the marriage wasn't working, she moved back home with her parents. She says of her relationship with her husband, "Love shouldn't hurt and I was always feeling hurt." Pat's husband returned to Nigeria and she continued to live with her parents. One day she returned from work to find him sitting on the stoop: "He came in, we talked, and he suggested going on a date the following day. My sister told me, 'Whatever you do, don't have sex.' One month later I didn't see my period. I got pregnant at 23."

Pat thought her husband would be happy because he had always wanted them to have a baby, but from the moment he knew, "his whole aura changed. He asked me, 'What are you going to do?' " The last time during her pregnancy that she saw him she was in her fifth month. Her parents took care of her and paid her hospital bill. She says that while she didn't feel it was going to work out between them, she did think he would be in their child's life.

Pat talks about the issues she was dealing with during those months:

My husband stopped paying his bills, so I was getting calls about his credit cards, payment for his car, etc. They said I was responsible since he wasn't paying. And my mother, she was into "What will the neighbors think?" Here I am pregnant and there's no man around. When I had the baby and my mother came to visit me in the hospital, she brought pictures of my wedding to show the *stranger* in the next bed— to make sure this woman knew I was married!

I took the baby back home and thought I would never see my husband again. His parents and relatives were in London and Africa. But he showed up after six weeks. I was furious! My parents told me he was there and that the baby really liked the time he spent with him. He brought the baby a gold bracelet, which he put on his arm. I was so angry that I ripped the bracelet off the baby and threw it out. The whole pregnancy he was not there for me. My sister was my birth coach. The whole pregnancy I was making up lies at work about where he is. Some people knew but not most, so I told lies to my co-workers to keep up appearances. And my mother is snooty, so she wasn't happy if people thought I had no husband.

Pat lived with her parents for six years. Her mother cared for the baby when Pat was at work; when she came home, her mother went to work. Recalling this period, she says, "You're always at somebody's mercy because you need their help. It really sucks!" Her husband gave her money "occasionally." She says she did not seek a divorce or regular child support because she feared he would take their son to London or Nigeria. Pat talks about being a single mother:

> Being a single mom is really hard. I never felt so fat or so black as when I was around other moms with children. I think they assumed I had a lot of kids and was on welfare. At school my child was quiet. His first-grade teacher, a young woman, told me, "I think something is wrong with him. I think maybe he needs to be in special ed." I was in tears and while I'm upset, she's checking her face and her eye makeup. And she's telling me my son should be in special ed!
>
> They assume I'm some ghetto fabulous chick. My son is a smart kid. We talk at home; we have fabulous conversations. I had him tested and we went to school to discuss the results. The room had a rectangular table. All the professionals sat on one side and my son's father sat on that side next to the professionals. That was profound. That really told me something. He didn't want to sit near me. And the testing found that no way did this child belong in special ed.

Pat and her son currently live with her older sister and her brother-in-law. She also works for her brother-in-law as a counselor in a group home. She says that her son is really not comfortable living in his aunt and uncle's house, and that he would like the two of them to move into a place of their own. Noting that she is always cleaning up, Pat continues, "Whenever I go into my house, I'm on pins and needles because I always think he [her brother-in-law] is judging me. Sometimes I wonder, where did I go so wrong?" For many years, she was three credits shy of her B.A. degree. Her son's father told him, "You're never going to get a college degree because your mother doesn't have one. You're going to be cleaning people's asses, too." Now, Pat reports, her son doesn't even want to speak to his father.

Pat is clearly dissatisfied with both her work and her living arrangements. She feels exploited by her sister and her brother-in-law but seems stuck, powerless to make any fundamental changes in her life. As she says, having to rely on family can be very difficult. Family members are often slotted into specific roles—the smart one, the dependent one, the one who always gets in trouble, and so on—which are then subtly and sometimes not so subtly reinforced both by circumstances and by other relatives. Without a college degree, Pat felt limited in the kind of work she could obtain. Since our interview, she has completed the three credits and obtained her degree, but the job market she now faces is a very difficult one. Her agreeing to marry someone who "wasn't the right guy" to help him stay in the United States and her getting pregnant after their separation so many years ago were clearly turning points in her life. An intelligent, savvy woman, she not only has been the victim of racism and, in all likelihood, class bias but has also consistently underachieved and disappointed both those close to her and, more important, herself.

Diana Suarez, another intelligent, insightful young woman, experienced an extraordinarily traumatic childhood and is now coping with a difficult adult life as well. A 23-year-old, articulate Latina woman, she lives in Connecticut just outside New York. Diana recounts the disastrous events of her childhood in a flat, matter-of-fact manner:

> I was born in Bridgeport [Connecticut] but I was raised in Puerto Rico. I came back here when I was 8 with my father's mother. My father was incarcerated and my mother was a crack addict. I never knew her at all until I got a call from her when I was 10. She said she was living in a beautiful house, and two weeks later I started living with her. A year and a half later, we had an argument and I left.
>
> While I was living there my [maternal] grandmother was on dialysis and my mother had AIDS. I usually helped my grandmother with her medical problems. One day she was sleeping in the basement and she had a heart attack and died. I was 10 and a half and I found her.
>
> Six months later me and my mother had an argument. So my mother took a frying pan and swung it at me. Because I turned away, it just hit me on the shoulder. The police came, took me away, and put me in a shelter. I was the youngest one there. I was only 11.

Then my other grandmother took me back to Puerto Rico. A few months later, someone blurted out that my mother had died. I was almost 12.

I lived in Puerto Rico for a year and a half, but there were lots of arguments so my grandmother and I came back here. But then I started fighting in school so I was placed in residential living. Some of the kids there were suicidal. I was never suicidal; my grandmother gave me a lot of love.

Diana went to school while she was in foster care and although she was originally placed in the lowest level (because she is "Hispanic," she feels), by the time she left she was in the highest level and doing very well. Moreover, she feels that the residential placement taught her "structure" and "responsibility." She lived there from age 14 to 16.

Diana then moved into a group home, lived with a cousin who is a social worker before going into another group home, and by 18 finally had her own apartment. She became pregnant at 16 but had an abortion because her cousin refused to have the baby in her home. After graduating from high school at 17, Diana began attending community college. When she was 18, her father came out of jail but then went right back in. She says simply, "He was in jail my whole life."

Diana continues,

Then I met my daughter's father. I had sex with him and the third time I got pregnant. I went through the whole pregnancy by myself. I made two appointments for an abortion but I couldn't go through with it. I should have done it. I love my daughter but I haven't accomplished anything.

I have no relationship with her father. He is seeing someone else. He now pays child support but owes me for the first year. I brought him to court and the DNA was positive for his being her father. He doesn't see his daughter at all; he has only seen her four times. He has two other children—a 5-year-old daughter and an 8-year-old. He should take all his kids out—at least once a month. The child support is taken out of his paycheck—$70 a week. Once she goes to day care when she's 3, he needs to pay half.

Currently, Diana is going to school studying chemistry because she is "going for nursing. This is the third time I'm taking it [chemistry]. I've got to pass it or I'll kill myself." She's also looking for a job. At the time of our interview, she had applied to Sprint, had taken the drug test, and was supposed to hear any day. She feels that being bilingual is an asset in finding work. If she does get a job, she'll need to find someone to take care of her two-and-a-half-year-old daughter—perhaps one of her friends' mothers.

Diana discusses her current life:

> My daughter is the main thing. It's really hard. You know, I'm married. When I was pregnant, I had nowhere to live so I got married—to an alien. He's from Morocco. He's really not bad-looking. He's a little light-skinned. He owns the corner store. He works from seven in the morning to eleven at night.
>
> My daughter is in the terrible twos. She doesn't pay any attention to me. I'm not having any more children. I have to do something with my life. My husband—I don't really like him but I just couldn't pay the bills. I get unemployment—$48 a week plus the child support. If I kick my husband out, I can't pay my rent. My husband also pays for my school. I always have to hustle it. I never have any money—not since I had my daughter.

Before our interview ended, Diana said she wanted to give some advice to other young women: "Wait to have kids. Wait until you finish school. Wait until your career is established 'cause you have your own life to live. Wait until you're 21, until you're legal. Have a real paying job first. Try to have a car. You don't want to be walking with a stroller in the winter to the doctor."

What seems amazing about Diana is that she survived at all. Her multiple childhood losses would have felled a person with less courage and resilience; perhaps Diana is correct in crediting her grandmother with giving her enough love to withstand the many traumatic experiences she endured. But still she cannot pay her rent and feed herself and her daughter without marrying someone she says she does not like. With a few demographic changes, Diana could be a character in a nineteenth-century novel—dependent on marriage for her own and her daughter's day-to-day economic survival.

One of the most damaging aspects of single motherhood is downward mobility. When the marriage or relationship ends, when the father walks out or dies, when he is addicted or incarcerated, when the mother decides to separate, the woman and her children often find that their standard of living falls significantly. Frequently, they must manage only on the mother's salary, which tends to be the lower of the two that had previously supported them. Her need to care for the children may limit her to part-time work in jobs that both make far less money available to them and fail to provide health insurance and other benefits. As many of these interviews have shown, the father may well refuse to pay child support, forcing the mother and children to move to lower-cost housing in a less desirable neighborhood with less desirable schools. Indeed, they may end up utterly impoverished.

Judith Berman, her husband, and their children were living at a middle-class level; but when he walked out, she and the children fell into poverty and were forced to apply for welfare benefits. Jeri Miller had been supporting herself at a working- or lower-middle-class standard, but when her son was born and her male friend left, she, too, needed to seek help from the welfare department in order to attend college. Both Soo Hyun Park and Young Heoy Lee experienced significant economic hardship after making disastrous marriages (the result of choices that had seemed reasonable at the time) and ultimately having to care for their children on their own. Jeanne Gonzalez and Jennifer Soriano have both had serious economic problems, and Diana Suarez continues to barely get by even though she has married in order to pay the rent. Some of these women descend into poverty or near-poverty temporarily; when they obtain their education they will be able to support themselves and their children at a decent, if not lavish, standard of living. Others, however, may never recover from becoming what has been termed "the new poor"—people who did not grow up poor but whose circumstances drove them into poverty as adults.

Perhaps one of the most dramatic accounts of being precipitated into poverty by single motherhood was told by Doreen Cullen, a white, 46-year-old mother of eight whom I interviewed for my book *Women and Children Last*. Doreen and her husband were both 18 when they married. In twenty-three years of marriage Doreen had thirteen pregnancies; eight children survived. She spoke about her marriage:

> My husband was a devoted husband and father but we had very separate roles. He took care of everything outside of the home and I took care of everything inside the home. He handled all the financial matters. When I told him I wanted to go to get a job after twenty years of marriage, he didn't understand and told me everything had to be done around the house the same way even if I worked. No routines could be interrupted; all the meals must be ready on time and supper must be on the table at five o'clock every day.
>
> Meanwhile, I was losing myself. Not having my hair done. I had gained weight. I was losing myself and I didn't know it.[1]

On their twenty-third anniversary, Doreen's husband sent her flowers for the first time since she had given birth. Shortly afterward he took her dancing—another first. Within the next few weeks he told her he wanted to talk with her, and over coffee at McDonald's he told her he had fallen in love with a 28-year-old woman and that he was leaving her. His exact words, according to Doreen, were "I love you and I love the kids but I just can't live without Sandy." Doreen recalled, "I was devastated. I became suicidal. My self-esteem was a big, black zero."[2] Also dropping precipitously was the family's income, which fell from $70,000 a year to just over $7,000. Her husband paid no child support because he walked away from his job at the same time he walked away from his family. Doreen was working part-time as a homemaker/health aide and earning the typically low salary of those in human services. When the weather turned cold, she quickly ran out of heating oil. She sold her dishwasher and anything else she could do without. She lost their house because the bank foreclosed on the mortgage. By the time he had been gone a year and a half, her husband owed her $10,576. When she went to court for the divorce, the judge waived the $10,000 because her husband had no job. Doreen and the children had joined the ranks of the new poor.

Ironically, while many critics of single mothers, particularly poor single mothers, view them as irresponsible—irresponsible for having sex without using effective birth control, perhaps irresponsible for having sex outside of marriage, irresponsible for making bad choices about the men with whom they have relationships, and irresponsible for having and raising children without a partner or without sufficient income—many single mothers feel, to the contrary, that they are the responsible ones. On many levels they have been raised to act responsibly, to take care of others, to stand by their family members even when doing so is clearly not to their own benefit. In her illuminating and wrenching study of low-income girls and women in the Boston area, *Don't Call Us Out of Name*, Lisa Dodson points out that low-income women are socialized from a very young age to put the needs of others before their own. Many low-income daughters perform a significant amount of work around the homes in which they are raised. Generally, they do three kinds of work: child care, housework, and mediation and advocacy centered on their parents' problems. Dodson estimates that the girls in her study spent between sixteen and twenty hours a week on housework and child care—a time commitment equivalent to a part-time job. Clearly, as Dodson points out, "the demand for daughters' work is economic and the result of a lack of money. Where there are no nannies, no cars, no child-care centers, no washers or dryers or dishwashers, no vacations, no house cleaners, no takeout dinners, a daughter's labor must substitute." And rather than making decisions simply on the basis of what they want or what is best for them, "these women and girls were weighing the cost of their every move and the effect that it would have on a whole constellation of people to whom they were tied."[3] In contrast, more affluent young people are often encouraged to see their needs, their interests, their desires, and their goals as priorities. Family life often revolves around their soccer, ballet, music lessons, school, college aspirations, or social life rather than their obligations to their immediate and extended family.

Being socialized to put others' needs first has real consequences. As one 24-year-old African American woman observed, "If you are taught to put everybody before yourself, how do you ever get out? How do you achieve something?"[4]

Carol Stack, in her classic study of the survival techniques of impoverished African Americans in a midwestern city during the late 1960s and early 1970s, found that these city dwellers, many of whom were living at a "bare subsistence" level, adopted out of necessity "a variety of tactics in order to survive." Family members and friends helped one another by trading and swapping both goods and services. Establishing complex domestic networks, residents of The Flats entered into intricate reciprocal relationships that both enabled them to survive and, at the same time, kept them from moving out of the poverty in which they were enmeshed. When one couple inherited a substantial sum of money, "the information spread quickly to every member of their domestic network. Within a month and a half all of the money was absorbed by participants in their network whose demands and needs could not be refused."[5]

Moreover, while low-income women are often criticized for having sex and especially for bearing children outside of marriage, many of them see having and caring for their children as the responsible way to live. Studies indicate that middle- and upper-middle-class young women are also having sex, but with an important difference: they are more likely to be using contraception. Researchers from the Alan Guttmacher Institute who examined contraceptive use among U.S. women undergoing abortions in 2000–2001 report that women with higher incomes and those who are college graduates are significantly more likely than lower-income women and those with less than a college degree to use contraceptives. Moreover, the authors point out that economic disadvantage frequently makes obtaining contraception more difficult. As they note, "Whereas some higher-income women reported access problems, poor and low-income women were much more likely to do so."[6]

In my study of the attitudes, hopes, and dreams of girls and young women ages 14 to 26, *On Her Own: Growing Up in the Shadow of the Amer-*

ican Dream, I found that middle- and upper-middle-class females had very well-thought-out plans for their lives, plans that they were not going to see disrupted by early childbearing. Beth Conant is prototypical of a group of young women whom I labeled New American Dreamers. A 16-year-old high-school junior who lived with her mother, stepfather, and five brothers in an affluent New England town, Beth hoped to study drama in college—perhaps at Yale, "like Meryl Streep." She then imagined she would live and act in England for a while, "possibly doing Shakespeare," before living in New York in her own apartment or "condo" while acting and working at another job to support herself. By the time she was 30, her career would be "starting to go forth" and she would be getting good roles. By 35, Beth thought she would most likely have a child ("probably be married beforehand"), be working in New York, and have a house in the country. Eventually she hoped to "make one movie a year."[7]

But the young women did not need to be upper-middle-class like Beth to have such definite plans for their lives. Jacqueline Gonzalez, a 19-year-old Mexican American woman, was a sophomore at a community college in Southern California when I interviewed her. She described her father as a "self-employed contractor" and her mother as a "housewife." The second youngest of six children, Jacqueline was the first in her family to attend college; only one sibling had even finished high school. Her goal was to go to law school and then into private practice. She saw herself as eventually married with "one or two children," but stressed that she also expected to be successful at work and have an upper-middle-class lifestyle. Angela Dawson, a 16-year-old high-school junior, also from Southern California, summed up the views of many of the young women who had very definite dreams and expectations of their lives and believed that their future was in their own hands: "It's your life. You have to live it yourself. You must decide what you want in high school, plan your college education, and from there you can basically get what you want. If you work hard enough, you will get there. You must be in control of your life, and then somehow it will all work out." These young women absolutely believed in the ideology of the American dream and felt they need only make it apply to females as well as males. A baby was definitely not part of the scenario for these women. They had things to do, educations to complete, professions to master, consumer goods to buy before they would be ready, in Beth's words, to be "tied down."[8] If one of these young women became pregnant accidentally, they might well find their way to Planned Parenthood, have an abortion, and preserve the future that they envisioned.

While the New American Dreamers I interviewed for *On Her Own* assumed that their plans would probably come to pass, they were in the minority: millions of young women do not plan out their lives expecting that all their dreams will come true. Some recognize that life is a balancing act, particularly for women, and that they will have to choose their path as they go along. This middle group, whom I called Neo-traditionalists, recognized that they would probably have to work out their dual roles of caregiver and high-achieving professional. A third group, the Outsiders, took for granted that their dreams would in all likelihood never materialize. They saw themselves as outsiders—outsiders within their family unit, within their community, or within the wider society. Race and class as well as gender may play a significant part in their feelings of outsiderness, but another key question relating to their feelings of alienation is whether they are transitory emotions associated with adolescence or are more deeply rooted in the young women's social status, and in their psyche. Perhaps Linda Smith, a high school dropout from North Carolina, summed it up best when she said, "I don't plan. I don't look to the future. I can't plan, 'cause my plans never work out."[9]

Toni Morrison has written a compelling description of what it is like to be a true outsider:

Outdoors, we knew, was the real terror of life. . . .
    There is a difference between being put *out* and being put out*doors*. If you are put out, you go somewhere else; if you are outdoors, there is no place to go. The distinction was subtle but final. Outdoors was

the end of something, an irrevocable, physical fact, defining and com-
plementing our metaphysical condition.[10]

Single motherhood seems to hit hardest those who truly feel like outsiders—girls and young women who have no place to go for help, those
who live on the margins of society economically and socially, and those
who cannot see their way clear to solving the fundamental problems of
providing day-to-day care for their children and functioning adequately
in the outside world so that they can pay the rent and put food on the
table. Might these "outsiders," because they often have so little belief in
themselves, also be most at risk of an abusive relationship with a man or
with family members? Is this why Pat Clarke married not for love but to
enable someone to solve his immigration problem? Is this why Soo Hyun
Park, an obvious outsider in the affluent, white, professional community
in which her husband lived and worked, was nearly paralyzed by her abusive marriage in a strange land? Young Heoy Lee, a Korean American,
was clearly comfortable with the customs and culture of New York City;
but once she and her husband moved back to Korea, she became an outsider economically, emotionally, and culturally as her husband distanced
himself from her and the children while her in-laws ostracized her for not
producing a male heir. Moreover, problems are often compounded. As
one unfortunate decision leads to another or to a circumstance that seems
to require one more stopgap measure, events soon take on a life of their
own. And we have not even added to the mix the toll that hopelessness
and depression take—the feeling that there is indeed no way out, or that
one is simply not equal to the challenge of finding a workable solution.

Despite the serious and often devastating consequences of unplanned
pregnancy, abortion is anathema to many girls and young women. In the
interviewing I did for *On Her Own*, many young women expressed negative views about terminating their pregnancies. One African American
teenage mother in Arizona said, "Abortion? My mother would kill me!"
Another, a 17-year-old mother of two, told me, "In our family we don't
believe in abortion. My grandmother would disown anyone who had an

abortion."[11] To put these views into context, we must keep in mind that almost half of U.S. pregnancies are unintended and more than one-fifth of all pregnancies end in abortion. According to a recent article titled "Abortion Incidence and Services in the United States in 2000," the number of abortions has "declined from a high of 1.61 million in 1990 to 1.36 million in 1996, the last year for which comprehensive abortion incidence data were collected." In the past, the U.S. abortion rate has been significantly higher than the rate in other industrialized countries; but following its recent decline, the U.S. rate (21.3 per 1,000 women ages 15–44 in 2000), while still higher, is within the range of rates found in a few other developed countries, such as Sweden (18.7) and Australia (22.2). Furthermore, "U.S. rates vary by women's ethnicity and socioeconomic standing: the rate among white non-Hispanic women is in the middle range of other developed countries, but other ethnic groups have higher rates. Moreover, poor and near-poor women have rates roughly twice as high as their wealthier counterparts." The authors suggest that "increased economic pressures are discouraging greater numbers of lower-income women from having children, or that it is more difficult for them to avoid unintended pregnancy because of decreased access to contraceptive services."[12]

The women interviewed for this study, by definition, chose not to abort (or chose not to abort the children under discussion) and many of them had conflicted or negative feelings about abortion. When Pamela Curtis learned she was pregnant, her boyfriend suggested she have an abortion but she says she didn't want to. She "had visions of never being able to live with it." Several women speak of making appointments to have an abortion but not being able to go through with it. Karen Morrison was so upset about being pregnant and having to tell her parents that she couldn't even figure out how to "form my mouth to tell them"; yet she could not bring herself to keep any of her three appointments to have an abortion. Cicely Franklin believes that "every woman should have a choice" but states firmly, "It was not an option for me." Jeanne Gonzalez's mother suggested she have an abortion but she says she was too afraid. "Not knowing what [was] going to happen" to her if she had an abortion, she decided she would "just have the baby." Keisha Johnson recalls that her mother wanted her to have an abortion but "I couldn't do it. It was not the right thing to do." And she adds that her grandmother, with whom she was particularly close, agreed with her. The pattern of the young woman's mother encouraging her to have an abortion but the daughter resisting was frequent. Sandra Mason responded to a question about abortion by saying, "Abortion? I never even thought of it. My mother was not overjoyed that I was pregnant. There was some tension between us at that time."

Moreover, many of the young women in Dodson's study did not see the decision to go ahead with motherhood as "an easy way out" or as evidence of irresponsibility but rather "as an act of responsibility." Motherhood is viewed as an important, valued role, one that they had been training for all their lives. When Dodson asked some of the girls if it wouldn't be better, if it wouldn't make a difference if they waited to get pregnant, the common response was, "Wait for what, what's coming anyway?"[13]

Many in middle- and upper-middle-class America, in criticizing young women for having children without a stable partner to help with finances, child rearing, and the problems of daily life, implicitly assume that girls and young women would have more control over their lives if they deferred motherhood—that they would have more opportunities in education, in work, in making a better life; but low-income young women rarely see such choices as open to them at all. That is what they mean when they ask, "Wait for what?" All too often they do not experience the rituals marking the growing-up process that higher-income young people experience—the driver's license, perhaps even a car of their own, the senior prom, graduation from high school, summer and after-school jobs, moving on to college, and then entering the workforce. All these steps gradually mark the transitions from adolescence to adulthood for millions of Americans—but not for young people whose families have meager resources and who may live in areas lacking adequate schools, job opportunities, and the social and financial capital needed to participate in these rites of passage. As Dodson notes, in this world of scarce resources and roles, "Motherhood is valued for the position, the clear and tangible role, it offers."[14]

In addition, single motherhood is the result of the other symbol of growing up, of moving on to a new stage of life—the boyfriend. Dodson describes young girls' longing for love, longing for a boyfriend, longing for "someone who is there for me." Having a boyfriend yields enormous status, is a key way of belonging and a symbol of moving from girlhood to womanhood. And with the boyfriend comes the pressure to have sex. As one girl said, "If you want him to stay, you don't have a choice. If you're not giving to him, someone else will."[15]

But once they become pregnant and give birth, many young women find themselves living in extreme isolation. As we have seen, mothers of single pregnant girls are frequently both angry and bitterly disappointed that their daughters will, in all likelihood, be prevented from finishing their education and enjoying the more comfortable life that their mothers had envisioned for them and often had made significant sacrifices so that they might achieve. In their anger, some mothers order their pregnant daughters to leave home. Without family support, without boyfriends sharing the experience with them or friends to lend a hand, the young women Dodson interviewed "speak of searing solitude, of days and nights trapped in shabby rooms with a needy baby. They recall not hearing a single kind word come to them for weeks on end and somehow trying to pass on some little joy to babies." Polly, a 24-year-old mother of three from a working-class Greek family who shunned her because her children's father was Latino, recalled the dark days of trying to care for three very young children: "I was alone in a two-room apartment with my three babies. I spent my days figuring out how to get to the grocery store on foot or using a shopping cart I had stashed in the back, stuffing three kids in it. I washed diapers in the bath tub and hung them on a line in the hall. The windows were so loose that the wind blew through, and I couldn't keep the apartment warm. My kids were sick all the time."

Dodson summarizes the situation of many impoverished young women: "Where there is no special support, no money, nor adequate educational preparation for college and career, the role of mother is simply the next tough part of life."[16]

Adding significantly to the extraordinary difficulty of single motherhood for some women is the widespread problem of men who will not or cannot be effective partners to these women and of course the corollary—men who will not or cannot be effective fathers to their children. Many of the women whom I interviewed for this book described both situations. Women who have made incredibly successful new lives for themselves and their children, women who seem stuck in the morass of single motherhood, and women whose lives have fallen apart because of their experiences all speak of men who walked away, both literally and figuratively, from their relationships and responsibilities. The following chapter will discuss some of these experiences and the factors that contribute to the very different expectations, attitudes, and actions of women and men as they deal with their roles as parents and providers.

7

"I Really, Really Believed He Would Stick Around"

Conflicting Conceptions of Commitment

When I was pregnant, I was truly in love. I thought marriage
would come later. . . . When we broke up, I was shocked. I
thought we would work things out. But he said, "I want to have
my own life."   **Shirika Simmons**, 31-year-old mother of one

Sam's father left a little before my eighth month. I came home
and saw his clothes and few things weren't there. . . . The whole
feeling in the apartment was different; the weight had shifted. . . .
     I have never, ever, ever been so totally in love. The minute I
held him. . . . To bring something into the world that is completely dependent. I just wanted to stare at him forever.

Jeri Miller, 54-year-old mother of one

Something powerful must happen between the seventh and eighth
months of pregnancy. Perhaps it's an outgrowth of the physical changes
in the body of the pregnant woman, or possibly the psychological
changes in either partner; but when men suddenly realize that they are
about to cross the border into new territory, into a new world, many of
them walk away. Often they give no reasons; they just disappear. Some
withdraw more gradually, but the message is clear: many women and
their husbands, boyfriends, or partners differ profoundly in attitudes, expectations, and behavior regarding both the nature of their own relationship and their commitment to the parent-child relationship. Some

men are unfaithful; others are harsh, punitive, and sometimes abusive. Many seem to view the women as their possessions, whom they can treat in any way they see fit, and some reject the parental role outright. When they learn about their partner's pregnancy or when the birth is imminent, a surprising number simply leave. Others withdraw from their parental role when their relationship with the mother deteriorates. Still others, according to the women, have inappropriate expectations for their children's behavior and treat them with undue severity or even violence. Listening to the women's stories, one sometimes has the sense that men and women are still socialized to have almost opposite views both of romantic relationships and of parenting. Invariably, the women consider caring for their children a central responsibility and commitment of their lives; in contrast, many men do not perceive parenting as their responsibility at all, and others see it as a peripheral obligation at best. A few of the men who had walked away when the children were born or when they were young developed relationships with their daughters and sons as they grew older, but the mothers were always there.

Jeri Miller, a 54-year-old white woman, talks about her relationship with her son's father:

> We split before Sam was born. My expectations were different. The father walked out. The "putative" father—he was Jamaican—and I had been living together off and on in my apartment. We were arguing off and on. I was not interested in getting married. During the pregnancy he was getting more conservative about his expectations. One day there was a movie on that I really wanted to watch so I told him that was what I was going to do. He was in the room ironing shirts. He said, "What's wrong with this picture?" I said, "I don't even do that for myself!"
>
> I had imagined we'd be together and that he would do the right thing, but I had expectations of a full-time father—twenty-four hours a day— all the way or nothing. In my parents' marriage she did everything— including work—and he came home and sat on the Barcalounger. And it was now the late '70s; I really thought that the world had changed.
>
> Sam's father left a little before my eighth month. I came home and saw his clothes and few things weren't there so I thought, I guess we're

not going out for dinner tonight. So I picked up the phone, ordered Chinese food, sat down to eat and read a magazine. The whole feeling in the apartment was different; the weight had shifted.

When Sam was born, I called his mother. She said she didn't know where he was so I left a message that the baby had been born but I never heard anything. When Sam was about 2 years old, I went to a jazz club with a friend and from one end of the bar, from the back of his head I saw his ear. I went down to talk with him. We spoke a few words and I went back to my friends. I saw him one other time—crossing the street on the Upper West Side. I had the baby in one of those huggie things and he was coming toward us. He saw us and dashed across the street in the traffic [to avoid them]. It was a wonder he wasn't killed.

A little later in the interview, while talking about how rarely she went out socially without her son, Jeri remembers: "I never wanted to leave him. I have never, ever, ever been so totally in love. The minute I held him. How unbelievably overwhelming it was. To bring something into the world that is completely dependent. I just wanted to stare at him forever."

Jennifer Soriano and her boyfriend had discussed what would happen if she got pregnant and she recalls, "I really, really believed he would stick around." He did—until she too was eight months pregnant; then he stopped coming by. When the baby was two months old, he was incarcerated. Now that their son is 6 years old, his father does "come around" but gives no child support and is emotionally abusive to Jennifer. Similarly, Jeanne Gonzalez describes the father of her son as "not part of his life." He dropped out of high school and was then in prison for several years. Although she was only 16 when her child was born, she has cared for him and his sister, coped with his severe medical problems, worked, and graduated from college. Neither she nor Jennifer walked away; both fathers did. According to Sandra Mason, the man with whom she was living was not ready for a mature, responsible relationship either with her or with their son. She felt she needed to do it all and was not prepared for such a one-sided arrangement.

Some of the women who were not married to the fathers of their children describe the fathers as being to some extent around and available for their children. Keisha Johnson recounts that her daughter's father contributes some child support and has something of a relationship with his daughter; Pamela Curtis states that while her daughter's father wasn't interested in marriage, he nonetheless has always recognized his parental responsibilities, particularly the need to help support his daughter financially. The father of Karen Morrison's older daughter contributed no child support and played a minimal role in her life until she was in her teens; at that point, they established a relationship.

Shirika Simmons, a 31-year-old African American who is a special education teacher and the mother of a 5-year-old son, describes how a relationship she felt was solid and in fact expected would lead to marriage dissolved in front of her eyes. She begins, "I grew up in Queens. I was raised by my maternal grandmother because my mother died when I was 15. She was a single mom. I have two sisters; we have different fathers. I have one father and they have another. I didn't have a relationship with my father until after my mother died." During her junior year at college in upstate New York, she met her son's father through a mutual friend. While they were both still in college (he in Virginia), they had a long-distance relationship; and when he returned home, according to Shirika, it became "more serious." She describes what happened next:

> My son was born in 1999 when I was 27. His father was younger than I was; he was too young. I was going to go along with the pregnancy—yes, it was unplanned. He had parents. I didn't have my mother and father, but since he did I thought it would be different—that his parents would want to keep the family together.
>
> He was on the road for his job a lot. He was not even there for the birth. I needed him around more. He never clearly stated that he didn't want to be involved but he was gone sometimes three months at a time and my son was growing up.

Shirika and her son still live with her grandmother in the house in which she was raised. She says her grandmother "thought a marriage would take place. He and I would speak about marriage. We talked about living together and moving in together." She adds,

> When I was pregnant, I was truly in love. I thought marriage would come later. I look back now and realize I never saw this coming. My family was shocked. He was at all our family functions; he would eat dinner with my family, stay overnight. And my grandmother was strict. I would not have gone against her wishes but he was like family. My grandmother accepted him, thought he was going to be part of the family. When we broke up, I was shocked. I thought we would work things out. But he said, "I want to have my own life." It's not another woman. He's a workaholic. But he still doesn't know what he wants to do with himself. Now he's applying to law schools.

Shirika and her son's father had a serious, long-term relationship. This was no casual one-night stand. They spoke of marriage, she knew his family well, and he was part of her family. What happened? Did he get cold feet? Was he just too young or too immature to take on the responsibility of marriage after fathering a child? Currently he sees his son about twice a week. She says he's involved, but sometimes she feels his involvement is "forced." He rarely does anything without being asked, comes by for quick visits, and never takes his son for weekends. Nor does he pay regular child support. But he does pay for day care and sometimes gives her money for the child's overall care. Shirika says she has never had a problem with their financial arrangements.

Was Shirika's relationship sidetracked by her unplanned pregnancy? Was her son's father simply not prepared to make a long-term commitment to marriage and parenthood? Only 24 when his son was born, he clearly wanted to do something with his life and was still figuring out which direction to take. In fact, five years later he still seems to be trying to figure it out.

This is a middle-class couple with professional aspirations. The accidental pregnancy turned their lives upside down. When I ask Shirika why she didn't have an abortion, she responds, "Yuh, I thought about it, but when I told my grandmother she let me know she was proud of me—that

I had accomplished all she had imagined. She was excited that I was pregnant. We never discussed abortion. It was as though the decision was already made for me." Shirika is not unusual in being heavily influenced by family members and lovers in making a decision about abortion. Did her grandmother want her to have the baby at least in part so that she, the grandmother, would have another child to love and to help raise? Was her grandmother so certain that Shirika and her long-term boyfriend would marry that she foresaw no problem? And Shirika herself, of course, assumed they would marry.

Shirika notes that her middle sister is a college graduate who has a master's degree from a prestigious university and "has had a long relationship with a nice guy. He comes from a good family. We think there'll be a marriage and then children. We say to her, 'Please keep him.' "

Susan Jackson reflects the same reality: after her sons were born, their father was not there for her—or for them. He wasn't even willing to care for them at night while she worked. The absence of men, particularly African American men, as active participants in the family unit has been noted and analyzed by sociologists, economists, psychologists, and, above all, by the women left to manage on their own. One black woman, an administrative assistant at Spelman College, describes the independence and self-reliance that African American women have been forced to acquire over the generations: "Men leave, we keep going. We don't miss a beat. Like later for them. That's basically the attitude my mother and grandmother had. . . . They assumed the role of both male and female." But this same young woman quickly drops her tone of bravado when she describes how difficult it is to be a single mother: "It's a constant battle. How to make enough to take care of the kids. What do I do to prepare them for their education? Where am I going to get the money from? How are we going to eat today? Where's the gas coming from for the car? You're working two jobs and you're getting maybe three hours of sleep a night and it's like this is crazy. I just feel so trapped but I'm like I can't give up."[1]

Unmarried fathers are not the only ones who leave. Men who have been married for several years and have developed relationships with their children may also walk away. When their relationship deteriorated and disintegrated, Hannah Alexander's husband ended the marriage and eventually, after the divorce, abandoned his responsibilities as a father as well. Because Hannah's daughter was 9 when they separated, he—unlike the men who leave before or just after their baby's birth—obviously had a relationship with his daughter. Nonetheless, he stopped giving child support and finally stopped seeing his daughter at all. Hannah puts it simply: "Not a phone call. I never forgave him for that."

Soledad Martinez's husband also had a relationship with his children. When she left him, he sued for custody of his son and daughter in a transparent attempt to force her to return to him. He even later admitted to her, "I was just doing it to get you back." Perhaps most remarkably, after custody was settled and the divorce became final, he did not see the children at all for a year and a half.

Cathy Morgan and her husband split up two months before their daughter was born. He moved out of state and didn't pay child support for years—until she took him to court. Judith Berman's husband had several affairs while they were together and then finally "walked out" on his wife and six children. He did so little to raise them that he acknowledged that he didn't even have the right to be proud of his son on the young doctor's wedding day. While Judith was forced to turn to welfare, food stamps, and Medicaid in order to survive, returned to college, obtained a graduate degree, and worked to care for and support her children, their father formed other relationships and played a minimal part in their lives.

Some fathers refuse to take on familial responsibilities even when they are still present. Jackie Watkins, a 26-year-old mother of a 7-year-old son, describes how she became a single mother:

> I was born in London. My parents were from Guyana. My father had gone to London to work when he was young but returned to Guyana to visit his mother. My mother and her family lived nearby. They met on Sunday, married on Tuesday. It was an arranged marriage. Then they went to London to live where my sister and I were born. We came

here [the United States] when I was eight and my younger brother was born here.

In high school I met this nice, dashing guy. He was very ambitious. We dated and when I was 17, I found I was pregnant. We used birth control but once the condom broke. I thought, "I'll be OK," but then I found I was late. I took a pregnancy test and learned I was pregnant.

I spoke to a cousin because I was so scared to tell my parents. I knew they were going to throw me out so I was all packed. When I told them, my mother jumped up from the sofa like she was going to come toward me so I jumped up to get away. My father said, "You have to have an abortion; you're too young," and I said, "No, I'm having this baby." I didn't even know that was coming out of my mouth. Then I left.

Jackie moved in with her boyfriend and his parents. While she was pregnant, she was not allowed to go to her parents' house or talk with her brother and sister. She recalls, "My father didn't speak to me for a long time." Her parents were also upset because they are Muslim and her boyfriend was Catholic. The young couple married three months before their son was born. They moved into a one-bedroom apartment and she stayed home to raise their son. At first, her husband was a "great provider"; but after a while she began to see that "he wasn't really involved. His only responsibility was working. One day we were going out so I said, 'You watch Robert and I'll lock the door.' I locked the door and heard a crash. Robert had fallen down the stairs and hit his head. He couldn't even watch him for a minute."

After a while, her husband didn't even feel like going to work some days. When they didn't have enough money to pay the rent and Jackie tried to discuss their financial problems with him and offered to go to work, his response was "Oh, we'll be fine." Jackie eventually learned that her husband was "cheating" on her—in fact, he had cheated on her "with many girls—even while I was pregnant." When she spoke to him about it, he suggested that they "see other people." Though she acknowledges that she perhaps should have worked harder on the marriage, she believes that they had different concepts of marriage and parenthood. She always felt a lot older than he—even though he was 21 and she was 18 when their son was born. She describes him as "very needy," requiring "a lot of attention": he "wanted someone to do *everything* for him."

They divorced when their son was 3. According to Jackie, her husband was "very nasty" during the divorce. He said he didn't want to see Robert. He was supposed to pay $100 in child support every two weeks but never did so. In fact, he deliberately stopped working so that he couldn't be forced to pay. Since they divorced, he has given his son a total of $110 and has seen him three times. The last time he saw Robert, two years before our interview (and two years after the divorce), he stepped outside to smoke a cigarette and somehow Robert cut himself on his forehead right above his eye and required thirteen stitches. When Jackie arrived at the hospital and saw what had happened, she told her ex-husband, "He's never coming to see you again." After that incident he never called to find out how Robert was doing and hasn't seen him since.

Jackie and her son had to move back to her parents' home. She has a good position at a prestigious retail store and has hopes of advancement. The family members all help take care of Robert, but Jackie admits that she is very disappointed with herself for being dependent on her parents. They do tell her "We told you so" and "You should have listened to us," but at the moment she does not see how she can afford to move into her own place.

Other husbands withdraw emotionally even while they are still physically present. Carolyn Miller describes her husband's gradual withdrawal from family life while they were all living together: "There was a detachment. He retreated. He never was very engaged with the kids." He didn't go to parent-teacher conferences or to back-to-school nights. He came home after the children's bedtime. Eventually he refused to eat with them or go on vacation with them. Finally, he emptied their joint bank accounts and left.

Mary Giordano, a white, 39-year-old mother of one daughter, says her husband was unsure whether he wanted children. She feels he changed toward her when she became pregnant—as soon as "I started showing." She continues, "He was degrading me—commenting on how big I was and asking how big I was going to get. I knew it was going to be a problem but I said to myself, 'I'll make it work.' " He left her alone in the hospital at the time of a "very difficult" delivery, and after their daughter was born, the baby was "just this thing to him." He "didn't take to her. She was very healthy, beautiful, had no complaints. I couldn't understand it." Mary recalls that he didn't even want to hold the baby; he seemed not to want to spend money on her, didn't want her toys on the floor, just "didn't want a baby in the house." When their daughter was a little over 2, Mary and her husband separated. Though he initially resisted, he has paid child support regularly and eventually developed a relationship with his daughter.

A particularly interesting example of paternal participation is described by Nancy Mendez. Nancy and her husband had early problems in their marriage and had difficulties with birth control; when she accidentally became pregnant, her husband wanted her to have an abortion. When she found she "could not go through with it," he left, saying, "Oh yeah? Well, that's going to be your baby." Notwithstanding their contentious relationship—she repeatedly returned to family court to force him to pay child support—her ex-husband assumed the role of father that he had rejected for years when she found she had breast cancer. Acknowledging his shortcomings as a parent, he offered to take over the care of their son, then 16, while she was undergoing treatment and getting back on her feet. Nancy not only speaks of her gratitude for the support and for what it meant to her son but says that it led her to forgive him for all he had put her through—for "all those years of being a single parent."

While many of the women detail how they and the fathers of their children disagreed totally on what their roles should be, others describe fathers who are remarkably devoted to their children. Carolina Delgado and her husband share custody amicably despite the profound problems in their marriage. She describes her life as a single mother of three as a "constant race—getting them on the school bus, going to work, picking them up, getting them to and from soccer practice and religion classes. And then I have to fit in the supermarket and errands. During the week I'm exhausted by the time we're done with the homework. I'm often in bed by ten o'clock with them." But Carolina is quick to say that her husband, from whom she is separated, cares for the children every Tuesday and Thursday as well as every other weekend. In her words, "Daddy's there for them." Moreover, if a problem at work prevents her from picking them up, she can call him and he'll do it. She and her husband also get together with the children and her in-laws at celebrations and holidays; in many ways they still function as a family.

Perhaps the most unusual arrangement among my interviewees was the one created by Cicely Franklin and the father of her son. Though they are not married and do not now have an intimate physical relationship, they live together with their son as a nuclear family. Members of their extended families on both sides are actively involved in helping to care for the child. Despite the stigma of giving birth outside of marriage, Cicely decided that pregnancy was not itself a good enough reason to marry; she has instead chosen to put her own romantic life on hold so that she might focus on creating a loving, caring environment for her son. And her son's father is clearly part of that environment. Unlike most of the fathers described by these women, he shares expenses as well as responsibility for day-to-day living and decision making.

The causes of the sometimes dramatically different attitudes and behavior of men and women are undoubtedly complex. Today, in the first decade of the twenty-first century, all the explanations commonly suggested—biology, very different socialization of girls and boys during childhood, varying cultural expectations and norms as women and men become young adults, profound changes in family structure, and structural or economic conditions—are likely at work in different degrees in creating the wide gap in values and priorities. The gender divide has actually gotten so wide that the political scientist Andrew Hacker currently finds a "mismatch" between many men and women.[2] Generalizations about the United States' diverse society, particularly as exemplified by the metropolitan New York City area that is home to these women, in which a multitude of social patterns, values, and norms exist side by side, are problematic. Nonetheless, many young girls apparently are still being socialized, possibly from birth, to see themselves at some point in their lives as caregivers. Walking down the streets of New York, alongside the children riding tricycles and bicycles, playing ball, or swooping by on their scooters, are little girls pushing little strollers with even smaller dolls inside. The message is clear: along with all the other opportunities open to many of them if they are lucky, these girls will take care of babies. Girls may play soccer, study a musical instrument, excel in school, go to college in greater numbers than men (in the year 2000, 57.2 percent of all bachelor's degrees were awarded to women), and even go on in significant numbers to law and medical schools (in 2000, 45.9 percent of the degrees in law and 42.7 percent of the degrees in medicine were awarded to women);[3] but women are still expected to care for their children. Even if they hire someone else to perform the day-to-day care, mothers are ultimately responsible. In some families, fathers share responsibility, but their caregiving is usually added to that of a mother, not substituted for it. The exceptions to this pattern are the growing numbers of fathers raising children on their own. In 2000, 20.7 percent of single parents were fathers, almost double the figure in 1970 (10.8 percent).[4]

But while all of the women in this study have been and are committed to caring for their children, many of them have also been committed to personal achievement, to making a contribution to the wider society, to achieving upward mobility. Many have sought out work and educational opportunities and have been publicly recognized for their professional accomplishments. Many are also actively involved in civil society—in their churches, in activist organizations, in professional associations. Several of these women are thus successfully taking on multiple parts: caregiver, provider, and often community activist. In sociological terms, they are playing both the expressive and the instrumental roles.

Dramatic changes within the family and in the working conditions and opportunities for women and men alike have helped widen the gulf between male and female aspirations and commitment to family. As the sociologist Terry Arendell notes, "Although the family has never been static . . . , the pace and array of changes experienced in this [twentieth] century are staggering."[5] American families have been transformed from units largely of production to units of consumption, have moved from farms and small communities to urban centers and larger communities, have shifted from the model of the male breadwinner to the two-earner family, from separate spheres of authority for men and women, a system that assumes the ultimate authority of males, to the ideal—if not always the reality—of shared decision making and authority. In recent decades, structural changes in the economy have led to declining or stagnant wages for male workers, except for the best educated and most highly paid. The proportion of U.S. jobs in the more highly rewarded manufacturing sector has declined while jobs in the significantly less well rewarded service sector have grown. During the 1970s and 1980s, according to Kathleen Gerson, "Men under 45 working year-round full-time, as well as white males serving as their families' only breadwinners, [were] especially hard hit." She adds, "The stagnation of wages and the decline in job security have eroded men's ability to earn family or living wages on a consistent, predictable basis." These changes have "undermined men's economic dominance along with their role as family breadwinners. The economic support of wives and children has become more difficult and less attractive to a growing proportion of men."[6]

Between 2001 and 2003, following the economic boom of the 1990s, nearly 2.6 million jobs disappeared. Approximately 90 percent of the lost jobs were in manufacturing, and government data show that black workers were hit harder than white workers. Some of those laid off were employees of many years. As textile production has shifted to China and India, tens of thousands of experienced workers in the South have lost jobs. According to Bruce Raynor, the president of the union that represents textile workers (now UNITE HERE), during the early 2000s thousands of workers lost their jobs in mills in North Carolina, Georgia, and Virginia. Most are black men and women who had been earning $11 an hour; if they found new employment, the replacement jobs paid far less.[7]

Not only are jobs that pay decent wages disappearing but millions of workers are underemployed, able to find only part-time work and not full-time jobs with benefits. According to the Bureau of Labor Statistics, the numbers of Americans working "part time for economic reasons" rose from 3.1 million in 2000 to 4.8 million in July 2003. Moreover, underemployment is likely to be self-perpetuating. People who are forced to take jobs with lower pay must often work two jobs, leaving them little time to look for something better. And skills can quickly deteriorate if workers are away from technological jobs too long.[8] In addition, between 2000 and 2004 there has been a sizable growth in the number of "discouraged" workers—those who do not have jobs and are not looking for them. According to the Bureau of Labor Statistics, the number of nonworkers, or adults "not in the labor force," increased by about 4.4 million to a total of 66.6 million.[9] These discouraged workers or nonworkers are not included in the official unemployment statistics. In June 2004, for example, 8.2 million people were officially considered unemployed. If we take into account people with "hidden" unemployment—those working part-time who really want full-time employment—and the "marginally attached" unemployed workers who are left out of the official total because they are not currently looking for work, the number jumps to 14.3 million.[10]

The erosion of male earning capacity has been accompanied by a sharp increase in female employment outside of the home. For mothers with children under the age of 18, for example, employment rose from 53 percent in 1980 to 70 percent in 2001. Of those mothers employed in 2001, 52 percent were working full-time. Divorced mothers were most likely to work full-time (72 percent); the rates for never-married mothers (52 percent) and married mothers (49 percent) were significantly lower. In 2001, black mothers were most likely to be employed (73 percent), followed by white mothers (70 percent) and Hispanic mothers (58 percent). Black mothers were also most likely to be employed full-time (63 percent).[11]

These fundamental changes in the economic status of both men and women have had a substantial impact on male-female relationships and on family life. As Kathleen Gerson observes, "On the one hand, women's growing economic independence has given men greater freedom to avoid commitment or to leave relationships without feeling economically responsible for the people left behind. On the other hand, independent sources of income give women more leverage in relationships. They, too, possess the option to leave."[12] We have seen both trends illustrated in these interviews—men who walked away, leaving a working mother to provide for the family, and women who felt that the relationship was no longer working and ended it. But we have also seen men walk away when it was not at all clear how the mother and her child or children would manage. Jeri Miller's male friend left when she was eight months pregnant; she was working in an office, but how she would both work and care for an infant was not at all clear at the time. Jeanne Gonzalez and Jennifer Soriano also had no clear plan for managing when their male friends walked away. Hannah Alexander's husband abandoned not only his marriage but also a daughter he had helped raise. Gerson describes men who engage in this kind of behavior as having an "autonomous orientation," of distancing themselves from family commitments and instead seeking freedom. She argues, "As social change has eroded men's breadwinning abilities and sent legions of women into the workplace, men have had to develop new responses to the historic tensions between freedom and sharing, independence and interdependence, and privilege and equality."[13] Arendell describes these omnipresent conflicts slightly differently: "Tensions persist between the values of separation and commitment, competition and cooperation, autonomy and intimacy, utilitarian individualism and love, and obligation and freedom." She then quotes the authors of *Habits of the Heart:* "Most Americans are, in fact, caught between ideals of obligation and freedom."[14]

The same tension is discussed by Daniel Mendelsohn in his review, published in the *New York Review of Books*, of the HBO production of *Angels in America*: "The action of the first part, 'Millennium Approaches,' is organized around a series of abandonments and escapes which are meant to make us think about the issues of responsibility and love and freedom; the second part, which is organized around a series of unexpected scenes of forgiveness, shows the consequences of those flights and is meant to make us think about change and redemption."[15] These themes are central to the narratives in this study. Many of the men who walk away may be seeking their freedom and independence from obligations that they do not wish to meet or feel they cannot meet, but their flight has clearly led many of the women to feel truly abandoned, often at a time of great need. Only occasionally have we seen "scenes of forgiveness." Generally, the women simply must find the capacity and the courage to move on with their lives.

Yet another factor significantly affecting relationships is the nature of the communities in which many Americans live today. Because many of us are highly mobile and dwell in large cities where we live virtually anonymous lives, often at a considerable distance from our extended families, the power of social pressure and social stigma has been considerably eroded. Even in smaller communities, attitudes toward so-called deadbeat dads seem to have little power over male behavior. Carolyn Miller's husband left her and their two children, yet he remains in the relatively small, upper-middle-class suburb in which they live. Her friends may think he's a "shit," but their opinion evidently does not materially alter his behavior. And in some communities, that men have weakened or even nonexistent ties to their children is almost the norm.

Andrew Hacker suggests that men's commitment to family life remains markedly different from women's. He states that men "feel entitled to retain much of their freedom and independence . . . [and] feel they can allocate only so much of themselves to a marriage, lest they impair the powers they will need to take on the world." In contrast, he sees women as "willing to relinquish more for love," because "often they expect that through their marriage they will find new facets and dimensions of themselves," while men "don't expect they will have to alter their identity." Women thus want more from marriage than do men. "Indeed," Hacker argues, "it is not an exaggeration to suggest that today's women actually want more from life than men do."[16]

In her book *Stiffed: The Betrayal of the American Man*, Susan Faludi analyzes what she calls the "male predicament" or the "male crisis." While the "prevailing American image of masculinity" is the man "controlling his environment," "in the driver's seat, the king of the road forever charging down the open highway," the reality, according to Faludi, is that men "are being mastered, in the marketplace and at home, by forces that seem to be sweeping away the soil beneath their feet." Faludi writes of "men's loss of economic authority," of public betrayals of their loyalty, of private betrayal and desertion by their fathers, and, above all, of their having to find meaning in a world in which personal worth is judged by image and by "winning" rather than by substance or "meaningful social purpose."[17]

It is therefore perhaps not surprising that many of the interviews of single mothers for this book strikingly portray the gap between the dreams and goals of the women and those of their husbands or male friends. This stark difference in attitudes about the importance of parenting, their aspirations for the future, and the kinds of lives they hope to live was, in several instances, the cause of the unmendable rift between the parents. Eva Sanchez saw that there was another kind of life she could live but her husband didn't see it, couldn't imagine it, wasn't willing or able to work with her toward it. She truly seems to want more from both marriage and life than her husband could imagine. Soledad Martinez, too, envisioned a different life for herself and her children. She was unwilling to continue to be emotionally abused and controlled by her husband; she obtained her education and walked away. Susan Jackson wanted a very different life than her partner was able to sustain. Yet another woman, married to an affluent, high-achieving man who had a severe drinking problem, earned her Ph.D. and then decided to separate. Though she had tried getting help for him and they had tried couples counseling, he continued to drink excessively. She decided she could no longer live and raise their three children with the constant burden of his drinking and the personality changes it caused. There is little doubt that her professional degree and her ability to work in a field to which she is committed contributed significantly to her decision to separate.

This divergence in values and aspirations for the future is painfully and beautifully depicted by Paule Marshall in her timeless novel, *Brown Girl, Brownstones*. Marshall tells the poignant story of the Boyce family— the mother, Silla; the father, Deighton; and two daughters, Selina and Ina. Immigrants from Barbados who live in Brooklyn, they are struggling to make ends meet in the late 1930s and 1940s. Silla works day and night and yearns to put down roots in their new country and to be part of the American dream by purchasing a brownstone. The Barbadian community recognizes that owning property is a key route out of poverty, particularly for blacks, during this time of economic hardship and persistent racism. Her romantic, somewhat unfocused husband has dreams of one day returning to his homeland and building a fine house there. Deighton cannot quite find an occupation that suits his dreams and spends his money frivolously on dapper clothes and women. Selina is torn between her parents' opposing goals and battered by her mother's rage toward her father. The parents see the world from very different perspectives. At one point, uttering what could be the book's epigraph, Silla expresses to a friend her amazement and incomprehension at the injustice of life: "In truth . . . there don seem to be no plan a-tall, a-tall to this life. How things just happen and don happen for no good reason. I tell you, it's like God is sleeping."[18] Predictably, the conflict ends in tragedy for the entire family.

But often conflicting dreams and worldviews are not all that keep men and women apart. Elliot Liebow's classic anthropological study, *Tally's Corner*, sheds light on the impact of unemployment and underemployment on men's relationships with women and with their children. Using the research methodology of participant-observation, in the early 1960s Liebow studied low-income black men who spent the bulk of their days in and around the New Deal Carry-out shop on a street corner of downtown Washington, D.C. Liebow describes the men as living "in a sea of want" and points out that "living on the edge of both economic and psychological subsistence, the streetcorner man is obliged to expend all his resources on maintaining himself from moment to moment." For such a man, according to Liebow, "the job is not a stepping stone to something better. It is a dead end."[19] Such dead ends have significant repercussions on these men's relationships with their children: as Liebow points out, in all likelihood the men are failing to provide for their children, a failure that "contaminates" their performance as father as well. Liebow could be describing several of the relationships depicted in this study when he states that few of these men "do in fact support their families over sustained periods of time. Money is chronically in short supply and chronically a source of dissension in the home." Because "marriage is an occasion of failure," to remain with one's family is to be faced by that failure day after day.[20] Today, living with the mothers of their children is an "occasion of failure" for unemployed and underemployed men; every time they walk into the family home, they are keenly aware of what they cannot provide.

In recent years the damaging effects of the low economic status of black men and its impact on their intimate lives have appreciably worsened for a substantial segment of the black community. A study done by the Center for Labor Market Studies at Northeastern University in Boston found that "by 2002, one of every four black men in the U.S. was idle all year long. This idleness rate was twice as high as that of white and Hispanic males." According to the lead author of the study, their count was "conservative," since they did not include those men who were homeless, in jail, or in prison. Most economists agree that the recession of the early 2000s hit black men particularly hard. As Bob Herbert notes in his *New York Times* column citing the labor study, "Things fall apart when 25 percent of the male population is jobless. . . . Men in a permanent state of joblessness are in no position to take on the roles of husband and father. Marriage? Forget about it. Child support? Ditto."[21]

But black men are not simply jobless; millions are caught in some way within the criminal justice system. Lani Guinier and Gerald Torres offer sobering statistics: "Among black men between the ages of 18 and 30 who drop out of high school, more become incarcerated than either go on to attend college or hold a job." According to 1999 data, among black men aged 22 to 30 who had dropped out of high school, 41 percent were incarcerated; among their white peers, 6 percent were incarcerated. As Guinier and Torres observe, "In the United States, if young men are not tracked to college and they are black or brown, we wait for their boredom, desperation, or sense of uselessness to catch up with them. We wait, in other words, for them to give us an excuse to send them to prison. The criminal justice system has thus become our major instrument of urban social policy."[22] The sociologist Loic Wacquant puts the current role of prisons in historical perspective, noting that prisons are the latest in the "historical sequence of 'peculiar institutions' that have shouldered the task of defining and confining African Americans, alongside slavery, the Jim Crow regime, and the ghetto."[23]

In New York State, for example, blacks and Latinos constitute 25 percent of the population but make up 83 percent of the inmates in state prison, and 94 percent of those incarcerated for drug offenses. Guinier and Torres point out that "while blacks represent only 15 percent of all drug users and 33 percent of those arrested for drug possession, they make up 55 percent of those *convicted* for drug possession and 74 percent of those sentenced to prison for nonviolent drug offenses" (emphasis theirs). At the same time, prison construction has become—next to defense-related industries—America's major public works program. Over the past two decades, New York has opened thirty-eight new prisons, all in rural, primarily white areas. Although two-thirds of black and Latino prisoners come from New York City, three-quarters serve their time in facilities located at least three hours away from the city.[24] And as the money spent for prisons has skyrocketed, the resources allocated to higher education have declined.

According to a report released by the U.S. Bureau of Justice Statistics in November 2004, the number of inmates in state and federal prisons increased 2.1 percent during 2003, rising to 1,470,045 even as violent and property crime fell in the United States. When the inmates in city and county jails and the incarcerated juvenile offenders are included, the total number of American men and women behind bars on December 31 was 2,212,475. The report estimates that 44 percent of state and federal prisoners in 2003 were black, 35 percent were white, 19 percent Hispanic, and 2 percent of other races: almost 10 percent of all American black men between the ages of 25 to 29 were in prison in 2003.[25]

Disturbing as such data are, Johnnetta Cole and Beverly Guy-Sheftall do not believe that economic hardship and incarceration wholly explain the disastrous state of relations between black men and black women. In *Gender Talk: The Struggle for Women's Equality in African American Communities*, they suggest that hostile gender relationships are "embedded in the very structure of Black society."[26] They cite the sociologist Orlando Patterson, who describes relationships between black men and women as "fraught with distrust and conflict," declaring that "Afro-Americans are today the loneliest of all Americans," and another sociologist, Delores B. Aldridge, who calls them relationships "in chaos." She continues, "tears come to my eyes when I think about the deterioration we've experienced over the past several decades. There are communication problems and serious respect issues among our men and women."[27]

The critic and historian of hip-hop culture Kevin Powell connects the theory of "the endangered Black male" with the deterioration of black male-female relationships: "There's something about Black manhood which every day of our existence makes us feel we're under siege. Does that justify being oppressive, being sexist, being misogynistic? Definitely not. But I think there's a feeling with a lot of Black men that I know . . . that we are under siege. . . . It's like Zora Neale Hurston said, 'women are the mules of the earth' and y'all the easiest, as sisters, as Black women, to oppress because we can't do nothing to nobody else." Powell adds that men of color are strongly influenced by white patriarchal ideas about manhood, which stress that "the way to be a man is to have power." Because so many black men find most routes to power blocked, Powell

claims that within that subculture "power translates into material possessions, provocative and often foul language, flashes of violence, and
blatant objectification of and disrespect for women."[28] Such objectification and disrespect, which contribute to the alienation between the
sexes, are most clearly discernible in rap lyrics, which are frequently violent and women-hating. The constant labeling of women as "bitches"
and "hos" has taken hold so deeply that some black girls and women even
refer to themselves by these epithets.[29]

Sarita, a 22-year-old woman interviewed by Tricia Rose for her book
Longing to Tell: Black Women Talk about Sexuality and Intimacy, criticized
the portrayal of black women in black film and music videos, particularly
those featuring hip-hop artists:

> In this music video by the rapper Redman, he is on his rooftop, and
> down on the street there are scenes of prostitutes. They are black with
> blond wigs on, short shorts and halter tops and really slimy outfits. The
> camera is showing their asses and their breasts. They are proposition-
> ing men in cars and talking to police in very sexual ways. . . . That's not
> what we look like; and when I go into any black neighborhood I don't
> see prostitutes. I don't see women dressed like that in any black neigh-
> borhood I've been in, in my entire life.
>
> I don't understand that. Why is it that you can represent me like
> that? Why are you representing me like that to the world? It really
> pisses me off, because I feel like, "Damn, I birth you, I raise you, and
> I break my back to feed you all your life"—which I am sure every sin-
> gle one of the rappers' mothers did—"and then this is the thanks I
> get?" I have a lot of anger about it; it directly affects the way black men
> treat black women because we're seen as objects, commodities.[30]

The current denigration and devaluation of black women clearly
grows out of the violence and commodification to which they have long
been subjected in the United States. Beginning in the time of slavery, according to Cole and Guy-Sheftall, "Black women have always occupied
a precarious social space in American society."[31] They still do.

The pressures and circumstances that have so strained gender relationships among African Americans also affect other groups in American society. Joblessness, underemployment, low wages, drugs, alcohol, and imprisonment take a toll on all families but most especially minority families, all of whom also suffer discrimination. As the sociologist Maxine Baca Zinn has observed, "Racial and ethnic groups occupy particular social locations in which family life is constructed out of widely varying social resources. The uneven distribution of social advantages and social costs operates to strengthen some families while simultaneously weakening others."[32] The harm done to Native Americans, for example, by poverty, discrimination, and marginalization has been well documented. Moreover, Latino, Asian American, and other immigrant families often must balance beliefs deeply rooted in their countries of origin with contemporary American ideas and norms. The result is frequently conflict, sometimes leading to irreconcilable differences within families and even their breakup. In thinking about the specific problems of a wide variety of families, we must relinquish the assumption that all families must mirror, in Zinn's words, the "White middle-class ideal . . . [and] abandon all notions that uphold one family form as normal and others as 'cultural variations.' "[33]

What do families—both single-parent and two-parent—need so that they can effectively care for their children and for themselves and construct rewarding, meaningful lives? What do family members need from one another, from their communities, and from the larger society? These are the issues that the final chapter will consider.

8

An Agenda for the Twenty-first Century

Caring for All Our Families

━━━━━━━

The good we secure for ourselves is precarious and uncertain . . . until it is secured for all of us and incorporated into our common life.   **Jane Addams**, *Twenty Years at Hull-House*

Without fundamental change in our thinking about the needs of all families, particularly mother-only families, and without fundamental changes in our family policy, all families in the United States will continue to suffer. We must recognize that the well-being of children and their families is the responsibility not only of the families themselves but of government at all levels and of civil society as well.

Single mothers and their children have all too often been seen as a breed apart, a subgroup that requires its own analysis, norms, criticism, and punishment. But the lives of the women interviewed for this book make clear that while single mothers indeed have special problems and vulnerabilities, they differ little from the vast majority of mothers in the United States. Though their burdens—financial, social, and emotional—are considerably greater than those of two-parent families, they face the same fundamental issues as other mothers face today. Both single mothers and mothers with partners must balance, often precariously, their work lives, their caregiving lives, their personal lives, and their lives as citizens.

Rather than being a breed apart, single mothers are, I suggest, the proverbial miner's canaries. It is a metaphor drawn on by Lani Guinier and Gerald Torres, who explain: "Miners often carried a canary into the mine alongside them. The canary's more fragile respiratory system would cause it to collapse from noxious gases long before humans were affected, thus alerting the miners to danger. The canary's distress signaled that it was time to get out of the mine because the air was becoming too poisonous to breathe."[1] People who are denigrated and marginalized are more sensitive to dangers in the environment that have the potential to hurt us all. Therefore, paying attention to the problems and needs of single mothers will help us more clearly understand the problems and needs of all families. The miner's canary alerts us to both "danger and promise"—making us aware of the severe problems the miners face day by day, but also pointing to the opportunities to "change the air in the mines."[2]

The lives of the women examined in this study plainly dispel the common stereotypes about single mothers. These women are hardworking, responsible, resourceful people who, no matter the circumstances, manage to care for their children. None of them intentionally became a single mother. All of them thought, assumed, or hoped that in some way the father of their children would be present in their lives or at least in the lives of their children. When it became clear that their life was not taking the course they had expected, that their plans for the future had to be drastically altered, many experienced feelings of loss—loss of a relationship, of financial support, of their future as they had imagined it, of their hopes and dreams. After spending some time in emotional and often social and financial limbo, they set about restructuring the various pieces of their lives. In order to think through what steps they needed to take, many of the women were forced to make adjustments—sometimes quite fundamental—in their images of themselves. Jeri Miller had to realize that she was smart, able to think creatively about complex ideas and theories and therefore able to play a very different role in the world than she had ever imagined. Linda Powell faced several tasks: to grow up, to continue with her education, to care for her small child, and to figure out a way to support them both. Both Barbara Tucci and Rose

Conti had to come to grips with the loss of their husbands to early death; the emotional, financial, and social turmoil that followed; and the end of the lives they had known and had assumed would long continue. Then, for the sake of their children and their own mental health, they needed to find the inner resources to play both the expressive and the instrumental roles within the family. Some of these women are still finding their way; it is not yet clear what directions their stories, their lives, will take. Others have reconstituted their lives in remarkable, even heroic ways, choosing paths no other people close to them have followed and taking significant emotional, social, intellectual, and financial risks. Many have courageously transformed their lives and the lives of their children in ways that would once have been unimaginable to them. The usual narratives and stereotypes that are endlessly reiterated, often with great hostility and venom, about the nature of single mothers and single motherhood obviously do not apply to any of these women; and, I suspect, they similarly fail to describe millions of other single mothers. To the contrary, many of these women have fashioned lives that are the opposite of the stereotypes.

Part of the problem in how we perceive single mothers is our tendency to hold them responsible not only for being single parents, with all the negative connotations associated with that status, but also for becoming single mothers. The woman, the mother, the teenage girl is still, at the beginning of the twenty-first century, more likely than the man to be blamed for a relationship breaking up or a marriage not working, for the man walking out, and particularly for becoming pregnant in the first place. But clearly, the woman is not solely responsible for any of these events, including pregnancy.

Controlling fertility is a delicate issue, but a number of the interviewees discuss it. Eva Sanchez, a married woman, was so concerned about having two children in two years and fearful that the pattern would continue that she had a tubal ligation when she was only 21. Nancy Mendez talks about her problems using birth control, her accidental pregnancy, her reluctance to have an abortion, and her husband's subsequent statement that her choice made the baby hers—not his, not theirs. None of the women in this study who was single when she conceived intended to get pregnant when she did; in fact, each states flatly that the pregnancy was unplanned. Several of them recall that their parents had never spoken with them about sex, reproduction, or birth control. Linda Powell readily admits that she didn't even really know what sex was when she and her boyfriend skipped school and inadvertently and dramatically changed her life. Others received contraceptive advice from friends or used techniques that left them at high risk for pregnancy. Once the women learned they were pregnant, several considered the possibility of abortion. When describing how they made their choice, many indicated that their boyfriends or family members had substantial input into the decision-making process. Linda Powell's 15-year-old boyfriend told her definitively that she was not having an abortion because his family did not believe in it. Others recall that their mothers' or grandmothers' opposition to abortion kept them from seriously considering it. One young woman who lives with her grandmother was told that she had accomplished everything that the older woman had hoped she would accomplish, a statement that seemed to imply that there was therefore no reason to terminate the pregnancy—and that focused on her grandmother's expectations, not on her own. More typically, the women's mothers were extremely disappointed and in some instances angry about the pregnancy and its implications for the future lives of their daughters. Pamela Curtis, whose parents were upper-middle-class executives, recalls her mother's profound disappointment when she became pregnant between her freshman and sophomore years at college. Indeed, becoming a single mother has changed the course of Pamela's life and forced her to scale back her professional aspirations—exactly what her mother must have feared when she learned about the pregnancy.

For several of the young women, lack of knowledge about abortion as well as reproduction made their decisions even more complex, haphazard, and poignant. Jeanne Gonzalez speaks of her fear of the procedure itself. She knew women survive childbirth every day, but because she had no clear picture of how abortion is performed she was extremely fearful of it. Having little understanding about sex, how to prevent pregnancy, what abortion involves, and the process of childbirth is obviously an enormous hindrance to making informed decisions. It is almost inconceivable to many adults that teenagers—despite their classes in sex education in public schools and their massive cultural exposure to sexuality at ever-younger ages through fashion, music, advertisements, videos, movies, and television programming—still lack a genuine understanding of sexuality, human reproduction, how contraception works, and how early childbearing would affect them. Their accounts indicate that young women often hear nothing in the home about sexual matters, beyond perhaps being told not to engage in sexual activity and get pregnant. Girls and young women frequently are largely ignorant of the mechanics of sex when they have their first sexual encounter. By the time they gain knowledge, they may have inadvertently changed the course of their lives for many years to come.

Confusion about sex and pregnancy arises in part because of the large number of myths that have persisted through generations of teens. When they hear "You can't get pregnant the first time," "You can't get pregnant standing up," "You can't get pregnant if you drink ice water because your reproductive system will be frozen," and "You can't get pregnant if you don't enjoy it," young people are lulled into complacency about the possibility of getting pregnant and their need for birth control. An equally powerful belief that the use of contraceptives, particularly the condom, significantly diminishes the man's pleasure undoubtedly contributes to unwanted pregnancy and to the spread of AIDS and other sexually transmitted diseases.

Moreover, many teenagers fall into adolescent risk taking, or what has been called "magical thinking," believing "Nothing bad will ever happen to me." They think they are invincible, indestructible, immune from disaster. They think they can experiment with drugs and not become addicted, smoke and stop any time they choose, drive at high speeds and never crash, engage in binge drinking without affecting their health, and have sex without protection and not become pregnant. According to one professional who works with teen mothers, "Ninety percent never thought it would happen to them. They never, ever, thought they would get pregnant!"[3]

A nurse-practitioner who works with young women in New Jersey suggested to me that this gap in comprehension exhibited by otherwise rational young people is "developmental." She feels that many adolescent women do not yet have the conceptual ability to put the facts together and understand, in a way that will motivate them to action and overcome their reticence or embarrassment or pattern of deference to males, that sexual intercourse without contraception is likely to lead to pregnancy. In addition, being prepared for sex can damage a young woman's reputation: using contraception may earn her the label of "slut." That old epithet, redolent of the 1950s or even earlier, has been resurrected to disparage young women who are responsibly protecting themselves against pregnancy or sexually transmitted diseases. In contrast, young men who are having sex are called "macho" or "studs" or "real men." As college students at the University of California who were volunteering as health advocates told me in the early 1990s, the conventional thinking is that "only bad girls plan for sex."

Despite these widespread attitudes, teenage pregnancy rates in the United States have declined appreciably in recent years; data compiled by the Alan Guttmacher Institute show a fall nationally of 28 percent between 1990 (the peak year) and 2000. During that decade, the rate among black teenagers declined even more dramatically—by 32 percent.[4] In New York State, births to unmarried mothers of all ages dropped from 95,033 in 2000 to 89,840 in 2002. Analysts disagree on the reasons, but Dr. Allan Rosenfield, dean at Columbia University's Mailman School of Public Health, credits what he calls a "significant increase in contraceptive use among teenagers, particularly the growing availability of emergency contraception," and points to growing awareness of how to avoid AIDS and other sexually transmitted diseases. Moreover, women who have unprotected sex in the middle of their menstrual cycle can now receive injections to prevent unwanted pregnancy, a form of contraception uncommon before 2000.[5] Others attribute the drop in teenage and out-of-wedlock births to a new culture of restraint on the part of teenagers, an increase in the importance of religion and conservative values in young people's lives, programs stressing abstinence, the substitution of oral sex for intercourse, and changes in welfare policy. A complex blend of factors seems to be at work; as the reporter Nina Bernstein puts it in the *New York Times*, "In their topsy-turvy world of explicit sex and elusive intimacy, young people yearning for human contact are distilling new codes of conduct from a volatile blend of sex education, popular culture and family experience."[6]

While rates of teenage pregnancy have dropped in the United States, studies indicate that adolescent childbearing is still notably more common here than in other developed countries. According to a cross-cultural study published in *Family Planning Perspectives* in 2001, 22 percent of women in the United States reported having had a child before age 20, compared with 15 percent in Great Britain, 11 percent in Canada, 6 percent in France, and 4 percent in Sweden. The authors explain the disparities: "Although all five focus countries have a high per capita income and are highly developed and industrialized, they differ in their extent of social and economic inequality, in their government policies and programs that address inequality, in their health care systems and their provision of services to teenagers, and in their societal attitudes concerning sexuality and adolescents. All of these factors are likely to affect adolescent reproductive behavior."[7] In a second article published at the same time, the authors suggest that socioeconomic disadvantage is central to "early age at first intercourse, less reliance on or poor use of contraceptives, and lower motivation to avoid, or ambivalence about, having a child."[8] In addition to the high rate of disadvantage in the United States directly affecting sexual and reproductive behavior, the "social exclusion" that is a common outgrowth of socioeconomic disadvantage strongly predicts adolescents' risk-taking reproductive behavior and choices.

My interviews with these single mothers strikingly illustrate the extent to which individuals in modern America are able to alter their values, their priorities, their lifestyle, even their sense of their own identity. Robert Jay Lifton, author of *The Protean Self: Human Resilience in an Age of Fragmentation*, observes, "We are becoming fluid and many-sided. Without quite realizing it, we have been evolving a sense of self appropriate to the restlessness and flux of our time. This mode of being differs radically from that of the past, and enables us to engage in continuous exploration and personal experiment." Lifton states that this evolving self is rooted in confusion, in the "widespread feelings that we are losing our psychological moorings . . . that we are buffeted about by unmanageable forces and social uncertainties." These forces, he feels, lead us to "change ideas and partners frequently, and do the same with jobs and places of residence." Since the self is flexible and changes as conditions change, it "turns out to be surprisingly resilient."[9] This phenomenon is hardly new in the United States; the frontier was an opportunity for many to reinvent themselves. As *Harper's* editor-in-chief Lewis Lapham has written, "The American is always on the way to someplace else." Or as the columnist Richard Reeves puts it, "We are a nomad people, always have been, leaving almost everything behind when we move on—place, family, job, religion, friends."[10] And clearly, a central task for millions of immigrants in the past and for the millions who continue to migrate to this country is adjusting to a very different world than the one they left. Not only must they often reinvent themselves but their children and their children's children are expected to carry on the process—to "move to geographic, spiritual and economic places denied to their parents." This process frequently exacts a high cost, which Lifton finds expressed in the final lines of a poem written by an immigrant pants presser: "A stranger am I to my child / And stranger my child to me."[11]

Maintaining long-term relationships or marriages, never easy, becomes even more difficult during such a period of rapid social and personal change. Several of the women in this study married when they were quite young. In fact, a number of the interviewees met their future husbands, fell in love quickly, and married within a few months. As they came to know their husbands better and as they gradually discovered who they themselves were and might become, they often found a gulf between them that grew ever wider. Some of the women went on to college while they were married and their children were young, and this experience further changed them. Problems clearly occur when individuals move in different directions. Soledad Martinez described her husband as extremely controlling—both of herself and of the children. At the same time, she was attending college and then graduate school, undoubtedly developing new perspectives and seeing herself in different ways than she had ever imagined when she married. The result—she finally took the children and left. Like several of the women who similarly had married young, Soledad later married a man whose values, personality, and interests better matched the woman she had become.

In addition, the women in this study seem considerably more upwardly mobile than their original husbands, partners, or male friends. Despite their domestic and child-rearing responsibilities, they were far more likely to struggle to continue their education and, in some instances, to go on to become professionals; in contrast, their husbands often remained in working-class or lower-middle-class jobs. They seem to support Andrew Hacker's claim that women have higher expectations than do men, not only of marriage but also of life. This pattern seems to be reinforced by the gradual loss of opportunities for many men over the past thirty years—the decline of male-dominated jobs, particularly in manufacturing, and the decline of male wages—even as women's participation in the workforce and their wages were increasing. Moreover, many of these women are members of minority groups and, as we have seen, women of color are far more likely to pursue higher education and to be upwardly mobile than are men of color.

In discussing the supports that have helped them survive the difficult years of single motherhood, many of the women focus on the extraordinary contributions of family members. They often vividly describe the help of mothers, of siblings, occasionally of their fathers, and, perhaps most movingly, of their grandmothers. Several of the women have or have had very special relationships with their grandmothers. Jeanne Gonzalez describes her and her children's relationship with her grandmother as being one of mutual love, mutual respect, and mutual aid. They are a true family, supporting each other: her grandmother helps Jeanne take care of the children and Jeanne helps her grandmother take care of herself. Keisha Johnson was particularly close to her grandmother; now that her grandmother is dead, she has a more ambivalent relationship with her aunt and uncle. Cicely Franklin was raised by her grandmother, whom she clearly still reveres, although she is now unusually close to her mother. Shirika Simmons was also raised by her grandmother and still lives with her son in her grandmother's home. These grandmothers provide not only love, support, help with child care, meals, and sometimes housing and emotional sustenance to these young women but often the guidance for the crucial decisions these young women must make.

In addition, many of the women credit their religious beliefs with offering key support during difficult times. Several cite the belief in a personal god, someone who is watching over them and looking out specifically for their well-being, as critical to their survival and their ability to thrive. This conviction that God is there for them, particularly at crucial moments, crosses age and class lines. Several women speak movingly of their church, of support groups within the church, and of the roles they play in the church organization as the foundation of their strong sense of self-esteem, sense of purpose, and feelings of belonging. Sandra Mason emphasizes the importance of her religious beliefs in raising her son—she says she needs the external validation to withstand rampant materialism, racism, and negative cultural influences on her son. Naomi Martin discusses the influence her religious group has had on her personal behavior and on her child rearing, pointing out how much more sensitive she is toward her children's feelings and needs since she has become an active participant in her church. While women from diverse backgrounds speak of their belief in a personal god and their activities within the church, most of those who spoke with the deepest feeling about their religious involvement and described religion as a center of their lives were African American.

The other external involvement cited as key to their development is participation in social movements. Both Hannah Alexander and Judith Berman recall the energy and the feeling of being part of something transformative, something larger than self, when they discuss their involvement in anti–Vietnam War activities or in the women's movement. As Hannah says, it was as though she was waiting for a movement to happen. Other women allude to the impact of the women's movement on their thinking; a few talk about the importance of small support groups at their children's preschools in broadening their views, offering meaningful suggestions, and providing networking opportunities and an important friendship group.

As several researchers have documented, low-income mothers often have social networks that are insular and encourage the mothers to remain within the local community, where their resources—emotional, social, and material—frequently are desperately needed. The ethnographers Silvia Dominguez and Celeste Watkins point out that there are two types of social networks or social capital: those that provide social support and those that provide social leverage. As they state, "ties that offer *social support* help individuals to 'get by' or cope with the demands of everyday life and other stresses. . . . Networks composed of ties that offer *social leverage* help individuals to 'get ahead'. . . promote upward mobility by providing access to education, training and employment" (emphasis theirs).[12] We have seen many examples of social support. Several of these women stated outright that they didn't know how they would have survived otherwise, particularly emphasizing the help of their mothers or their grandmothers. The religious beliefs and affiliations that many of the mothers discuss so movingly are, I believe, sources of both support and leverage. Their belief in a personal god who is looking out for them, their reliance on the teachings of the Bible, and their adherence to a specific belief system give them comfort and certainty in an often chaotic world. But their religious involvement frequently brings them more than that. By becoming active participants within the religious community, some of them learn new skills and gain confidence in their ability to take on new roles in the larger society. The other parishioners whom they meet and with whom they often become very close also provide them with new ways of thinking and a friendship group beyond their usual community.

Several of the women have benefited enormously from relationships outside their immediate support networks. Jeri Miller's life was dramatically changed by her relationship with her therapist, who not only perceived Jeri very differently than she perceived herself but also understood the workings of the education system and the human service structure and had the power to mobilize their resources on Jeri's behalf. This interclass relationship provided Jeri with both the support and leverage necessary to enable her to make a very different life for herself and her son. Eva Sanchez similarly made connections at every stage of her life with people who provided social leverage—from the older woman with whom she lived when she first returned to New York as a teenager to her friend who was head of her agency and from whom she learned about everything from work to food to cars. People reached out to Eva and she reached out to them; through that interaction, plus her hard work and personal characteristics, she evolved from a poor girl in Mexico to an upper-middle-class professional woman in a suburb outside of New York City. Linda Powell and Lourdes Soriano also connected with people from very different backgrounds and levels of expertise than theirs, people who both encouraged them to set higher educational and career goals and offered specific advice on how to accomplish them. Both Hannah Alexander and Judith Berman were active in social movements that provided emotional support and an alternate vision of what was possible—for them personally as well as for the wider society.

What about the women whose lives seem somewhat bleak, perhaps even damaged beyond repair? Soo Hyun Park had support both from family members who lived far away and eventually from knowledgeable community leaders in the New York area, but the life she endured after coming to the United States to live with her new, unknown husband may have left her too traumatized both physically and emotionally to fully recover. Others such as Pat Clarke and Diana Sanchez also seem trapped in their current lives, looking for alternatives but clearly having difficulty finding a way out.

Despite their strong ties with family, friends, fellow churchgoers, associates in social movements, and members of support groups, several of the women feel that in the long run, they are solely responsible for themselves and their children. When decisions, particularly financial ones, must be made, the women believe they are fundamentally alone. One woman, widowed with two sons, had to figure out how to send her sons first to college and then to graduate school on a limited budget. A single father writes movingly about bearing sole responsibility for a child when there is no other parent with whom to share decisions, both big and small: "But now even the most mundane parenting decision becomes fraught with significance because it reminds me I have to make every decision on my own: nobody else to consult, commiserate with or blame."[13]

Work is a major concern for the vast majority of single mothers. Virtually all the women I interviewed need to work in order to earn their living, to provide for their children, and, in some instances, to engage in challenging and rewarding activity. Many of the fathers—both those who were married and those who were unmarried—pay little or no child support and therefore the burden of economic support falls squarely on the mothers. As has been demonstrated in previous chapters, many of the women continued with their education in order to move into more rewarding and higher-paying jobs; but many others are not so fortunate and find themselves locked into low-paying, monotonous, repetitive jobs that all too often are humiliating as well. Moreover, at the current federal minimum wage of $5.15 an hour, it is extraordinarily difficult if not impossible for millions of women to meet even the minimal expenses of daily life. In their book, *Making Ends Meet: How Single Mothers Survive Welfare and Low-Wage Work*, Kathryn Edin and Laura Lein demonstrate how difficult it is for unskilled single mothers to earn an income sufficient to cover the rent, put food on the table, and pay for transportation and other necessities. The sociologist and the anthropologist interviewed a sample of 379 low-income single mothers in four cities: Chicago, Boston, San Antonio, and Charleston, South Carolina. Two hundred fourteen of the women (the "welfare reliant," to use their term) were receiving cash welfare benefits; 165 mothers (the "wage reliant") instead had low-wage jobs paying between $5 and $7 an hour. In neither group, they found, could the mothers generate sufficient income to meet their families' basic needs. This research was done before the 1996 legislation abolished Aid to Families with Dependent Children (AFDC), the federal program that had guaranteed aid to poor children since the passage of the Social Security Act of 1935: it was replaced by a state-controlled program, Temporary Assistance for Needy Families (TANF), which has forced millions of welfare recipients to go out to work.

More than one-third of their wage-reliant mothers worked at technical and skilled jobs as "secretaries, receptionists, licensed practical nurses, cosmetologists, maintenance workers, licensed health care workers, restaurant cooks, and teacher's aides." The other two-thirds worked at "unskilled or semi-skilled jobs [as] . . . cashiers, stock clerks, general office clerks, nurse's aides, and child care workers." No working mother in Edin and Lein's sample could meet her expenses through her earnings alone; all needed supplemental income. In fact, they found that their working mothers suffered more material hardships than did their welfare-reliant mothers. Twenty-four percent of the former experienced food shortages, between one-third and one-half reported that they had needed to see a doctor during the previous year but could not afford to do so, 20 percent had no health insurance for their children, and an equal number had no insurance for themselves even though they worked full-time, full year. In short, Edin and Lein declare, "Working did not protect these women from the deprivation and financial insecurity one normally associates with welfare-reliant families. In fact, working often increased a family's financial pressures, by raising the costs of child care, health care, commuting, and clothing."[14] One welfare-reliant woman speaks for mothers of both groups when she describes some of the problems of economic deprivation in an extraordinarily rich society: "You know, we live in such a materialistic world. Our welfare babies have needs and wants too. They see other kids going to the circus, having toys and stuff like that. You gotta do what you gotta do to make your kid feel normal. There is no way you can deprive your child."[15]

In *Nickel and Dimed: On (Not) Getting By in America,* the social critic and activist Barbara Ehrenreich tells what trying to both pay the rent and eat on the salary of a low-income job is really like. In three cities—Key West (her hometown); Portland, Maine; and Minneapolis—she worked in 1999 and 2000 as a waitress, as a house cleaner and nursing home aide, and at Wal-Mart, rarely earning enough to get by. Holding rent, food, and miscellaneous expenses to a minimum and permitting herself to keep only her car and her health insurance from her real life, Ehrenreich undertook difficult, physically demanding work for very little pay. The jobs were also often accompanied by high levels of frustration and indignity. She describes cleaning rich people's toilets, the right of employers to search waitresses' purses at any time for any reason, routine drug testing (sometimes with employees stripped down to their underwear and forced to urinate into a cup in the presence of a technician or an aide), rules against " 'gossip,' or even 'talking,' " and the possibility of being summarily fired at any time, particularly for union organizing. Ehrenreich observes, "When you enter the low-wage workplace—and many of the medium-wage workplaces as well—you check your civil liberties at the door, leave America and all it supposedly stands for behind, and learn to zip your lip for the duration of the shift." The only time she achieved "a decent fit between income and expenses" was in Portland, when she was holding down two jobs (one of which provided free meals) and working seven days a week.[16] And she didn't have any children to worry about—children who need to be fed and clothed, placed in day care and after-school programs, bathed and read to at the end of an exhausting day.

Economic conditions have deteriorated significantly since Ehrenreich and Edin and Lein completed their studies. According to the Bureau of Labor Statistics, between 2001 and 2003, the years during which most of the interviews for this study were conducted, nearly 10 million workers lost their full-time jobs. By July 2004, 45 percent of them were working again in a full-time job; but of those 4.4 million workers, over half earned less than they had at their previous jobs.[17] According to the U.S. Department of Labor, 57 percent of those who had found work, either full-time or part-time, were earning less than they did in their previous jobs. Moreover, as of December 2003, four out of ten displaced factory workers had yet to find a new job.[18]

Frank Levy, a professor of economics at the Massachusetts Institute of Technology, emphasizes the widening gap between people with different levels of education: "You want to think of two job markets . . . one for college graduates and the other for high school graduates." He continues, "The market for college-grad jobs over the last four years has been expanding. . . . But the market for high school graduates has been deteriorating, with production and clerical jobs shrinking and being replaced by lower-paying service sector jobs."[19] This analysis underscores the importance of the decision made by some of my interviewees to obtain a college degree, and in some cases a graduate degree as well. Their higher education enables them to earn a somewhat more adequate income and perhaps provides them with greater economic security as well. But many of the other women are grappling with low-status, low-income service jobs.

Middle-class families have suffered from the recent downturn in the economy as well. Elizabeth Warren, a Harvard Law School professor and the co-author of *The Two-Income Trap: Why Middle-Class Mothers and Fathers Are Going Broke*, puts their situation in stark terms: "This year [2003], more people will end up bankrupt than will suffer a heart attack. More adults will file for bankruptcy than will be diagnosed with cancer. More people will file for bankruptcy than will graduate from college. And, in an era when traditionalists decry the demise of the institution of marriage, Americans will file more petitions for bankruptcy than for divorce."[20] Women have been particularly hard-hit. Not only have single mothers had to cope with recent job losses, the shift from higher-quality positions to lower-paid and part-time work, and disproportionate increases in the cost of housing, health care, and other essentials, but the median annual earnings of full-time, year-round women workers declined by 0.6 percent between 2002 and 2003[21]—the first fall in women's real earnings since 1995. Moreover, the gap between men's and women's pay has persisted, though, according to the Institute for Women's Policy Research, it had narrowed by 2004 to 76.5 percent, both because of the continuing stagnation of men's income and because of the rising educational attainment of women who work full-time.[22]

Several factors keep women's wages below men's: the dual labor market, which locks women more often than men into low-skilled, low-paying work, particularly service jobs; women's concentration in part-time work, either because those are the only jobs they can find or because they must spend considerable time on domestic tasks; and mothers' tendency to drop out of the workforce, sometimes for years, to raise their young children. Single mothers usually do not have the option of withdrawing from the labor force even temporarily, but their need to be available to their children—when their children are sick, during school vacations, after school, even for special events during the school day—limits their job choices. The average woman spends 1,498 hours a year in paid work outside the home; the average man, 2,219 hours.[23] In 2004 part-time jobs represented 18 percent of the overall job market, the highest level since 1997. According to a study done by the Employee Benefit Research Institute in Washington, only 19 percent of the 25 million part-time workers in 2003 had employee health benefits. An additional 37 percent, or 9.2 million workers, were covered as dependents of other family members; 44 percent (11 million) had no health care benefits at all.[24] Single mothers are obviously more likely to be in the latter group, since they are usually the sole wage earner in their family.

Although large numbers of women have entered formerly male-dominated professions such as medicine and law, sex segregation is still common across the country: only 15 percent of women work in jobs typically held by men, such as engineer, judge, or stockbroker. Conversely, fewer than 8 percent of men hold typically female jobs, such as nurse, salesperson, or teacher. The persistence of this dual labor market translates into significant income differentials. For example, between 1983 and 1998 male college dropouts earned an average of $36,000 a year while female college graduates earned only $35,000. In addition, during the same period of time women with a graduate degree averaged $42,000; men with comparable training averaged nearly $77,000.[25]

Perhaps the single most important step that could be taken to immediately improve the economic status of single mothers would be raising the minimum wage, which has been unchanged since 1997. At $5.15 an hour, the current federal minimum wage is a poverty wage, yielding an annual full-time income of about $11,000. Today, according to Beth Shulman, author of *The Betrayal of Work: How Low-Wage Jobs Fail 30 Million Americans*, the "minimum wage represents a 21% cut in purchasing power from 1979." As Shulman points out, "Millions of Americans are working hard every day, yet their jobs fail to provide the means for a decent life." One in every four workers—more than 30 million men and women—work at jobs that pay less than $8.70 an hour. Thus, if they work full-time, they earn less than the government-defined poverty line for a family of four. Contrary to widespread myths, most of these low-paid workers do not work in fast-food establishments but rather hold service jobs throughout the economy: "They are nursing home workers and home health workers who care for our mothers and fathers. . . . They are retail store workers who help us in department stores, grocery stores and convenience stores. They are hotel workers who ensure that the rooms we sleep in on our business trips and family vacations are clean. . . . They are security guards that help make us safe. They are ambulance drivers. . . . And they are child care workers and educational assistants who educate and care for our children."[26]

Moreover, most low-wage workers receive no health or retirement benefits or sick leave, are the most likely to be injured on the job, and are the least likely to qualify for unemployment insurance. Low-wage occupations—food service worker, wait staff, janitor and nurse's aide, orderly and attendant, and so on—are predicted to have the largest real job growth through the year 2012. Though many people believe that most of these workers are teenagers, illegal immigrants, or high school dropouts, in reality the majority are white women with family responsibilities (though blacks and Latinos are overrepresented compared to their numbers in the labor force). Most have a high school education, one-third have some postsecondary education, and 5 percent have a college degree. Twenty percent of white workers earn below $8.70 per hour, as do 31.2 percent of blacks and 40.4 percent of Latinos. In addition, according to Shulman, "Immigrants generally work in the lowest rungs of the low-wage workforce. They are more likely than natives to be food-preparation workers, sewing machine operators, parking lot attendants, housekeepers, waiters, private-household cleaners, food processing workers, agricultural workers, elevator operators and janitors. . . . These occupations have the greatest number of jobs that pay below $8.70 per hour." And because workers holding such jobs are the least likely to advance, the result is "a caste-like system, with women, minorities, and immigrants at the bottom of this labor force."[27]

According to the Fiscal Policy Institute, approximately 700,000 New Yorkers earn between $5.15 and $7.10 an hour. These workers are, for the most part, dishwashers, gas station attendants, baggers in supermarkets, and haircutters. During the summer of 2004, New York's legislature voted to raise the state minimum wage to $7.15 an hour by January 2007, and in December 2004 the bill became law after the legislature overrode Governor George E. Pataki's veto.[28] But even $7.15 an hour is not sufficient for a family to survive. In 1997, the year their book was published, Kathryn Edin and Laura Lein estimated that mothers with two children would need to earn at least $16,000 a year—$8 to $10 an hour—in 1991 dollars to make ends meet (the equivalent in 2005 would be close to $23,000 a year). These figures assume that the families would have "very modest child care or health care costs." Greater costs would require that they earn considerably more income or else, in the words of Edin and Lein, "put their children at serious risk."[29]

Some progressive activists and economists seeking to increase low salaries have become proponents of the living-wage movement. Living-wage ordinances, usually adopted at the city or county level, establish a wage floor above the prevailing minimum wage. As of February 2004, there were about a hundred such ordinances in effect across the country and some seventy campaigns under way to pass similar measures. The ordinances vary considerably in what categories of workers, firms, or employers are covered and what that coverage entails. Jared Bernstein and Jeff Chapman, economists at the Economic Policy Institute, describe one common model of living-wage legislation: "Under these ordinances, private firms under contract with the city to provide a service—cleaning streets, maintaining public areas, etc.—are mandated to pay the wage level specified in the ordinance, typically a few dollars above the minimum wage. Many ordinances allow employers to take a dollar or more off the mandated living wage level if they provide health insurance."[30]

For example, in Alexandria, Virginia, a living-wage ordinance applies to all nonconstruction contracts exceeding $50,000. Firms that have contracts with the city must pay their workers a minimum of $10.89 an hour, a wage indexed to inflation. The living-wage model has recently been applied in university settings, most notably at Harvard University; there, after an aggressive campaign by students on behalf of Harvard's low-income workers, an agreement was signed that covers dining service workers, custodians, and security guards. These local ordinances often reflect the circumstances of their specific area. Thus the living wage in San Jose, California, is relatively high, while in Santa Fe the required minimum wage is $8.50 for workers who are employed by the city.[31]

In addition to improving the wages of both female and male workers, the United States must create additional jobs at livable wages that offer all workers the possibility of advancing. Study after study has clearly demonstrated that unemployed and underemployed men have far weaker ties to their families than do men who have decent jobs at decent wages with at least some job security. If we truly want men to be active in parenting their children, we must provide appropriate job training to displaced, discouraged workers and make sure that jobs for them exist when their training period is completed. By investing in jobs, particularly for those without college degrees, we as a society are actually investing in our families.

What supports are essential if single mothers and their children are to live decent lives in the United States? What supports are essential for all families? What is the experience of other industrialized countries and what can we learn from them? The role of the larger society in contributing to the well-being of children and families is complex and multifaceted, determined largely by political ideology and by a broad view of the nature of the social contract between the individual and society. Are children primarily the responsibility of their parents, or does society as a whole have a clear and well-defined responsibility to provide at least a minimum standard of living for its children? Does society also have a responsibility to ensure that the basic necessities required by all children and their families are equally available at an equal quality? If so, what are those necessities that must be guaranteed to all families regardless of their class, race, ethnicity, work status, or place of residence? Should mother-only families be entitled to special consideration because their status is even more precarious than that of two-parent families?

Most industrialized countries answer these questions very differently than does the United States. Many, particularly in Europe, have established comprehensive family policies not just for the neediest but for all families. As Lee Rainwater, a sociologist, and Timothy Smeeding, a professor of public policy, note in *Poor Kids in a Rich Country: America's Children in Comparative Perspective*, "Child allowances are nearly universal in rich countries."[32] That is, the state gives families a set sum for each child, regardless of income. The amounts are often not large—in many countries equivalent to approximately $100 per month per child—but the guaranteed income contributes to the economic well-being of children and demonstrates the nation's commitment to treat children as the responsibility of society as a whole, not of the individual family alone. Parental sick leave, which allows parents to take time off from work when their children need them and is separate from the leave to which workers are entitled when they themselves are sick, is universally guaranteed in nearly all European countries and many other countries as well. In addition, in many countries workers are entitled to parental leave when a child is born or adopted. In Sweden, for example, fathers as well as mothers, whether the couple is married or not, are encouraged to take paid leave around the time their baby is born or adopted. Of particular consequence to single mothers is a program in some countries guaranteeing that when the absent parent does not pay the required child support, the government makes the payment. In Sweden and Norway, for example, these "advance maintenance payments" contribute significantly to the income of mother-only families; more than 80 percent of children receive child support either from the absent parent or from the government. An indication of the importance of these three programs—child allowances, parental leave, and child support—is that their combined value, per capita, averages almost half the poverty level in Sweden and Norway.[33] And none of these programs is means-tested; in other words, they are available to all, regardless of income. Families do not need to undergo the often humiliating investigation into their financial status, their work status, and their personal lives endured by generations of poor women in the United States.

Another universal benefit crucial to the well-being of all families and available in virtually all industrialized countries is health insurance. According to the U.S. Census Bureau, in 2003 the number of people in the United States lacking insurance against the cost of medical care climbed to 45 million, or almost 16 percent of the U.S. population. For those working full-time, the percentage uninsured rose from 16.8 percent in 2002 to 17.5 percent in 2003, an increase of more than 1 million people. Moreover, more than 80 million Americans were without health insurance for some period during 2002–03. More than four out of five people who were uninsured were either working or were looking for work. And though low-income people are more likely to be uninsured, also without coverage were about 25 percent of workers with family incomes of $56,000 to $75,640.[34] In addition, more than 8 million children are uninsured—most of them poor children, whose number rose to 12.9 million in 2003. While it is generally assumed that poor children are covered by Medicaid, in many states a full-time, minimum wage worker in a family of three earns too much to qualify for Medicaid. And such lack of health insurance has real consequences. According to statistics published by the Centers for Disease Control and Prevention, only about half of uninsured children had a health checkup in 2003 and uninsured children are nine times more likely than insured children to be without a regular health care provider.[35]

The United States must recognize that the individual and the nuclear family cannot go it alone in this complex, unpredictable world. One of the main reasons that American society is so ready to blame single mothers for nearly all the problems faced by the American family is the myth that individuals are largely in control of their destiny—that teenagers knowingly get pregnant, that most single mothers have made a "lifestyle" decision to raise children on their own, that the impoverished are simply not working hard enough. As these interviews and myriad other studies demonstrate, for the most part these assumptions are false. Rather than simplistically blaming individuals, we must recognize that their behavior is strongly influenced by widespread economic and social trends. People without health insurance are less likely than those who are insured to have access to the health care system. The omnipresence of sexuality in American culture clearly influences the behavior of both adolescents and adults. The critical shortage of jobs that pay a living wage, particularly for workers without a college degree, has a direct impact on male commitment to their families and especially their children. Those who are marginalized or excluded from mainstream society obviously suffer profound social, emotional, and economic consequences. Furthermore, we must recognize that social or family policy has a direct impact on individuals' behavior.

Most of the single mothers I interviewed describe a mixture of private and public solutions to their day-to-day problems and to the overall challenge of developing a positive, balanced life for themselves and their children. Many are fortunate to have close relatives able and willing to help with child rearing and other domestic responsibilities. But even those who can rely on parents, siblings, grandmothers, and other extended family members find they must also draw on community resources: day care, after-school care, food stamps, WIC (the Special Supplemental Nutrition Program for Women, Infants and Children), welfare benefits, and health care and special educational services for children with special needs. Several of the mothers report using such services for low-income people, at least temporarily. Although she refused to call it "welfare" because she felt it had little to do with the word's traditional sense, "well-being," Jeri Miller received AFDC for a period of time when she was going to college. Judith Berman also was on AFDC as well as food stamps while she was continuing her education. Lourdes Garcia received financial aid when she was laid off or unable to work, and both Jeanne Gonzalez and Diana Suarez are currently receiving some financial support. These women illustrate a crucial use of financial aid for single mothers—tiding them over when times are especially hard and providing support while they go to school, thereby making it possible to move from bare survival to genuine middle-class status and to vastly improve the life chances of their children and themselves.

If we truly want to strengthen families—both single- and two-parent—we must recognize that they need support from the wider society. The United States must seriously consider adopting several of the policies already in place in other comparable industrial societies. Clearly, we must find a way of providing health insurance for all Americans. We must also have a serious debate on the value of establishing other universal supports for all families, such as children's allowances, parental leave at the time a child is born or adopted, and parental sick leave when a child is ill. Moreover, if either the federal government or state governments were to guarantee child support when the father refuses or is unable to pay, the lives of single mothers and their children would be significantly improved. Given the national political climate during the first decade of the twenty-first century, the first steps toward establishing universal supports for families are likely to be taken in new programs at the local or state levels. Legislators and policy analysts can then assess the efficacy, cost, and impact of such pilot programs to judge their suitability for use at the national level. Also, assuming they are effective, such policies will in time develop a constituency willing and perhaps eager to work toward their implementation nationwide.

Of primary importance in securing the well-being of all children, particularly the children in mother-only families, is the provision of first-rate, accessible, affordable preschool care and after-school care. Several women I interviewed stress how vital this is. Lourdes Garcia recalls innovative neighborhood-based day care without which she feels she could not have worked while caring for her small children. The first step Jeri Miller's therapist took to help her go to college was to place her young son in quality day care. And beyond ensuring the children's well-being, day care often also provides information and networking for the mothers. After-school care is of equal importance. Millions of children lack adult supervision between the end of the school day and the time a parent returns home from work. The need to occasionally leave children alone is a source of considerable anxiety and shame for several of the women. Susan Jackson feels that it must remain her "secret." Another mother similarly described herself as "ashamed" to admit to having "a latchkey child. When he comes home from school, he locks himself in the house and waits for me to come home. In the summertime, he can go outside, but only if he calls me to check in every hour. I had to get him a little watch with a timer so that he would remember to check in with me. If I don't get that call, I leave work to go find him."[36]

And, of course, we must pay child care workers a living wage if we hope to avoid high turnover and inadequate care. Today, millions of child care workers earn incomes below the poverty line; if we truly value our children and are concerned about their well-being, we must treat their caregivers with respect and provide the remuneration and working conditions that will keep them in the field. At the same time, the expense to families must be contained. According to the Institute for Women's Policy Research, low-income families spend more than 28 percent of their income on child care services, while higher-income families spend 5 percent. Infant care is the most costly. A national study has found that infant care costs more than public college tuition in every state—in some states, more than twice as much.[37] In her article "Children Left Behind," Stephanie Mencimer calls for a national child-care program for families at all income levels. Pointing to the rapid influx of mothers of preschool children into the workforce, she argues for more child care subsidies to individual families and the expansion of preschool and after-school care programs. According to Ruby Takanishi, president of the Foundation for Child Development, "Most people view child care as a private matter," but they are only partly right.[38] The availability of child care affects the stability of millions of members of the current workforce, and quality child care can benefit the nation by educating and nurturing the future workforce.

As a result of growing numbers of women in the United States working outside the home in a society in which preschool and after-school care are still grossly inadequate—far less adequate than in comparable European countries—and in which most men still do not participate adequately in either caregiving or domestic work, women from the third world are increasingly being recruited to do what is still thought of as "women's work." Millions of female workers in search of higher wages have migrated from poor countries to rich ones to care for the children, the elderly, and the sick and to clean the homes of those too busy to do the caring and the domestic work themselves. As Barbara Ehrenreich and Arlie Hochschild note in *Global Woman: Nannies, Maids, and Sex Workers in the New Economy*, "While the European or American woman commutes to work an average of twenty-eight minutes a day, many nannies from the Philippines, Sri Lanka, and India cross the globe to get their jobs."[39] Moreover, many of the women who migrate to the United States,

England, and other first world countries are leaving behind families and children of their own. In addition to the hardships caused by traveling great distances to very different cultures and having to learn new customs and often a new language, significant numbers of these women also experience downward mobility. And because many were professionals in their own country—teachers, midlevel administrators, and nurses and other health workers—filling the "care deficit" in rich countries means creating a "care drain" in poor countries.

This removal of mothers from their countries of origin and from their own families has serious consequences for their own children. Although the money they send back home provides essential resources for the family and the nation they left behind, the personal loss to their children can be extremely difficult to bear. In studying the Philippines' "care crisis," Rhacel Salazar Parreñas has interviewed young adults who grew up in "transnational" families in the Philippines. One young woman described her feelings about the absence of her mother, who was doing domestic work in New York: "There are times when you want to talk to her, but she is not there. That is really hard, very difficult. . . . There are times when I want to call her, speak to her, cry to her, and I cannot. It is difficult. The only thing that I can do is write to her. And I cannot cry through the mails." Another young woman, whose mother returns for vacation only rarely, called her family "broken": "When my mother is home, I just sit next to her. I stare at her face, to see the changes in her face, to see how she aged during the years that she was away from us. But when she is about to go back to Hong Kong, it's like my heart is going to burst. I would cry and cry. . . . I ask myself, how many more years will it be until we see each other again?"[40]

In today's global economy, major shifts in labor force participation in the first world accompanied by societal neglect of essential services reverberate thousands of miles away, reshaping not just the lives of children and families but also the social structures of the third world. Ehrenreich and Hochschild offer a cogent comparison: "The First World takes on a role like that of the old-fashioned male in the family—pampered, entitled, unable to cook, clean, or find his socks. Poor countries take on a role like that of the traditional woman within the family—patient, nurturing, and self-denying. A division of labor feminists critiqued when it was 'local' has now, metaphorically speaking, gone global."[41]

The interviews with the single mothers in this study also indicate that the United States must do a much better job educating young people about sexuality, reproduction, contraception, abortion, and sexually transmitted diseases. Many teenagers are woefully uninformed about these matters, but many adult women as well have difficulty with family planning. The current emphasis on abstinence-only programs—granted nearly $170 million by the Bush administration in 2005—may help some young people postpone having sex, but such programs do not educate them about sexuality, reproduction, or how to protect themselves from HIV-AIDS and other sexually transmitted diseases. Moreover, several of these groups have been criticized in a congressional report for providing "false, misleading, or distorted information."[42] Oversimplifying sexuality and the crucial choices related to sex will not serve young people well. Rather, we must recognize the complexity of decisions made about sexuality and fertility and acknowledge how choices and actions are powerfully influenced by older family members, by male friends, and by women's goals and what they perceive as possibilities for their future. We must work to demystify sex and reproduction and, at the same time, make sure that young people truly understand that sex has consequences—sometimes life-changing ones. Above all, we must make sure that women have access not only to knowledge but to appropriate, confidential gynecological services.

For some critics, the solution to the problems of single mothers is to promote marriage, especially for low-income women. In January 2004 the Bush administration announced an initiative intended to provide at least $1.5 billion for training to help couples, particularly poor couples, develop interpersonal skills in order to sustain "healthy marriages."[43] Such efforts to promote marriage have been ongoing since the 2000 election; they are seen as a way of completing the unfinished business of the welfare legislation of 1996 that forced millions of the poor off the welfare rolls and into the workforce. Some analysts have raised questions about the efficacy of encouraging poor, single women to marry. In an op-ed piece in the *New York Times,* Michael Tanner of the Cato Institute cites William Julius Wilson's conclusion that there are "relatively few marriageable men" in high poverty areas. He also draws on a study of census data done by researchers at Columbia and Princeton to point out that "more than a third of fathers of children born out of wedlock lacked a high school degree; 28 percent were unemployed; and 20 percent had incomes of less than $6,000 per year. Roughly 38 percent had criminal records."[44] If they should marry, would these men really be able to help their female partners out of poverty?

In 2002 Katherine Boo, a writer for the *New Yorker,* observed a three-day seminar given at a local church to encourage marriage among poor women who live in Sooner Haven, a public housing project in Oklahoma City. She focused on Kim Henderson, a 22-year-old who was trying to figure out how "to live a life less indigent and criminal than the one in which she was raised," and her best friend, Corean Brothers, a 49-year-old mother of five. While Kim recognizes that "Two parents means two paychecks," Boo notes that "Kim's experience with males, like that of the other women in the class, pointed toward a more complex calculation." Boo adds,

> None of the women were on welfare, and all were determined not to be. And while they wanted men for companionship, sex, and the sort of honest, intimate conversation they were enjoying in marriage class, they weren't entirely sure that men were useful to their efforts at self-improvement. All but one of the women in the room had grown up without a father in the home. At least two had been sexually abused in the first ten years of their lives. Those who had children had been left by the children's fathers. Three had been beaten by men they had loved, and two had been involved with violent criminals. In short, it required an imaginative leap to believe that a committed relationship with a man would rescue a woman from poverty. At Sooner Haven, relationships with men were often what stopped an ambitious woman from escaping.[45]

When the article leaves Kim and Corean, they are no closer to marriage, but the pastor of the church is conducting another marriage seminar and hoping that this training would produce its first wedding.

Kim and Corean do not need seminars on interpersonal skills and the importance of marriage. What they and millions of other women and men need are decent jobs at decent wages; adequate, affordable housing; health insurance and access to first-rate health care; human services that support their efforts to improve their lives; financial support for those in need; and finally, opportunities to continue their education. As the interviews reported in this study have frequently demonstrated, education—whether the completion of high school, vocational training, attendance at community college, or a degree from a four-year college or even a graduate or professional school—is the surest way to move out of poverty, to expand one's opportunities, and to put together a rewarding life for oneself and one's children. Education must be affordable and welcoming to people of all classes and backgrounds. We as a society must be truly committed to education at every level and support all who want to study and learn to follow their dreams and become fully contributing members of society.

In her book *Brave New Families*, Judith Stacey describes how attending reentry programs at a local community college affected low-income women in Silicon Valley during the 1970s. They began to see themselves differently and consequently began to see their lives and their relationships very differently. One woman characterized the change as "self-respect" and attributed the women's new sense of self-esteem to the supportive relationships they experienced in the classroom. Such programs clearly affect the participants on multiple levels.[46] Two examples of innovative programs specifically designed to enable those who have traditionally been underserved by higher education to pursue additional study and eventually play new roles in their communities are the Urban College of Boston and the Access Project of Hamilton College in upstate New York. The Urban College offers a two-year program that grants associate degrees in early childhood education, general studies, and human service administration. Providing internships and other hands-on opportunities, the college serves more than 700 students each semester and has graduated 237 students since its inception in 1994.[47]

The administrators of the Access Project describe it as "a demonstration educational, social service, and career program that assists profoundly low-income parents in central New York in their efforts to move from welfare and low-wage work to meaningful and secure career employment through the pathway of higher education."[48] Begun in 2001, the project has enrolled students living below the poverty line, many of whom have depended on social service benefits for two or more years. Some have had to overcome homelessness, medical emergencies, domestic violence, and family crises but nevertheless have stayed with the program and have thrived. The Access Project provides a full range of support services as it prepares these students to matriculate at two- and four-year colleges. Its director, the sociologist Vivyan Adair, points out the transformation that can and often does take place among poor parents who are given the chance to profoundly change their lives and declares, "Supporting low-income parents who are earning college degrees makes moral, intellectual, cultural, and fiscal sense."[49]

A brief examination of income and wealth inequality in the United States may shed light on the question of whether the country has the resources to provide these opportunities and support services to our families. In 2003, the lowest 20 percent of households in the United States received 3.4 percent of the nation's total household income, the smallest percentage on record. That same year the richest 20 percent of households received almost half of all household income (49.8 percent), the second highest level on record. At the same time, the middle 60 percent, the middle classes, received 46.9 percent of total household income, the third smallest share on record. The disparities between high-income and middle-income households and between high-income and low-income households were either the largest on record or tied with those in the year 2000 for the largest on record. The Congressional Budget Office offers a slightly different angle on these disparities: according to its figures, between 1979 and 2001, after adjusting for inflation, the average income of the top 1 percent of the population rose by $408,800, or 139 percent. During that same twenty-two-year period, the average income of the middle 20 percent rose $6,300 (17 percent) and the average income of the bottom 20 percent rose just $1,000 (8 percent).[50] The wealth gap is equally significant. In 2001, for example, a year when the economy was in a recession, the wealth of the top 10 percent of households surged much more than that of families in any other group. Between 1998 and 2001, the net worth of these families jumped 69 percent, from $492,400 to $833,600. In contrast, the net worth of families in the bottom 20 percent rose 24 percent to $7,900. Through most of the 1990s, the median net worth of families at the top was about 12 times that of lower-middle-class families; in 2001, the median net worth of the top earners was about 22 times as great.[51]

The United States has the resources; we just need to allocate them more equitably. This may seem like a daunting task in today's political climate, but it is one we need to undertake if we are to create a just and caring environment for all Americans. We could begin to reduce the current massive inequalities in American society by expanding the Earned Income Tax Credit, making the child tax credit refundable for working families with no federal income tax obligations, and making federal tax policy more progressive rather than more regressive.

Moreover, we must accept that single-parent families are here to stay. A significant number of marriages will inevitably dissolve, whether through separation or divorce. And tragic, untimely deaths of spouses will continue to occur. Children will also continue to be born outside of marriage. In some cases, the couples will marry; in others, one or both of the partners will reject the idea of marriage. Some men will walk away, while others, to varying degrees, will remain in the mother's or the child's life. Rates of teenage pregnancy have declined considerably, and in the future they can be lowered even further if young people are given better reproductive education, greater access to gynecological services, and improved educational and employment opportunities. Nonetheless, single teenage mothers are also a permanent part of our constellation of families.

As we attempt to understand the complex strategies that these women employ to balance their multiple responsibilities, it might be helpful to keep in mind some of the larger forces and beliefs that have permeated American culture over the centuries. In his analysis of the prevailing attitudes of Americans from colonial times through the early nineteenth century, the social historian John Demos points out that the settlement generation of the 1600s viewed the world in terms of tradition and cycles. The cycles of days and nights, of the moon and the seasons, of marriage and reproduction dominated their lives. Home and hearth were the physical and emotional center of the settlers' lives. By the time of the American Revolution, however, the traditional was being replaced by the "new"—the "new man," "new ideas," "new opinions."[52] Perhaps Thomas Paine best expressed the spirit of the times in his pamphlet *Common Sense:* "We have it in our power to begin the world over again. A situation similar to the present has not happened since the days of Noah till now. The birth of a new world is at hand."[53]

One major change was that life was beginning to be seen as more linear than cyclical. According to Demos, liberalism's "central affirmations—free choice, free inquiry, individual autonomy, rational self-interest—were typically expressed as a *quest:* an unfolding, a moving forward, and (in some versions at least) an idea of progress" (emphasis his). By the nineteenth century, autobiographical writings reveal that the notion of life as an individual's journey toward the future had taken hold. Education was key to the journey, as was the belief in opportunity and the "acknowledgment of personal agency and ambition." As the "cult of the self-made man" became dominant, "moving away from one's point of origin"—moving metaphorically away from one's family and background toward self-improvement and success—became the ideal. Demos observes, however, that "the rise of the linear" was "primarily a *male* phenomenon" (emphasis his).[54] In fact, male opportunity and success was dependent in part on women's maintaining the cyclical traditions of the family and the home.

The women in this study seem to be engaged in both kinds of thinking—the traditional and the modern, the cyclical and the linear. Some of them are devoted and committed to the families who raised them and from whom they receive continuous sustenance. Yet this relationship, while nourishing and often essential to their and their children's survival, is sometimes fraught with conflict. Other women have gone the more linear route—moving away from their own families' patterns (often by acquiring advanced education) and discovering in themselves talents, skills, preferences, and a capacity for success they had never previously imagined. And many of the women combine the two ways of thinking and being. They are committed to their original family members and see them as role models, but at the same time they embark on a quest, a journey to establish a different life that moves in new directions, toward new goals. They combine the patterns of both circles and lines—connectedness and personal transformation.

Rather than isolating and marginalizing them, rather than denigrating and stereotyping them, rather than blaming them for problems that befall a wide variety of families, we as a society must recognize that most single mothers are strong, courageous, and uncommonly hardworking. We must also recognize that many of them are truly heroines—caring for their children and often their extended family as well, frequently under extraordinarily difficult circumstances while remarkably remaking their own lives in ways that will provide a better future for the entire family. Moreover, we must acknowledge that single-parent and two-parent families are more similar than different in their circumstances, problems, concerns, and needs. Many of the issues common to all families require significant societal support: we must provide many more services and broaden opportunities for those who have less, and we must distribute income and wealth far more equitably. We are an astonishingly rich society. It is time for us to use our abundant resources to enable all families to care for and nurture their children, to find satisfying and productive work that pays a living wage, to live in relative harmony with other family members, friends, and neighbors, and to contribute meaningfully to the larger community. We can do no less.

Notes

Introduction

1. For further discussion of these issues, see Mimi Abramovitz, *Regulating the Lives of Women.*

2. For a fuller discussion of this period, see Ruth Sidel, *Women and Children Last.*

3. Charles Murray, quoted in Sue Woodman, "How Teen Pregnancy Has Become a Political Football."

4. See Jason DeParle, "The Clinton Welfare Bill."

5. Barbara Dafoe Whitehead, "Dan Quayle Was Right," p. 77.

6. Newt Gingrich, quoted in Katherine Q. Seelye, "Gingrich Looks to Victorian Age to Cure Today's Social Failings."

7. Nathaniel Hawthorne, *The Scarlet Letter,* pp. 89–90.

8. For a fuller discussion of the welfare legislation and its consequences, see Ruth Sidel, *Keeping Women and Children Last,* and Sharon Hays, *Flat Broke with Children.*

9. David T. Ellwood and Christopher Jencks, "The Uneven Spread of Single-Parent Families," pp. 12, 3, 5.

10. U.S. Department of Health and Human Services, *Trends in the Well-Being of America's Children and Youth 2003,* p. 51.

11. Ellwood and Jencks, "Uneven Spread of Single-Parent Families," p. 14.

12. Louis Uchitelle, "Gaining Ground on the Wage Front."

13. U.S. Department of Health and Human Services, *Trends in the Well-Being of America's Children and Youth 2003,* p. 77.

14. Ibid., pp. 81–82.

15. Annette Lareau, *Unequal Childhoods,* pp. 3, 5, 6.

16. Robert Haveman, Gary Sandefur, Barbara Wolfe, and Andrea Voyer,

"Trends in Children's Attainments and Their Determinants as Family Income Inequality Has Increased," p. 165.

17. Carolyn G. Heilbrun, *Writing a Woman's Life*, p. 18.

18. Robert Fulford, *The Triumph of Narrative*, pp. 14, 17.

19. Pirandello, quoted in Robert Jay Lifton, *The Protean Self*, p. 121.

20. Joyce Carol Oates, quoted in Anna Fels, *Necessary Dreams*, p. 74.

21. Gay Becker, *Disrupted Lives*, p. 17.

1. Moving Beyond Stigma

1. Barbara Dafoe Whitehead, "Dan Quayle Was Right," p. 77.

2. Vivyan Adair, *From Good Ma to Welfare Queen*, p. x.

3. John Ashcroft and Charles Murray, quoted in ibid., p. 13.

4. Michael Savage, quoted in "Right Is Wrong," p. 1.

5. "Speaking as a Father, Not a Son."

6. Quoted in Barry Glassner, *The Culture of Fear*, p. 90.

7. David Blankenhorn and Wade Horn, quoted in ibid., p. 96.

8. Adam Walinsky, "The Crisis of Public Order."

9. Matthew Wald, "Most Crimes of Violence and Property Hover at 30-Year Lows."

10. Rachel M. Brownstein, *Becoming a Heroine*, p. 16.

11. Kai T. Erikson, *Wayward Puritans*, p. 7.

12. James McBride, *The Color of Water*, p. 5.

13. Barack Obama, *Dreams from My Father*, pp. xvi, xii.

14. Adair, *From Good Ma to Welfare Queen*, pp. xvii, x–xi.

15. W. E. B. Du Bois, *The Souls of Black Folk*, p. 45.

16. Susan Stanford Friedman, "Women's Autobiographical Selves," p. 39.

17. William Julius Wilson, *The Truly Disadvantaged*, p. 8.

18. Whitehead, "Dan Quayle Was Right," p. 47.

19. David Popenoe, *Life without Father*, p. 25.

20. Patricia Hill Collins, *Black Feminist Thought*, p. 74.

21. Sara McLanahan and Gary Sandefur, *Growing Up with a Single Parent*, p. 28.

22. E. Mavis Hetherington and John Kelly, *For Better or For Worse*, p. 7.

23. Demie Kurz, *For Richer, For Poorer*, p. 13.

24. Linda J. Waite and Maggie Gallagher, *The Case for Marriage*, pp. 141, 144.

25. *The State of Our Unions, 2003*, p. 26.

26. Arlie Russell Hochschild, *The Commercialization of Intimate Life*, pp. 217, 2, 39.

27. Quoted in Ruth Sidel, *On Her Own*, p. 172.

28. See Sharon Hays, *Flat Broke with Children*.

29. *The State of Our Unions, 2001*, pp. 8, 6.

30. Allison Pearson, *I Don't Know How She Does It*, pp. 10, 18, 56–57.

31. Ibid., p. 6.

32. Brownstein, *Becoming a Heroine*, p. xv.

33. Lee R. Edwards, *Psyche as Hero*, pp. 5–6.

2. Genuine Family Values

1. The Personal Responsibility and Work Opportunity Reconciliation Act of 1996 ended poor families' entitlement to federal welfare benefits, an entitlement that had been in place since the passage of the Social Security Act of 1935. This "reform" gave control of aid to the states, set time limits on families receiving aid, required many recipients to work outside the home, and placed a lifetime cap on benefits received. For a comprehensive examination of the legislation's impact, see Hays, *Flat Broke with Children*.

3. Loss

1. Julie Moir Messervy, "Going for Grace," p. 84.

2. Gay Becker, *Disrupted Lives*, pp. 7, 4.

3. Mariane Pearl, quoted in Julie Salamon, "A Widow, But Spare the Pity."

4. Becker, *Disrupted Lives*, p. 6.

4. Resilience, Strength, and Perseverance

1. Roslyn Mickelson and Stephen Smith, quoted in Vivyan Adair and Sandra Dahlberg, "Welfare Class Identity and the Rhetoric of Erasure in Academia," p. 75.

2. Adair and Dahlberg, "Welfare Class Identity," pp. 75–76.

3. Ibid., p. 79.

4. Campbell, quoted in ibid., p. 81.

5. Lani Guinier and Gerald Torres, *The Miner's Canary*, p. 141.

6. Ibid.

7. Linda M. Hartling, *Strengthening Resilience in a Risky World*, p. 2.

8. Ibid., p. 3.

9. Ibid., pp. 3–4.

6. "I Have to Do Something with My Life"

1. Doreen Cullen, quoted in Ruth Sidel, *Women and Children Last*, p. 27.

2. Ibid., pp. 28, 27.

3. Lisa Dodson, *Don't Call Us Out of Name*, pp. 16, 41, viii.

4. Quoted in ibid., p. 43.

5. Carol Stack, *All Our Kin*, pp. 29, 36–37.

6. Rachel K. Jones, Jacqueline E. Darroch, and Stanley K. Henshaw, "Contraceptive Use among U.S. Women Having Abortions in 2000–2001," p. 302.

7. Beth, quoted in Ruth Sidel, *On Her Own*, p. 16.

8. Jacqueline Gonzalez, a 16-year-old, and Beth Conant, quoted in ibid., pp. 25, 17, 16.

9. Linda Smith, quoted in ibid., p. 55.

10. Toni Morrison, *The Bluest Eye*, p. 18.

11. Both quoted in Sidel, *On Her Own*, p. 137.

12. Lawrence B. Finer and Stanley K. Henshaw, "Abortion Incidence and Services in the United States in 2000," pp. 6, 14, 14–15.

13. Dodson, *Don't Call Us Out of Name*, pp. 88, 90.

14. Ibid., p. 89. For further discussion of these issues, see also Kathryn Edin and Maria Kefalas, *Promises I Can Keep*.

15. Girls quoted in Dodson, *Don't Call Us Out of Name*, pp. 52, 55.

16. Ibid., pp. 99, 113; Polly is quoted in ibid., 100.

7. "I Really, Really Believed He Would Stick Around"

1. Quoted in Johnnetta Betsch Cole and Beverly Guy-Sheftall, *Gender Talk*, pp. 61, 62.

2. See Andrew Hacker, *Mismatch*.

3. Ibid., p. 81.

4. Ibid., pp. 57–58.

5. Terry Arendell, "A Social Constructionist Approach to Parenting," p. 7.

6. Kathleen Gerson, "The Social Construction of Fatherhood," pp. 143–44.

7. Louis Uchitelle, "Blacks Lose Better Jobs Faster as Middle-Class Work Drops."

8. Janny Scott, "Working, but Barely Enough to Get By."

9. Edmund L. Andrews, "A Growing Force of Nonworkers."

10. David Leonhardt, "Slow Job Growth Raises Concerns on U.S. Economy."

11. U.S. Department of Health and Human Services, *Trends in the Well-Being of America's Children and Youth*, *2003*, p. 100.

12. Gerson, "The Social Construction of Fatherhood," p. 145.

13. Ibid., pp. 122, 123–24.

14. Arendell, "A Social Constructionist Approach to Parenting," p. 11.

15. Daniel Mendelsohn, "Winged Messages," p. 43.

16. Hacker, *Mismatch*, pp. 12, 13.

17. Susan Faludi, *Stiffed*, pp. 7–13, 595–98.

18. Paule Marshall, *Brown Girl, Brownstones*, p. 31.

19. Elliot Liebow, *Tally's Corner*, pp. 65, 63.

20. Ibid., pp. 131, 135.

21. Bob Herbert, "An Emerging Catastrophe."

22. Guinier and Torres, *The Miner's Canary*, pp. 260–61.

23. Loic Wacquant, quoted in ibid., p. 261.

24. Guinier and Torres, *The Miner's Canary*, pp. 263, 264, 265.

25. Fox Butterfield, "Despite Drop in Crime, an Increase in Inmates."

26. Cole and Guy-Sheftall, *Gender Talk*, p. xxii.

27. Orlando Patterson and Delores B. Aldridge, quoted in ibid., p. xxvi.

28. Kevin Powell, quoted in ibid., pp. 45, 184.

29. Cole and Guy-Sheftall, *Gender Talk*, p. 204.

30. Sarita, quoted in Tricia Rose, *Longing to Tell*, pp. 44–45.

31. Cole and Guy-Sheftall, *Gender Talk*, p. 200.

32. Maxine Baca Zinn, "Feminist Rethinking from Racial-Ethnic Families," p. 306.

33. Ibid., p. 312.

8. An Agenda for the Twenty-first Century

1. Lani Guinier and Gerald Torres, *The Miner's Canary*, p. 11.

2. Ibid., p. 12.

3. Quoted in Ruth Sidel, *On Her Own*, p. 132.

4. Nina Bernstein, "Teenage Rate of Pregnancy Drops in U.S."

5. Leslie Kaufman, "It's a Trend."

6. Nina Bernstein, "Behind Fall in Pregnancy, a New Teenage Culture of Restraint."

7. Jacqueline E. Darroch, Susheela Singh, Jennifer J. Frost, and the Study Team, "Differences in Teenage Pregnancy Rates among Five Developed Countries," p. 244.

8. Susheela Singh, Jacqueline E. Darroch, Jennifer J. Frost, and the Study Team, "Socioeconomic Disadvantage and Adolescent Women's Sexual and Reproductive Behavior," p. 251.

9. Robert Jay Lifton, *The Protean Self*, p. 1.

10. Lewis Lapham and Richard Reeves, quoted in ibid., pp. 32, 33.

11. Lifton, *The Protean Self*, p. 37.

12. Silvia Dominguez and Celeste Watkins, "Creating Networks for Survival and Mobility," pp. 112–13.

13. Brendan Halpin, "Dedicated to Two Women, Only One of Them Alive."

14. Kathryn Edin and Laura Lein, *Making Ends Meet*, pp. 101, 118.

15. Quoted in ibid., p. 30.

16. Barbara Ehrenreich, *Nickel and Dimed*, pp. 209–10, 210, 197.

17. Institute for Women's Policy Research, "Persistent Inequalities."

18. Edmund L. Andrews, "It's Not Just the Jobs Lost, But the Pay In the New Ones."

19. Frank Levy, quoted in ibid.

20. Elizabeth Warren, quoted in Bob Herbert, "Admit We Have a Problem."

21. Heidi Hartmann, Vicky Lovell, and Misha Werschkul, "Women and the Economy," p. 5.

22. Louis Uchitelle, "Gaining Ground on the Wage Front."

23. Aaron Bernstein, "Women's Pay."

24. David Koeppel, "When 'Job' Means Part Time, Life Becomes Very Different."

25. Bernstein, "Women's Pay."

26. Beth Shulman, "Low-Wage Work—America's Broken Promise," pp. 9, 1.

27. Ibid., pp. 1, 2.

28. Al Baker, "Over Pataki Veto, Minimum Wage to Rise to $7.15."

29. Edin and Lein, *Making Ends Meet*, p. 230. The figure for 2005 is taken from the Bureau of Labor Statistic's Inflation Calculator (available on the Consumer Price Index Home Page, http://www.bls.gov/cpi/home.htm).

30. Jared Bernstein and Jeff Chapman, "The Living Wage," p. 2.

31. Ibid.

32. Lee Rainwater and Timothy M. Smeeding, *Poor Kids in a Rich Country*, p. 123.

33. For a detailed comparison between family policy in the United States and that in other countries, see ibid., pp. 109–31.

34. "Rising Uninsurance Rates a Growing Problem for States."

35. "Census: 45 Million Americans Now Lack Health Insurance."

36. Quoted in Edin and Lein, *Making Ends Meet*, p. 134.

37. Colleen Henry, Misha Werschkul, and Manita C. Rao, "Child Care Subsidies Promote Mothers' Employment and Children's Development," p. 2.

38. Ruby Takanishi, quoted in Stephanie Mencimer, "Children Left Behind," p. 31.

39. Barbara Ehrenreich and Arlie Russell Hochschild, introduction to *Global Woman*, p. 3.

40. Both women are quoted in Rhacel Salazar Parreñas, "The Care Crisis in the Philippines," pp. 42, 50.

41. Ehrenreich and Hochschild, introduction to *Global Woman*, pp. 11–12.

42. Report quoted in Ceci Connolly, "Some Abstinence Programs Mislead Teens, Report Says."

43. Robert Pear and David D. Kirkpatrick, "Bush Plans $1.5 Billion Drive for Promotion of Marriage."

44. Michael Tanner, "Wedded to Poverty."

45. Katherine Boo, "The Marriage Cure," pp. 106, 109.

46. Judith Stacey, *Brave New Families*, p. 43.

47. *Urban College of Boston Viewbook & Catalogue 2004–2005*, pp. 12, 15.

48. *The Access Project*, p. 3.

49. Vivyan Adair, quoted in ibid., p. 6.

50. "Census Data Show Poverty Increased, Income Stagnated, and the Number of Uninsured Rose to a Record Level in 2003."

51. Edmund L. Andrews, "Economic Inequality Grew in 90's Boom, Fed Reports."

52. John Demos, *Circles and Lines*, p. 40.

53. Thomas Paine, quoted in ibid., p. 39.

54. Demos, *Circles and Lines*, pp. 49, 70, 78, 80, 76.

Bibliography

Abramovitz, Mimi. *Regulating the Lives of Women: Social Welfare Policy from Colonial Times to the Present.* Boston: South End Press, 1988.

The Access Project. Clinton, NY: Hamilton College, 2001.

Adair, Vivyan C. 2000. *From Good Ma to Welfare Queen: A Genealogy of the Poor Woman in American Literature, Photography, and Culture.* New York: Garland.

Adair, Vivyan C., and Sandra L. Dahlberg. *Reclaiming Class: Women, Poverty, and the Promise of Higher Education in America.* Philadelphia: Temple University Press, 2003.

———. "Welfare Class Identity and the Rhetoric of Erasure in Academia." *Public Voices* 5, no. 3 (Fall 2002): 75–84.

Addams, Jane. *Twenty Years at Hull-House.* 1910. Reprint, New York: Signet, 1961.

Andrews, Edmund L. "Economic Inequality Grew in 90's Boom, Fed Reports." *New York Times,* January 23, 2003.

———. "A Growing Force of Nonworkers." *New York Times,* July 18, 2004.

———. "It's Not Just the Jobs Lost, But the Pay in the New Ones." *New York Times,* August 9, 2004.

Arendell, Terry. *Mothers and Divorce: Legal, Economic, and Social Dilemmas.* Berkeley: University of California Press, 1986.

———. "A Social Constructionist Approach to Parenting." In *Contemporary Parenting: Challenges and Issues,* edited by Terry Arendell, pp. 1–44. Thousand Oaks, CA: Sage, 1997.

———, ed. *Contemporary Parenting: Challenges and Issues.* Thousand Oaks, CA: Sage, 1997.

Baker, Al. "Over Pataki Veto, Minimum Wage to Rise to $7.15." *New York Times,* December 7, 2004.

Becker, Gay. *Disrupted Lives: How People Create Meaning in a Chaotic World*. Berkeley: University of California Press, 1997.

Benstock, Shari, ed. *The Private Self: Theory and Practice of Women's Autobiographical Writings*. Chapel Hill: University of North Carolina Press, 1988.

Bergman, Barbara R. *Saving Our Children from Poverty: What the United States Can Learn from France*. 1996. Reprint, New York: Russell Sage Foundation, 1999.

Bernstein, Aaron. "Women's Pay: Why the Gap Remains a Chasm." *Business Week*, June 14, 2004, p. 58.

Bernstein, Jared, and Jeff Chapman. "The Living Wage: A Progressive Movement in Action." *Poverty & Race* 13, no. 1 (January/February 2004): 1–2, 6–7, 10–11.

Bernstein, Nina. "Behind Fall in Pregnancy, a New Teenage Culture of Restraint." *New York Times*, March 7, 2004.

———. "Teenage Rate of Pregnancy Drops in U.S." *New York Times*, February 20, 2004.

Blankenhorn, David. *Fatherless America: Confronting Our Most Urgent Social Problem*. New York: Basic Books, 1995.

Boo, Katherine. "The Marriage Cure." *New Yorker*, August 18 and 25, 2003, pp. 104–20.

Brownstein, Rachel M. *Becoming a Heroine: Reading about Women in Novels*. New York: Penguin, 1984.

Butterfield, Fox. "Despite Drop in Crime, an Increase in Inmates." *New York Times*, November 8, 2004.

"Census: 45 Million Americans Now Lack Health Insurance." *The Nation's Health*, October 2004, pp. 1–30.

"Census Data Show Poverty Increased, Income Stagnated, and the Number of Uninsured Rose to a Record Level in 2003." Washington, DC: Center on Budget and Policy Priorities, 2004. Available at www.cbpp.org/pubs/povinco4.htm (accessed June 14, 2005).

Chase, Susan E., and Mary F. Rogers. *Mothers and Children: Feminist Analyses and Personal Narratives*. New Brunswick, NJ: Rutgers University Press, 2001.

Cole, Johnnetta Betsch, and Beverly Guy-Sheftall. *Gender Talk: The Struggle for Women's Equality in African American Communities*. New York: Ballantine Books, 2004.

Collins, Patricia Hill. *Black Feminist Thought: Knowledge, Consciousness, and the Politics of Empowerment*. Boston: Unwin Hyman, 1990.

Connolly, Ceci. "Some Abstinence Programs Mislead Teens, Report Says." *Washington Post*, December 2, 2004.

Crittenden, Ann. *The Price of Motherhood: Why the Most Important Job in the World Is Still the Least Valued.* New York: Henry Holt, 2001.

Darroch, Jacqueline E., Susheela Singh, Jennifer J. Frost, and the Study Team. "Differences in Teenage Pregnancy Rates among Five Developed Countries: The Roles of Sexual Activity and Contraceptive Use." *Family Planning Perspectives* 33, no. 6 (November/December 2001): 244–50.

Demos, John. *Circles and Lines: The Shape of Life in Early America.* Cambridge, MA: Harvard University Press, 2004.

DeParle, Jason. "The Clinton Welfare Bill: A Long, Stormy Journey." *New York Times,* July 15, 1994.

Dodson, Lisa. *Don't Call Us Out of Name: The Untold Lives of Women and Girls in Poor America.* Boston: Beacon Press, 1998.

Dominguez, Silvia, and Celeste Watkins. "Creating Networks for Survival and Mobility: Social Capital among African-American and Latin-American Low-Income Mothers." *Social Problems* 50, no. 1 (2003): 111–35.

Du Bois, W. E. B. *The Souls of Black Folk.* 1903. Reprint, New York: Signet, 1969.

Edin, Kathryn, and Maria Kefalas. *Promises I Can Keep: Why Poor Women Put Motherhood before Marriage.* Berkeley: University of California Press, 2005.

Edin, Kathryn, and Laura Lein. *Making Ends Meet: How Single Mothers Survive Welfare and Low-Wage Work.* New York: Russell Sage Foundation, 1997.

Edwards, Lee R. *Psyche as Hero: Female Heroism and Fictional Form.* Middletown, CT: Wesleyan University Press, 1987.

Ehrenreich, Barbara. *Nickel and Dimed: On (Not) Getting By in America.* New York: Metropolitan Books, 2001.

Ehrenreich, Barbara, and Arlie Russell Hochschild. Introduction to *Global Woman: Nannies, Maids, and Sex Workers in the New Economy,* edited by Barbara Ehrenreich and Arlie Russell Hochschild, pp. 1–13. New York: Metropolitan Books, 2003.

———, eds. *Global Woman: Nannies, Maids, and Sex Workers in the New Economy.* New York: Metropolitan Books, 2003.

Ellwood, David T., and Christopher Jencks. "The Uneven Spread of Single-Parent Families: What Do We Know? Where Do We Look for Answers?" In *Social Inequality,* edited by Kathryn M. Neckerman, pp. 3–77. New York: Russell Sage Foundation, 2004.

Erikson, Kai T. *Wayward Puritans: A Study in the Sociology of Deviance.* New York: Macmillan, 1966.

Faludi, Susan. *Stiffed: The Betrayal of the American Man.* New York: Perennial, 2000.

Fels, Anna. *Necessary Dreams: Ambition in Women's Changing Lives*. New York: Pantheon, 2004.

Fineman, Martha Albertson. *The Neutered Mother, the Sexual Family and Other Twentieth Century Tragedies*. New York: Routledge, 1995.

Finer, Lawrence B., and Stanley K. Henshaw. "Abortion Incidence and Services in the United States in 2000." *Perspectives on Sexual and Reproductive Health* 35, no. 1 (2003): 6–15.

Fitch, Janet. *White Oleander*. Boston: Little, Brown, 1999.

Folbre, Nancy. *The Invisible Heart: Economics and Family Values*. New York: New Press, 2001.

Friedman, Susan Stanford. "Women's Autobiographical Selves: Theory and Practice." In *The Private Self: Theory and Practice of Women's Autobiographical Writings*, edited by Shari Benstock, pp. 34–62. Chapel Hill: University of North Carolina Press, 1988.

Fulford, Robert. *The Triumph of Narrative: Storytelling in the Age of Mass Culture*. New York: Broadway Books, 2000.

Gerson, Kathleen. "The Social Construction of Fatherhood." In *Contemporary Parenting: Challenges and Issues*, edited by Terry Arendell, pp. 119–53. Thousand Oaks, CA: Sage, 1997.

Glassner, Barry. *The Culture of Fear: Why Americans Are Afraid of the Wrong Things*. New York: Basic Books, 1999.

Goffman, Erving. *Stigma: Notes on the Management of Spoiled Identity*. Englewood Cliffs, NJ: Prentice-Hall, 1963.

Gordon, Linda. *Heroes of Their Own Lives: The Politics and History of Family Violence*. New York: Viking, 1988.

Guinier, Lani, and Gerald Torres. *The Miner's Canary: Enlisting Race, Resisting Power, Transforming Democracy*. Cambridge, MA: Harvard University Press, 2003.

Hacker, Andrew. *Mismatch: The Growing Gulf between Women and Men*. New York: Scribner, 2003.

Halpin, Brendan. "Dedicated to Two Women, Only One of Them Alive." *New York Times*, December 5, 2004.

Hartling, Linda M. *Strengthening Resilience in a Risky World: It's All About Relationships*. Work in Progress, no. 101. Wellesley, MA: Stone Center Working Paper Series, 2003.

Hartmann, Heidi, Vicky Lovell, and Misha Werschkul. "Women and the Economy: Recent Trends in Job Loss, Labor Force Participation, and Wages." Institute for Women's Policy Research publication no. B245, October 2004. www.iwpr.org/pdf/B245.pdf (accessed June 14, 2005).

Haveman, Robert, Gary Sandefur, Barbara Wolfe, and Andrea Voyer. "Trends in Children's Attainments and Their Determinants as Family Income Inequality Has Increased." In *Social Inequality*, edited by Kathryn M. Neckerman, pp. 149–88. New York: Russell Sage Foundation, 2004.

Hawthorne, Nathaniel. *The Scarlet Letter*. 1850. Reprint, New York: Penguin, 1986.

Hays, Sharon. *Flat Broke with Children: Women in the Age of Welfare Reform*. Oxford: Oxford University Press, 2004.

Heilbrun, Carolyn G. *Reinventing Womanhood*. New York: Norton, 1979.

———. *Writing a Woman's Life*. New York: Ballantine Books, 1989.

Henry, Colleen, Misha Werschkul, and Manita C. Rao. "Child Care Subsidies Promote Mothers' Employment and Children's Development." Institute for Women's Policy Research Publication no. G714, October 2003. www.iwpr.org/pdf/G714.pdf (accessed June 14, 2005).

Herbert, Bob. "Admit We Have a Problem." *New York Times*, August 9, 2004.

———. "An Emerging Catastrophe." *New York Times*, July 19, 2004.

Hetherington, E. Mavis, and John Kelly. *For Better or For Worse: Divorce Reconsidered*. New York: Norton, 2002.

Hochschild, Arlie Russell. *The Commercialization of Intimate Life: Notes from Home and Work*. Berkeley: University of California Press, 2003.

Hondagneu-Sotelo, Pierrette. *Doméstica: Immigrant Workers Cleaning and Caring in the Shadows of Affluence*. Berkeley: University of California Press, 2002.

Institute for Women's Policy Research. "Persistent Inequalities: Poverty, Lack of Health Coverage, and Wage Gaps Plague Economic Recovery." Institute for Women's Policy Research, news release, August 30, 2005.

Jacobson, Michael. *Downsizing Prisons: How to Reduce Crime and End Mass Incarceration*. New York: New York University Press, 2005.

Jones, Rachel K., Jacqueline E. Darroch, and Stanley K. Henshaw. "Contraceptive Use among U.S. Women Having Abortions in 2000–2001." *Perspectives on Sexual and Reproductive Health* 34, no. 6 (2002): 294–303.

Kaufman, Leslie. "It's a Trend: Births out of Wedlock Are Falling Statewide." *New York Times*, October 2, 2004.

Kimmel, Michael S. *The Gendered Society*. New York: Oxford University Press, 2000.

Koeppel, David. "When 'Job' Means Part Time, Life Becomes Very Different." *New York Times*, October 10, 2004.

Kurz, Demie. *For Richer, For Poorer*. New York: Routledge, 1995.

Lareau, Annette. *Unequal Childhoods: Class, Race, and Family Life*. Berkeley: University of California Press, 2003.

Leonhardt, David. "Slow Job Growth Raises Concerns on U.S. Economy." The Job Picture: The Overview. *New York Times*, August 7, 2004.

Liebow, Elliot. *Tally's Corner: A Study of Negro Streetcorner Men.* Boston: Little, Brown, 1967.

Lifton, Robert Jay. *The Protean Self: Human Resilience in an Age of Fragmentation.* Chicago: University of Chicago Press, 1993.

Marshall, Paule. *Brown Girl, Brownstones.* 1959. Reprint, New York: Feminist Press, 1981.

McBride, James. *The Color of Water: A Black Man's Tribute to His White Mother.* New York: Riverhead Books, 1996.

McLanahan, Sara, and Gary Sandefur. *Growing Up with a Single Parent: What Hurts, What Helps.* Cambridge, MA: Harvard University Press, 1994.

Mencimer, Stephanie. "Children Left Behind." *American Prospect*, December 10, 2002, pp. 29–31.

Mendelsohn, Daniel. "Winged Messages." *New York Review of Books*, February 12, 2004, pp. 42–47.

Messervy, Julie Moir. "Going for Grace." *Wellesley*, Fall 2004, p. 84.

Miller, Sue. *The Good Mother.* 1986. Reprint, New York: Delta, 1994.

Morrison, Toni. *The Bluest Eye.* 1970. Reprint, New York: Pocket, 1974.

Neckerman, Kathryn M., ed. *Social Inequality.* New York: Russell Sage Foundation, 2004.

Obama, Barack. *Dreams from My Father: A Story of Race and Inheritance.* 1996. Reprint, New York: Three Rivers Press, 2004.

Parreñas, Rhacel Salazar. "The Care Crisis in the Philippines: Children and Transnational Families in the New Global Economy." In *Global Woman: Nannies, Maids, and Sex Workers in the New Economy*, edited by Barbara Ehrenreich and Arlie Russell Hochschild, pp. 39–54. New York: Metropolitan Books, 2002.

———. *Servants of Globalization: Women, Migration, and Domestic Work.* Stanford: Stanford University Press, 2001.

Pear, Robert, and David D. Kirkpatrick. "Bush Plans $1.5 Billion Drive for Promotion of Marriage." *New York Times*, January 14, 2004.

Pearson, Allison. *I Don't Know How She Does It: The Life of Kate Reddy, Working Mother.* New York: Knopf, 2002.

Polakow, Valerie. *Lives on the Edge: Single Mothers and Their Children in the Other America.* Chicago: University of Chicago Press, 1993.

Popenoe, David. *Life without Father: Compelling New Evidence That Fatherhood and Marriage Are Indispensable for the Good of Children and Society.* Cambridge, MA: Harvard University Press, 1996.

Rainwater, Lee, and Timothy M. Smeeding. *Poor Kids in a Rich Country: America's Children in Comparative Perspective.* New York: Russell Sage, 2003.

"Right Is Wrong." *Notes from EMILY,* September 2004, p. 1.

"Rising Uninsurance Rates a Growing Problem for States." *The Nation's Health,* August 2004, pp. 1, 14.

Rose, Tricia. *Longing to Tell: Black Women Talk about Sexuality and Intimacy.* New York: Farrar, Straus and Giroux, 2003.

Salamon, Julie. "A Widow, But Spare the Pity." *New York Times,* October 6, 2003.

Scott, Janny. "Working, But Barely Enough to Get By." *New York Times,* August 24, 2003.

Seelye, Katherine Q. "Gingrich Looks to Victorian Age to Cure Today's Social Failings." *New York Times,* March 14, 1995.

Shipler, David K. *The Working Poor: Invisible in America.* New York: Knopf, 2004.

Shulman, Beth. "Low-Wage Work—America's Broken Promise." *Poverty & Race* 13, no. 3 (May/June 2004): 1–10.

Sidel, Ruth. *Keeping Women and Children Last: America's War on the Poor.* Rev. ed. New York: Penguin, 1998.

———. *On Her Own: Growing Up in the Shadow of the American Dream.* New York: Penguin, 1990.

———. *Women and Children Last: The Plight of Poor Women in Affluent America.* New York: Penguin, 1986.

Singh, Susheela, Jacqueline E. Darroch, Jennifer J. Frost, and the Study Team. "Socioeconomic Disadvantage and Adolescent Women's Sexual and Reproductive Behavior: The Case of Five Developed Countries." *Family Planning Perspectives* 33, no. 6 (November/December 2001): 251–58, 289.

"Speaking as a Father, Not a Son." The 2004 Campaign: Campaign Briefing—the States. *New York Times,* October 7, 2004.

Stacey, Judith. *Brave New Families: Stories of Domestic Upheaval in Late-Twentieth-Century America.* Berkeley: University of California Press, 1998.

Stack, Carol. *All Our Kin.* 1974. Reprint, New York: Basic Books, 1997.

The State of Our Unions, 2001: The Social Health of Marriage in America. Piscataway, NJ: National Marriage Project, Rutgers University, 2001. Available at http://marriage.rutgers.edu/publicat.htm (accessed June 14, 2005).

The State of Our Unions, 2003: The Social Health of Marriage in America. Piscataway, NJ: National Marriage Project, Rutgers University, 2003. Available at http://marriage.rutgers.edu/publicat.htm (accessed June 14, 2005).

Tanner, Michael. "Wedded to Poverty." *New York Times,* July 29, 2003.

Uchitelle, Louis. "Blacks Lose Better Jobs Faster as Middle-Class Work Drops." *New York Times*, July 12, 2003.

————. "Gaining Ground on the Wage Front." *New York Times*, December 31, 2004.

————. "It's Not New Jobs. It's All the Jobs." *New York Times*, August 29, 2004.

Urban College of Boston Viewbook and Catalogue, 2004–2005. Boston: Urban College, 2004.

U.S. Department of Health and Human Services. *Trends in the Well-Being of America's Children and Youth.* Washington, DC: U.S. Government Printing Office, 2003.

Waite, Linda J., and Maggie Gallagher. *The Case for Marriage: Why Married People Are Happier, Healthier, and Better Off Financially.* New York: Broadway Books, 2000.

Wald, Matthew. "Most Crimes of Violence and Property Hover at 30-Year Lows." *New York Times*, September 13, 2004.

Walinsky, Adam. "The Crisis of Public Order." *Atlantic Monthly*, April 1995, pp. 39–54.

Wallerstein, Judith S., Julia M. Lewis, and Sandra Blakeslee. *The Unexpected Legacy of Divorce: A 25 Year Landmark Study.* New York: Hyperion, 2000.

Whitehead, Barbara Dafoe. "Dan Quayle Was Right." *Atlantic Monthly*, April 1993, pp. 47–84.

Wilson, William Julius. *The Truly Disadvantaged: The Inner City, the Underclass, and Public Policy.* Chicago: University of Chicago, 1987.

Woodman, Sue. "How Teen Pregnancy Has Become a Political Football." *Ms.*, January/February 1995, pp. 90–92.

Young-Bruehl, Elisabeth. *Subject to Biography: Psychoanalysis, Feminism, and Writing Women's Lives.* Cambridge, MA: Harvard University Press, 1998.

Zinn, Maxine Baca. "Feminist Rethinking from Racial-Ethnic Families." In *Women of Color in U.S. Society*, edited by Maxine Baca Zinn and Bonnie Thornton Dill, pp. 303–14. Philadelphia: Temple University Press, 1994.

Zinn, Maxine Baca, and Bonnie Thornton Dill, eds. *Women of Color in U.S. Society.* Philadelphia: Temple University Press, 1994.

Index

abortion: and contraceptive use, 153; rates, 157; teen father stopping, 43, 57, 187; women choosing, 99, 148, 155. *See also* abortion not chosen by interviewees

"Abortion Incidence and Services in the United States in 2000," 157

abortion not chosen by interviewees, 25, 156–58, 187–88; Cicely Franklin, 115, 157; Diana Suarez, 135, 148; Jeanne Gonzalez, 82–83, 157–58, 187–88; Jennifer Soriano, 69; Karen Morrison, 108, 157; Keisha Johnson, 111, 158; Mary Giordano, 170; Nancy Mendez, 121, 186; Pamela Curtis, 140–41, 157; Sandra Mason, 158; Shirika Simmons, 165–66

abuse, 24; by fathers, 39, 40, 62–64, 68, 162. *See also* emotional abuse; physical abuse; substance abuse

academia, teaching jobs, 12, 45, 47, 55, 65–66, 72, 164. *See also* education

Access Project, Hamilton College, 213–14

Adair, Vivyan, 24, 36, 101–2, 214

Addams, Jane, 184

adoptions, 10, 13, 17, 136–37

affluence: single father, 21; women, 12. *See also* upper middle class

African Americans. *See* blacks

after-school care, 24–25, 28–29, 207, 208, 209

age: single mothers, 13; teen pregnancy, 8, 43, 69, 81, 155

Aid to Families with Dependent Children (AFDC), 2, 95, 96, 197, 207

Alan Guttmacher Institute, 153, 189

alcohol, children's father and, 138–39, 177

Aldridge, Delores B., 181

American Dream, New, 153–55. *See also* dreams

American ideal, self-made person, 58, 89, 216

Angels in America (HBO), 175–76

anger, strength from, 106, 126

Arendell, Terry, 173, 175

Ashcroft, John, 21–22

Asians, interviewees, 12, 60, 61–68, 156

Atlantic Monthly, 3

autism, 139, 140

bankruptcy, 199–200

Barbados, 125, 178

Becker, Gay, 77, 78

Becoming a Heroine: Reading about Women in Novels (Brownstein), 36–37

Bernstein, Jared, 203

Bernstein, Nina, 190

Compositor: Binghamton Valley Composition, LLC

Indexer: Barbara Roos

Text: 10/15 Janson

Display: Akzidenz Grotesk and Folio

Printer and binder: Maple-Vail Manufacturing Group